CANADA

CANADA

A Candid Travel Guide
by
Gerald Hall and John Brehl

William Morrow & Company, Inc.
New York, 1978

Printed in the United States of America

1 2 3 4 5 6 7 8 9 10

Library of Congress Catalog Card Number
78-56068

ISBN 0-688-03348-2

CONTENTS

To Margaret and Rita whose constant encouragement
has kept us on the road

O CANADA!

More than 400 years ago one of Canada's first tourists, a Frenchman named Jacques Cartier, sailed into the Gulf of St. Lawrence, took a look at Labrador's bleak shores and muttered that it looked like the land God gave to Cain.

That was just the first of a lot of things that have been said about Canada. Henry David Thoreau said that "what I got by going to Canada was a cold." Irish playwright Brendan Behan called Canada "barbaric without being picturesque." It has been said that "Canada is not so much a country as magnificent raw material for a country," and four centuries after Cartier's visit, Canada is still often referred to as "the unknown country."

Some nice things have been said too, of course. Author Hugh MacLennan called this land "one of the supreme surviving prizes of the earth." But then MacLennan is a Canadian.

The rest of us Canadians have always saved, and savored, the remarks other people have made about us. Not that we've always agreed with them, but we often feel deep down that maybe we are kind of laughable. And, after all, we have a fine comic tradition of lunacy, ranging from writer Stephen Leacock on down through comedians Wayne and Shuster to our politicians.

But is Canada still the unknown country?

Certainly, a lot of people are convinced they know things about Canada that simply aren't so. There are, for instance, the hoary tales of American tourists crossing the border with plans to ski on Hamilton mountain in July, when the temperature is in the 80s.

And then there are the widespread impressions of Canada as, oh, that quiet backwater up north, with lots of mountains and lakes and Mounties – a land where life is slower-paced and everybody has that sane back-to-the-earth outlook, and costs are low, and "you'd be surprised how far your money goes though we hate to say it but the people are stodgy and Sundays are hell."

It just isn't so. At least not most of it.

Oh, there is magnificent scenery in much of Canada, although there are wide areas where you wouldn't be mean enough to send your tax accountant.

But life in this "stodgy" land is hilarious politically, incomprehensible economically and exciting socially. It is a fun place and a funny place.

In recent years about 200,000 immigrants a year have come to Canada, bringing their customs, foods, cultures. Yet Canada has never been a melting pot – "more like a tossed salad," as one writer has said.

Toronto, that "slow-paced" town which used to be ranked with Philadelphia in the comic lexicon – "I spent a week in Toronto last Sunday" – is the second busiest theater city in North America, one of the temples for jazz and approaching the status of a center for gourmets on a level with New Orleans or Montreal.

And Toronto's just a sample. There's Winnipeg, where a century ago editor Bob Edwards got off a train and said drily: "So this is Winnipeg; I can tell it's not Paris." So can one still, but now it's famous for ballet . . . and body rub parlors that make house calls.

And Canada's not cheap anymore. It costs more to buy a house in Toronto than in Los Angeles, more to buy a gallon of gasoline in oil-rich Alberta than in New York state.

But for the visitor there is one great piece of news.

The Canadian dollar, long at a premium in terms of its U.S. counterpart, has been devalued. In early 1978 it was worth just 90 cents U.S.

But even at that it costs $10 to $12 more for a single room at a top motel in remote Sault Ste. Marie, not the garden spot of Canada, than for one in the better motels in and around booming Atlanta.

Yet in many ways Canada is worth the premium price. It has mountains loftier than any in the Alps, wild, unmanicured peaks where bighorned sheep fight tong wars in the middle of the highway and black bears mooch for handouts.

It has more than a million lakes, some of them sadly polluted, but some of them so fresh, so untouched, that you get the idea you're the first to have fished them.

It has a wildlife show unrivalled this side of East Africa. Caribou still roam the Canadian north more than 100,000 strong, with some herds taking more than a day to pass a single point.

It has one city that bustled with activity a full century before the Pilgrim Fathers set sail and another where you can sit down for a meal in a building that has stood for three centuries. And the cities are still safe to walk through at night. In fact, though crime is on the increase here too, most big-city streets in Canada are safer at midnight that at noon because you're not as likely to get hit by a car then.

Its rock-ribbed east coast offers seascapes that will make you forget New England . . . or even the Riviera. And its west coast has fjords that will remind you of Norway.

And the highest tower erected by man is not among the skyscrapers of New York or Chicago but in once dowdy Toronto, a city U.S. magazines are likening these days to New York before it went bad.

But keep in mind that Canada is the second biggest

(after the Soviet Union) land on earth. Magnificent scenery is anything but continuous. In fact there are thousands of miles of roads leading you through flat, unrelieved boredom. So there isn't another country this side of the Orient where a tourist needs more help. We offer that help. Not perfect, mind you, but candid. It seems impossible in light of our lithe youthfulness but the authors of this book have been writing about Canada for a combined total of 49 years, most of it as reporters for Canada's largest daily newspaper.

Gerry Hall, veteran travel editor of the Toronto Star and a former president of the Society of American Travel Writers, has criss-crossed Canada by plane, train, bus and car – covering nearly 10,000 miles in one auto pilgrimage alone.

John Brehl is a well-known Star columnist whose earliest travel goes back to the days when twin-engined Dakotas were used by Air Canada and you could get a real bedroom on trains that ran where you wanted to go.

We have toured Canada on the job and with our families, seeking dining rooms with highchairs and restaurants with high cuisine. Brehl starts to salivate 50 miles away as he approaches Montreal's restaurants.

We're the first to admit that Canada is too big for any person to know intimately, and at times we get the eerie feeling we've just scratched the surface. But we have the advantage of having approached most parts of the country as a stranger – just as you will. We've found out through trial and error where the clipjoints are, where the fun is and where it isn't.

Money matters to us. We feel ashamed, angered when we've been taken in by the glossy appearance of a restaurant where the potatoes have been steaming since before we got hungry. We know you feel that way too.

Like all books this one will be biased but, we hope, biased in your favor. So here we go, starting in the place where the sun rises on Canada and heading for that blue Pacific, where it sets. But first, a nutshell account of all the little things you've always wanted to know about Canada but didn't know who to ask.

EVERYTHING YOU EVER WANTED TO KNOW ABOUT CANADA

CANADA IN A NUTSHELL Actually the big land doesn't fit in a nutshell too well. Sprawling over 3,851,809 square miles, it is second in size to the Soviet Union and covers almost as much territory as all of the countries of Europe put together. It stretches north and south from the shadow of the north pole to Pelee Island, on the same latitude as northern California. East and west it is strung out nearly 6,000 miles from the Atlantic to the Pacific, across seven time zones. Yet only 22.6 million people call it home. They live in 10 provinces (from the east) Newfoundland, Nova Scotia, Prince Edward Island, New Brunswick, Quebec, Ontario, Manitoba, Saskatchewan, Alberta and British Columbia, and two gigantic, far-north territories, the Yukon and Northwest Territories. Most of the population, however, lives within 100 miles of the U.S. border.

GETTING THERE By car, 35 million Americans come as tourists each year, arriving along some two dozen major highways that bring you to the border.

By plane, there is daily jet service from many major U.S. cities, from several European capitals and from the Far East. Montreal is the major designated gateway though Toronto gets more traffic.

By sea, in summer a steady stream of tourists arrives in Victoria and Vancouver on west coast ferries and cruise ships bound for Alaska. Montreal, a once busy cruise port, is much less active today though a Russian luxury liner cruises from there in summer.

Train service has sadly declined since World War II but some trans-border trains still roll.

Bus service is good, with daily runs between many U.S. and Canadian cities.

GETTING IN   For Americans it's usually painless and easy. Passports are not required of U.S. citizens, but they must have in their possession papers which will establish their citizenship, such as a birth certificate or baptismal card. Naturalized U.S. citizens should carry naturalization papers. Persons under 18 unaccompanied by an adult should have a letter from a parent or guardian authorizing them to travel to Canada. Citizens of other countries require a passport and from some countries, notably in Eastern Europe, a visa, too.

Canada Customs allows foreign travellers to bring in the following duty-free articles: wearing apparel and personal effects, up to 200 cigarettes, 50 cigars and two pounds of tobacco, 40 ounces of liquor or wine or 288 ounces of beer per adult, cameras with a reasonable amount of film, two day's food supply, sporting goods, including up to 200 rounds of ammunition, and a full tank of gasoline.

Drivers should have vehicle registration cards, written permission from the owner if the car is not theirs, and a copy of the rental contract in the case of a rental car.

You can bring gifts for friends so long as they don't exceed $10 in value. Prohibited from entry without special permission from the Collector of Customs at your entry point are pistols, fully automatic weapons and firearms less than 26 inches in length. Visitors 16

years or older can bring in sporting rifles and shot-
guns without a permit.

If you are bringing your dog with you, it must have
been vaccinated against rabies within the past 12
months and you must have a certificate from a licensed veterinarian to establish this.

You must declare all plant material to customs.
Much of it is prohibited without written permission
from the director of the Plant Protection Division,
Dept. of Agriculture, Ottawa. Smallpox vaccinations
are no longer required of visitors from most countries. However, if you come from an infected area of
the world, you may be required to be vaccinated on
arrival.

GETTING AROUND You'll find excellent highways – from 16-lane freeways and the 5,000-mile,
coast-to-coast Trans-Canada Highway on down.
There are good highways in every part of the country
except the far north and parts of Newfoundland.
Coastal highways are rare along the fjord-indented
seacoast of mainland British Columbia. Speed limits
have been lowered to 50 miles an hour in some parts
of the country since the gasoline crisis but you will
still find higher limits on some major highways. Be
forewarned that speeds in several parts of the country
are now posted in kilometers per hour instead of
miles. To convert multiply kilometers by .62 – thus 50
km per hour is close to 30 mph, 80 km is close to 50
mph and 100 km close to 60 mph. If that confuses
you, don't worry, we Canadians are still trying to
figure it out, too.

Train service has declined but not as badly as in
the U.S. There are still daily trans-continental trains
(featuring a trip through the Rockies) and high-speed
trains on the bustling Windsor-to-Quebec corridor.

Elsewhere service can be woeful though that may improve under a new government agency called VIA which has just taken over responsibility for all rail traffic in Canada.

Inter-city bus service is generally excellent, with several buses a day between major cities and to resort areas for summer fun and winter skiing.

Up in the blue, Air Canada and CP Air, the country's major international carriers, supply daily trans-continental service. Regional airlines are active in all parts of the country and in summer bush pilot-style operations take avid sportsmen to hidden lakes and wilderness lodges.

Canadian airlines don't offer as many discounted air fares for holiday travel as their U.S. counterparts. You can, however, lop as much as 50 per cent off cross-country air fares by flying on "nighthawk" or Charter Class Canada plans. (Nighthawk flights depart at ridiculously late hours and charter class seats must be booked at least 45 days ahead.)

These air fares and some discounted train fares can be used in conjunction with government-sponsored, budget-priced "See Canada First" travel packages introduced in 1978. Travel agents in Canada and the U.S. can supply details.

COSTS As we said at the start, Canada is not cheap. Toronto and Montreal sport New York style restaurant and hotel prices, though McDonald's and the Colonel are every bit as present in major Canadian cities as they are in the U.S. (In fact, Colonel Sanders himself moved to Canada many years ago.) Even in tiny Regina a couple can pay $37 a night for a hotel room and in Toronto or Montreal a double in a downtown hotel will usually cost between $40 and $65 a night.

Generally speaking, accommodation in small towns and cities is much more reasonable, especially in commercial type hotels. Rates in the Prairies, especially away from the Trans-Canada Highway, are the lowest in the country. Budgeting families can take advantage of $10-a-night, guest house accommodation in the Atlantic provinces and there's an excellent system of campgrounds in provincial and national parks and on private land, right across the country. Camping fees vary from $2.50 a day for a primitive site to $5 for sites with electrical hookups, nearby laundries, showers and swim pools.

Unfortunately, Canada lags far behind the U.S. in the development of economy motel chains. However, one of the U.S. giants in this field, Days Inns, has opened its first unit, near Toronto. In the U.S. these economy motels generally charge from $15 single to $17 double. They are expected to add a $2 premium in Canada. As things stand now, you should expect to pay from $16 up for a motel room for two, with many motels that carry automobile association endorsement charging from $20 up.

Make sure you look up the pertinent hotel section in chapters about any city you're visiting. We've been searching for hotel bargains for years and have found some surprising ones – right in downtown Toronto, Montreal and Vancouver.

Gasoline is expensive – but not as expensive as it looks at first sight. Don't forget that the Imperial gallon used across Canada is 20% larger than the U.S. gallon. In other words, 4 Canadian gallons equal 5 U.S. gallons. Expect to pay about 90 cents a gallon for regular in Ontario and Quebec, slightly less out west and 10 cents or so more in the Atlantic provinces.

HEALTH   Canada is all but free of unusual health hazards. However, the southern parts of Ontario and Quebec, especially the Toronto and Montreal areas, are as treacherous as many parts of the U.S. for hay-fever sufferers, from mid-August until first frost. Most other parts of Canada, notably the Maritimes and British Columbia, are real havens from hay fever.

Medications and patent medicines available in the U.S. usually can be obtained in Canada. However, drug laws do vary in some instances and it's a good idea to have specialized prescriptions filled before leaving home. Vistors to Canada can arrange for medical coverage through Blue Cross. Family coverage, including emergency hospitalization, in hospital and out-patient medical care, is available in Ontario, for example, for $36 for 21 days. You can get details from Ontario Blue Cross, 150 Ferrand Drive, Don Mills, Ontario, M3C 1H6.

WEATHER   Don't let those ultra low readings you see in Canada scare you. The whole country has switched to the metric system, with temperatures being given in Celsius rather than Fahrenheit degrees. A reading of 24 degrees in Canada means it's slightly over 75 degrees on the old scale. A reading of 4.4 is coolish – but still a bearable 40 degrees Fahrenheit.

You can't make generalized statements about Canadian weather. Toronto is often hotter than Miami in summer. Vancouver and Victoria are almost always warmer than New York in winter – in fact many natives of this southwest corner of Canada golf 12 months of the year. One thing you can say about the whole country, however, is that it does get four seasons and changes in the weather are frequent. That's really noticeable in the far north where summers feature the midnight sun and the odd heat wave while winters are gloomy and frigid – 40 below 0° is a norm.

Here are sample average daily highs in Fahrenheit from across the country: St. John's, Newfoundland, Jan., 33 degrees, July, 69; Montreal, Jan., 23 degrees, July, 79; Toronto, Jan., 31 degrees, July, 81; Winnipeg, Jan., 9 degrees, July, 80; Edmonton, Jan., 17 degrees, July, 75; Victoria, Jan., 43 degrees, July, 68, and finally Yellowknife in the Northwest Territories, Jan., minus 10 degrees, July, 69. (Dress for winter and snow when you come between Dec. 1 and the end of March to any part of Canada except the southwest corner of British Columbia.) Summer casuals – what you would wear in New York or Chicago are fine in July and August, though if you're heading to resort country a warm sweater is handy at night even then. Especially if you're camping.

While on the subject of dress, Canadians tend to be slightly more conservative than Americans – but the same rules for dining out, relaxing at a resort, or going to the theater apply here as in the U.S.

HOLIDAYS Canada celebrates several national holidays in common with the United States. New Year's Day, Good Friday, Easter Monday, Labor Day and Christmas Day fall on the same calendar dates. National holidays not shared with the U.S. include: Victoria Day (celebrated on the nearest Monday to May 24 and a day of fireworks displays across the country); Dominion (or Canada) Day on July 1; Thanksgiving Day, on the second Monday in October (instead of in November as in the U.S.); Remembrance Day, Nov. 11, and Boxing Day, Dec. 26. On the latter two days many businesses are open as usual but schools and banks close.

As well as these national holidays, a Civic Holiday

is celebrated in many parts of the country on the first Monday in August. It's not a holiday for the tourist, however, as major festivals are held in cities across the country on that date. In Quebec, June 24 is St. Jean Baptiste Day, celebrated with parades and rallies across the province. If you are anywhere in Canada on a national holiday it's worth making a phone check before heading out to any attraction. Usually they are open (except for Christmas and New Year's) but hours are often changed.

LIQUOR LAWS They are under provincial control and used to vary substantially from province to province. But in the last decade efforts have been made to make them more uniform across the country. The legal drinking age has been lowered to 18 in Prince Edward Island, Quebec, Ontario, Manitoba and Alberta. In the rest of Canada it's 19. Quebec still has the most liberal drinking laws in the country (one of our earliest memories of a visit there was a roadside café where two truck drivers were washing down their breakfasts with a quart of beer each).

Beverage rooms (where beer only is served), cocktail lounges and bars, and licensed dining rooms are found in cities across the country though they are hard to find in some backward areas. Liquor by the bottle is sold through government liquor stores only. They're found throughout the big cities and in most sizeable towns. In Quebec, beer to take home is sold at grocery stores; in Ontario only through large outlets called Brewers' Retail. In western Canada you can usually buy beer-to-go from beverage rooms. The Maritimes, once the most backward part of Canada when it came to having a drink, have made it reasonably available to tourists these days though "local option" generally still applies and you'll come on dry areas where you're lucky to be able to get a glass of beer on a warm day.

OFFICIAL HELP   Each province and territory will supply maps, accommodation guides, pamphlets and other detailed information for the asking. Addresses of provincial tourist offices are included in the pertinent chapters.

Another excellent official source of travel information is the Canadian Government Office of Tourism, 150 Kent St., Ottawa, Ontario, Canada K1A 0H6. Branches are located across the U.S. in Atlanta, Boston, Buffalo, Cleveland, Detroit, New York, Philadelphia, Pittsburgh, Washington, Chicago, Los Angeles, Minneapolis, San Francisco and Seattle. Other offices are located in Mexico City, Frankfurt, The Hague, London, Paris, Sydney and Tokyo.

HUNTING AND FISHING   The opportunities for both are enormous right across Canada. But a guide to them would require another book as thick as this one. This is one area, however, in which each province and territory has a ready supply of detailed information on regulations, seasons and prime areas. The official addresses are listed below.

SKIING   The same holds true for skiing. Although mention is made of prime areas in various chapters, you should definitely contact the province you are heading for to get detailed, up-to-date information on new lodges, hills and lifts. It should be noted, however, that world-class ski hills are found in Alberta's Rockies and in the mountains of British Columbia. Quebec has no peaks to match them but the après ski life there is superb, especially in the Laurentians north of Montreal.

WHERE TO WRITE:

British Columbia Tourism
1117 Wharf Street
Victoria, British Columbia
V8W 2Z2

Travel Alberta
10065 Jasper Avenue
Edmonton, Alberta
T5J 3B1

Sask Travel
P.O. Box 7105
Regina, Saskatchewan
S4P 3N2

Manitoba Department of Tourism
Tourist Branch
200 Vaughan Street
Winnipeg, Manitoba
R3C 0V8

Ontario Travel
Queen's Park
Toronto, Ontario
M7A 2E5

Québec Department of Tourism
Place de la Capitale
150 Saint Cyrille Blvd. (E)
Québec, Québec
G1R 2B2

New Brunswick Department of Tourism
Box 12345
Fredericton, New Brunswick
E3B 5C3

Nova Scotia Department of Tourism
Box 456
Halifax, Nova Scotia
B3J 2R5

Tourist Information Centre
P.E.I. Department of Tourism
Box 940
Charlottetown, P.E.I.
C1A 7N5

Tourist Services Division
Newfoundland Department of Tourism
130 Water Street
St. John's, Newfoundland
A0L 3E0

Travel Arctic
Government Northwest Territories
Yellowknife, Northwest Territories
X1A 2L9

Yukon Department of Tourism
Box 2703
Whitehorse, Yukon
Y1A 2C6

NEWFOUNDLAND

*"And if you get cranky without a silk hanky
You'd better steer clear of the squid-jiggin'
ground."*

Those words of warning from one of the most popular of all Newfoundland folk songs could apply to the whole of this island province. This is no place for the pampered pleasure seeker, no place to come looking for 20th century trimmings – or for the 20th century itself.

This is a rugged land, intimately involved with the sea that surrounds it. Yet its people, growing up in the splendid isolation that being 80 miles out to sea affords, are by far the friendliest in Canada. And their home is as different and delightful a corner of North America as you'll find.

But come prepared to put up with some creature discomfort. There are more tourist rooms in any of the large convention hotels of Toronto or Chicago than there are on this whole island. The government guidebook, *Where to Stay in Newfoundland*, is indeed one of the thinnest volumes in the English language. A restaurant guide, if there were one, would be even slimmer.

This lack of formal accommodation has its compensations, however. Newfoundlanders, or Newfies as they are almost always called by the rest of us Canadians, are used to putting up strangers in their homes. When a Newfoundland businessman travels across his island, he's as likely to stay at Mrs. Finnerty's tourist home as at a motel. It's a way of life on this island that has known so much hardship and poverty. Chances are the room he gets will be cleaner and more comfortable than the one at the motel down the way.

And for the traveller, staying in a Newfie's home is an excellent way to get past those barriers of formality and look-alike accommodations which impede us when we go exploring a new part of the world. Besides, the price is right. A room in the so-called "hospitality homes" that are sprinkled across the island will cost a couple about $10 a night.

You're not long on the island before you begin to see some of the ways in which this place and its people have been molded by isolation. Newfies don't talk like other Canadians or Americans. On the streets of St. John's, the capital, the man who gives you directions will sound as if he just got off the boat from Ireland. Yet, chances are his family has lived in Newfoundland for two centuries. In a fishing village just 20 miles away, the accent becomes pure Devonshire. For not only was Newfoundland largely cut off from the rest of the world, its communities were cut off from each other. Until a couple of decades ago, there wasn't even a road across the island.

Being on his own that way made the Newfie different from the rest of us. He lived from the sea and his garden, built his home with his own hands, hunted moose and caribou and amused himself to the extent that there were almost as many fiddlers here as there were fishermen. That's why the best English-language folk songs in Canada are the ones which have wafted their way out of this island province.

Even the place names have a homespun lilt to them. Come-by-Chance, Ha Ha Bay, Nancy Oh, Heart's Delight, Misery Point, Joe Batt's Arm and Jerry's Nose aren't unusual monickers – they're typical.

The everyday language of the island is just as different. A man's not a liar here; he's a stranger to the truth. "Lard Jeezus" precedes almost everything some Newfies say. A pancake is a "gandy" and a "rawny" person is thin because he doesn't get enough "gruel" in his "puddock" (stomach).

A man asks an old friend who has retired how he's "enjoyin' his grazin'." And the friend will reply that he's "as lonesome as a gull on a rock without the b'ys around."

Although it is Canada's youngest province, having joined the rest of the country in 1949 after making a financial flop of going it alone, Newfoundland is the most historic section of North America – at least as far as the white man's history is concerned. Some 500 years before Columbus "discovered" America, a small group of Vikings landed on the northern tip of the island and built a small settlement. Their discovery of the New World here was confirmed in the early 1960s when Norwegians Helge and Anne Ingstad and a team of archeologists unearthed the remains of seven Norse buildings, including North America's first blacksmith shop, at L'Anse-au-Meadow. Radiocarbon tests placed some of the materials found in the smithy's fireplace at about the year 1000.

This leads historians to believe the settlement may have been established by Leif the Lucky, who, the Icelandic Sagas tell us, discovered a new territory, which he called Vinland, about that time.

But that's ancient history. Newfoundland's modern age began in 1497, just five years after Columbus landed in the West Indies. John Cabot (alias Giovanni Gabotto) sailed into St. John's harbor under the English flag and told the world that the richest fishing waters ever seen lay around this sometimes fogbound island. Fishermen from all over Western Europe beat a path to its bays. But even after Sir Humphrey Gil-

bert claimed Newfoundland for Britain in 1583, colonization was discouraged. The summer catch was
to be brought straight home. Merchants in England
didn't want to see any rival businesses set up amid
these rich fishing grounds. If you were rude enough
to build a home over the crown's objections, there
was a law that prevented you from having a chimney.
Freeze, you disobedient devils!

This ban on colonization largely explains the
"outports" that gave Newfoundland its special character. These were little fishing hamlets, hidden in
coves, clinging to rocky cliffs away from officialdom's
prying eyes. There was no road into town; the sea
was the only highway for some 1,300 of these communities tucked away along 6,000 miles of rock-ribbed coast. Since Confederation with Canada, many
outports have been linked by road with the mainline
Trans-Canada Highway, which sweeps 565 miles
across the island and, with the help of a ferryboat
link to the mainland, continues almost 5,000 miles
across the country to another island capital, Victoria,
on the Pacific Ocean.

Many other outports have been abandoned but
even today on much of the south coast there are
fishing villages whose only link with the outside
world is an infrequent steamer.

The thing to keep in mind when you come here is
that the real Newfoundland isn't found along the
Trans-Canada Highway. You have to get off this
sometimes pot-holed main drag and take one of those
lonely roads down to the sea. Our best memory of
this island came from doing just that and ending up
in the former outport of **Salvage**.

Salvage is so old that no one is quite sure when it
was founded. But fishermen have plied their trade
around here for nearly four centuries, sometimes sailing off to Labrador (Newfoundland's mainland pos-

session) for a whole summer of fishing. When their schooners returned, the fishermen dried their catch on "flakes" or racks and sold the salted cod to merchants in St. John's for shipment around the world. Theirs was a way of life that died gradually, the victim of the Great Depression, which bankrupted the island; refrigeration, which made fish salting unnecessary; competition from foreign factory ships, and other less understandable forces.

The men of Salvage (it rhymes with rage) knew it was dead for sure when a quintal of fish (112 pounds) that had once brought $18 would fetch only $3. Once 600 people called Salvage home; today fewer than half that number remain. Yet it's a sight to remember, a place you keep cheering for, years after you've left.

Pick a color and you'll find it among the rainbow of neat clapboard houses that surround Salvage's almost circular harbor. Each house is perched on a rock, many with small fenced gardens, enclosed not so much to keep anything in as to keep out the flocks of sheep that wander about the village. A roller coaster of a dirt road promenades past the houses until it runs out of steam about three-quarters of the way around and turns into a footpath. Across the road, by the water's edge, you find the lobster traps, weatherbeaten fishing shacks, piers, drying racks and overturned dories that are workaday Newfoundland.

When we tired of wandering, we asked a fisherman working on his nets about food and he directed us to the home of an old fishing captain whose wife put up the best meal we've had in three visits to the island. Cod tongues, seal soup, boiled moose, four vegetables and a swig of homemade rhubarb wine. "If I 'ad knowed you was comin' I would 'ave 'ad time to soak the 'ard bread to make you some brewis," the woman of the house told us. The tab for the meal came to

$2.50 each and there was no embarrassment involved in paying for it. In this Eastport Peninsula area, many householders make pin money by taking in guests for dinner. It's the only chance most summer visitors have to taste typical Newfie fare.

Just across the road, a fisherman working on his boat agreed to take us out "jiggin' for cod" for $5. "People are some proud when they catches one," he said. "But last summer I took out one man who wanted to know why we didn't have a machine to make the line jig up and down."

As we said, if you get cranky without your silk hanky, stay home. Now here's a rundown of things you should know before heading this way:

WEATHER   There's often more rain than a vacationer needs. But days in July and August are beautifully air conditioned, with temperatures rarely climbing above the low 70s (low 20s Celsius) and always dropping by 20 degrees at night for comfortable sleeping. Winters aren't unbearably cold but they're frigid enough in January and February when, even at high noon, temperatures rarely make it above the freezing mark. Weather in spring and autumn is chancy at best.

HOW TO GET THERE   By air, with either Air Canada or Eastern Provincial from the Maritimes. Most frequent service is from Halifax. But most people come by way of the Canadian National car ferries from North Sydney, Nova Scotia, to Port-aux-Basques where the Newfoundland portion of the Trans-Canada Highway begins. The nine-hour trip, 80 miles out to sea, can be expensive, especially in summer when rates go up. The 1978 summer rates were $18 one-way for your car and $6 for each adult, $2.50 for children 5 through 12. There's a CN bus at Port-aux-Basques that takes car-less passengers across the island to St. John's.

WHAT TO SEE St. John's, the capital, is the easternmost city in North America and one of the most historic. It was bustling with activity for a century before the Pilgrim Fathers set sail for New England and as early as 1528 a merchant named Bute had set up shop there.

But unless you're a history buff, you won't want to spend much more than a day here. To our way of thinking, the outports offer more fun for a family of explorers. If history is your bag, however, St. John's can hardly fail to grab you.

Water St., which borders part of the city's magnificient, almost landlocked harbor, claims to be the oldest shopping street in either Canada or the U.S. English and Portuguese fishermen were trading goods on a beach that this street now runs through, at the same time Michelangelo was splashing paint on the ceiling of the Sistine Chapel.

But there is one major problem with St. John's as a history-laden treasure house. Through the years it has been sacked in wars between the French and the English and during peacetime levelled by a series of disastrous fires. The last one in 1892 left 13,000 people homeless and wiped away forever places which otherwise might have become the sort of shrines one finds in Boston, Quebec and St. Augustine. The fact that St. John's was – and continues to be – mostly a city of wooden homes and buildings resulted from its destruction being so complete.

However, on each occasion it has quickly risen from the ashes and today it remains a remarkable sight for any visitor. You see it best by driving to the top of a grey peak known as **Signal Hill** which looms relentlessly above the city and harbor. You look down on an almost landlocked harbor which at times shelters and supplies ships from around the world. Hills plunging down toward the water are lined with wooden houses of every color imaginable, huddled together against the cruel sea and rolling off over more distant hills into endless valleys. That view is St. John's at its best, with the twin towers of the **Basilica of St. John the Baptist** dominating the skyline despite the incursion of a handful of ugly highrise office buildings.

When you set out to explore the city on foot, you find that it's far less beautiful, much more ramshackle close up. Most streets in the old section are lined with two-storey row houses, none the same color as its neighbour. Deep blue screams at shutter green. Yellow, mauve, purple, red and pink feud along a single block. Houses begin right at the sidewalk's edge – no lawns to cut and no gardens to admire. Yet this is a city where history was made. Up there on Signal Hill, Marconi received the first trans-Atlantic wireless message in 1901. And people started to take the airplane seriously in 1919 when Alcock and Brown took off from St. John's on the first successful nonstop trans-Atlantic flight. And just beneath the imposing **War Memorial** on Water St. you'll find a plaque authored by no less than Rudyard Kipling that picks up on another one of St. John's great moments: "Close to this commanding and historic spot," it proclaims, "Sir Humphrey Gilbert landed on the fifth day of August, 1583, and in taking possession of the new found land in the name of his Sovereign Queen Elizabeth thereby founded Britain's overseas empire."

This is a plaque-happy city but, if you're a real history buff, an absolutely invaluable pocketbook is

Paul O'Neill's *Everyman's Complete Guide* to St. John's which can be picked up in any Newfoundland bookstore for $2.50. Much less illuminating is the **Newfoundland Museum** on Duckworth St., one of the most disappointing you'll find anywhere in Canada. Sometime during your stay find a spot to park along **Harbor Drive** to take a stroll along the quayside where ships from around the world are familiar sights. If you're lucky you may even come upon a quayside soccer game.

You should climb the ridge that dominates the city for a look inside the **Basilica of St. John the Baptist,** (Harvey Rd.,) completed in 1855 on a site originally intended for the island's penitentiary. The star-studded ceiling of the church, restored in 1955, is one of the most heavenly you'll see anywhere in Canada. The nearby **Anglican Cathedral** (Gower St.,) a Gothic structure, is worth a momentary pause although it is unfinished and never really recovered from the Great Fire of 1892 which completely gutted it.

The **Confederation Building,** seat of the provincial government since union with Canada, stands on a height of land overlooking the city. It has an interesting military museum with replicas of the old forts around which the city grew up. Nearby is **Memorial University,** a newish 120-acre campus with a moderately interesting gallery of Canadian paintings. You can usually get permission to visit the university's excellent **Marine Science Lab** on the shore of nearby Logy Bay where all manner of sea life is on display. The old seat of island government, the **Colonial Building** on Military Rd., now houses the Newfoundland Public Archives.

The **Art and Culture Centre,** a contemporary complex built to celebrate Canada's 100th birthday in 1967, features a 1,000-seat theater, art gallery and library. Name stars who come to the island play here.

It's one of the few theaters anywhere in which performances are sometimes fogged out because the featured performer's plane was unable to land.

Cabot Tower, perched on the crest of Signal Hill, was built in 1897 to commemorate the 400th anniversary of the founding of the city. For many it's the symbol of Newfoundland and the center of the hill's national historic park. There's a good interpretation center down the hill from the tower, where the big moments of both Newfoundland and St. John's history are recounted through audio-visual displays.

Nearby **Cape Spear**, which can be reached in a 10-mile drive from downtown St. John's over one of the world's worst roads, is the most easterly point in North America. Ireland, 1,640 miles east, is actually closer than most of Canada to the cape. The road to Cape Spear ends at a clifftop lighthouse, said to be the oldest in North America. At the base of the cliff are rusting artillery gun barrels and a rabbit warren of bunkers where Canadian soldiers huddled for warmth through winter nights of World War II. This is the very spot upon which the sun rises on North America. Interestingly enough, its first rays touch two grave markers of soldiers who died accidentally there during the war.

WHAT ELSE TO SEE The **Avalon** peninsula on which St. John's stands is an absolute showstopper as far as scenery is concerned. You'll see enough sheer cliffs, roaring seas and fishing boats to last you a lifetime by following the **Marine Drive** to Pouch Cove. Take Routes 30 and 20 out of the capital.

Terra Nova National Park, 150 miles west of St. John's and straddling the Trans-Canada, is 156 square miles of marvellous wilderness – rocky headlands overlooking the sea, numerous inland lakes and streams, virgin forests, sheltered coves are all features. Camping sites, nature trails, tourist cabins and docking facilities are available, but be forewarned that this is the most popular of all recreation sites on the island. Getting a campsite can be difficult in summer. Moose, caribou and black bear are protected here. Schools of whales and harbor seals are often spotted. The other national park on the island, **Gros Morne** on Highway 73, is still under development. It will be spectacular when completed, lying as it does among the 2,000-foot-high Long Range Mountains. There are also campsites at some three dozen provincial parks. Outdoors types should keep in mind that while there are fine ocean beaches in Newfoundland the waters surrounding the island are ... well, frigid enough that icebergs are often sighted. Newfies usually swim in lakes and so should you on this island.

L'Anse-au-Meadow where the Vikings landed about the year 1000 is now the site of a national historic park. Trouble is it's located 230 miles off the Trans-Canada and you have to drive over unpaved road to get there. Then there's not much to see. If you're still game also stop at **Port-au-Choix**, midway along Highway 73, to see the Indian burial ground dating to 2340 B.C. There are a couple of motels and guest houses at nearby St. Anthony for those making it to the Viking finds.

As you drive the Trans-Canada to St. John's, you come on **Corner Brook,** the island's second-largest city and the site of an immense and smelly pulp and paper mill. We've never found a good reason to stop at Corner Brook. **Gander** is also on the route. It was famous in the days before jet travel began because the piston-engined planes set down here on their way across the Atlantic. Now planes almost always overfly unless weather forces them to stop. If that happens to you, too, there's an interesting **Aviation Museum**, but little else, there.

The French islands of **St. Pierre** and **Miquelon** can be visited from Newfoundland on regular ferry service from the port of Fortune. CN steamers also visit remote fishing outports along the south coast of the island and along the Labrador coast. But cabins are booked as much as two years in advance so you must plan ages ahead. Contact Canadian National in St. John's for details.

WHERE TO STAY   That is a problem. As we said before there are more rooms in most metropolitan convention hotels than there are on this entire island. Moreover, hotels and motels tend to be overpriced and overrated, if only by the people who run them. We think they're the worst bunch of hotels you'll find in Canada. An especially unfortunate aspect of this situation is that while the natives of Newfoundland are among the friendliest Canadians you'll find, we found the people who run the hotels to be almost as indifferent as New York cab drivers. We suggest staying at guest houses, called hospitality homes here, and leaving the hotels to businessmen on expense accounts.

In St. John's, the best known establishment is the tired, old **Hotel Newfoundland**, whose only claim to fame is that it stands on the site of Fort William, a bastion which almost always succumbed to enemy attack. It's still a loser today and should have been retired when its owners, Canadian National, retired the Newfie Bullet, its equally ineffectual passenger train.

Rooms are noisy, plumbing ancient and only one elevator serves the 134 rooms. Rates run from $29 single to $38 double. The good thing about the Hotel Newfoundland is that it's in the heart of town, within walking distance of everything you came to see. Better bet for intown location is the **Battery Inn** just below Signal Hill. Rates from $28 single to $33 double. Largest hotel is the **Holiday Inn** on Portugal Cove Rd., just outside town. Its 200 rooms rent from $25 single to $30 double. The **Skyline Motel** ($20 to $30), and the **Traveller's Inn** ($22 to $37), both on Kenmount Rd., the **Kenmount Motel** on Elizabeth Ave., ($22.50 to $27.50) and the **Airport Inn** on Airport Rd., ($28 to $33) are newish suburban spreads.

Outside St. John's you have to depend on the government booklet, *Where to Stay in Newfoundland*, available free from the Newfoundland Department of Tourism, Confederation Building, St. John's. It gives a priced list of hotel, motel and tourist home accommodation.

Two warnings: If you're coming in July or August confirm reservations before leaving home. Rooms are in short supply any time of the year. Also keep in mind that there's a hefty 10% tax added to room rates.

WHERE TO EAT   Also a problem. Along the Trans-Canada, diners feature hot turkey sandwiches and too little else. Ask for a poached egg for breakfast and you'll get a blank stare. Having lived on fish much of their lives, Newfies find it hard to accept that seafood is a big treat for us landlubbers. Even in St. John's good restaurants are as scarce as hens' teeth.

Consistently best, in our opinion, is the **Woodstock Colonial Inn,** seven miles out of town on Topsail Rd. The **Starboard Quarter**, overlooking the harbor from the heart of downtown, has the best view but we found the fish dinners disappointing. **Sergio's** on Water St. has the best wine cellar and the highest prices. **Act III** in the Arts and Culture Centre has the nicest atmosphere, so-so food. **The Galley**, next door to the Starboard Quarter, is the best bet for budgeters. Keep in mind that in small Canadian cities and towns, Chinese restaurants usually offer the best value. The **Kenmount Restaurant** on Kenmount Rd., is tops for Chinese fare in St. John's. We think the **Hotel Newfoundland** and **Battery Inn** offer the best hotel dining.

WHERE TO SHOP   Stores here are more expensive than on the mainland. Handmade jewelry and knitted goods are worth a look. Best places to do this are the **Cod Jigger** and the **Newfoundland Weavery**, both on Duckworth St.

HUNTING AND FISHING   An estimated 40,000 moose still roam the woods of Newfoundland and Labrador. Personally, we'd like to see them stay there. Nonetheless, the island has become perhaps more famous as a hunter's paradise than a spot for an ordinary tourist. Caribou, rabbit, ducks, geese and ptarmigan are also bagged. Fishermen get salmon, trout and tuna in abundance. You need a licensed guide to fish for salmon – except within a quarter mile of the Trans-Canada Highway. Guidebooks for both hunters and anglers are available free from the Newfoundland Department of Tourism, 130 Water St. St. John's.

LABRADOR   We haven't said much about this mainland section of the province, even though it's twice as large as the island itself and increasingly important to the island's economy. It's a last frontier and won't get many pleasure travellers for some years to come. A $950 million hydro-electric power development is taking place at Labrador's Churchill Falls and Labrador mines produce 40% of all the iron ore produced in Canada.

THE NEWFIE JOKE   They're told across Canada, like Aggie jokes in Texas and Polish jokes in Chicago. And the simple Newfie fisherman is usually the butt. But as Newfies have the best sense of humor in Canada, they tell the best ones on themselves. This one is typical: "Why can't they make ice cubes in Newfoundland? Because the only man who knew the recipe died." Or the two Newfies who went fishing and came on a spot where the fish were really jumping. The one put an "X" on the side of their rented dory to mark the spot. "That's stupid," said his friend. "Tomorrow we may get a different boat."

WHERE TO GET HELP WITH YOUR TRIP   The Newfoundland Department of Tourism, 130 Water St., St. John's is the best source for maps, accommodation guides and specialized information pamphlets. Give them plenty of lead time – they run the pokiest tourist office in Canada.

If your trip is going to take you to other parts of Canada too, contact the Canadian Government Travel Bureau, 150 Kent St., Ottawa K1A 0H6.

THE MARITIMES

"Why, good heavens man! Pugwash is right there between Shinimicas and Tatamagouche!"
    Industrialist Cyrus Eaton about his Maritimes hometown.

For a family of landlubbers in search of the sea there is no sweeter corner of North America than Canada's Maritimes. Made up of the provinces of New Brunswick, Nova Scotia and Prince Edward Island, the Maritimes are compact enough (at just over 45,000 square miles) to be seen comfortably in a couple of weeks yet varied anough to make it worth the trouble of seeing all three.

Much of the coast of Nova Scotia, for example, is a Captains Courageous sort of place; rocky and rugged and dotted with fishing villages where weatherbeaten wood is as much of a shade of paint as the snowy white stuff that invariably covers the local church. Prince Edward Island, on the other hand, is surrounded by a gentler sea, circled with sandy beaches and lapped in summer by the warmest waters north of the Carolinas. New Brunswick has a little of both, but seems much more a mainland place, heavily forested and filled with strange quirks of nature.

Before we take a look at these three provinces in detail, a glance at the weather is very much in order. It's contrary, to say the least. As in any other place so intimately involved with the sea, the Maritimes often put a little more rain into your holiday life than you can readily appreciate. Yet when much of the rest of North America reported "the lousiest summer ever" in 1976, all three Maritimes were drenched in sunshine almost daily. Summer is very much the time to come here, especially if you want to do some swimming. Days are mostly in the 70s and nights invariably air-conditioned enough for gentle slumber. But pack a raincoat in the trunk, just in case.

Which brings up a second major point about the Maritimes. It's ideally suited for a motoring holiday, not nearly so well adapted to other kinds – though bus and airline tours are available. Its real beauty and most of its fun lie outside its cities. Cocktail lounges and licensed dining rooms have made a belated appearance but this section of Canada still should be regarded as a place that is short on nightlife and long on family fun, a place to explore, to dilly and dally on nobody's schedule but your own.

Your treasured memories of a trip to the Maritimes are much more likely to center around a beachside feast of lobster you cooked up in seawater than any restaurant meal you experienced. Your favorite place is almost certain to be a seaside discovery you made on your own, a fishing village that wasn't even mentioned in a guidebook, not even this one.

NOVA SCOTIA

"Sweetheart of the sea."

Poet Bliss Carman

We're doing this province first not so much because it's the easternmost of the three but because it's by far the most interesting – geographically, historically, any way you want to look at it. It may have been seen first by Europeans in 1497, just five years after Columbus "discovered" America. It's not clear from the skimpy details surrounding John Cabot's voyage to the New World whether he landed on Nova Scotia's Cape Breton coast or in Newfoundland. Most Canadian historians lean toward the latter but few Nova Scotians do. At any rate it is well established that a permanent settlement was begun in 1605 at Port Royal by the great French explorer Samuel de Champlain and a colorful character named Pierre du Guast. To keep their settlers happy over those first lonely winters, Champlain set up American's first social club, the Order of the Good Time, in which members tried to outdo each other by preparing a more sumptuous feast than their neighbors. The club's still going strong – though now mostly as a tourist gimmick. If you stay at least three days in Nova Scotia and register with the province's tourist information offices at entry points on the way in or out, you can get a certificate that makes you a member in good standing – but not a guest at a feast.

Almost from the beginnings of that first settlement, now known as Annapolis Royal, the French and the English were to quarrel over Nova Scotia, ceding it back and forth as part of the settlement of their continuing squabbles in Europe. It finally reverted to Britain in 1713 under the terms of the Peace of Utrecht and this later gave rise to one of the most shameful episodes in Canadian history: the expulsion of the Acadians (as the French Nova Scotians were known). British settlers never really understood or trusted the French (some say they still don't) and in 1755 they simply booted some 7,000 of them out, usurping their lands and piling them aboard ships heading south. The story is familiar to anyone who has read Longfellow's *Evangeline*. There's a statue of Evangeline at Grand Pre in Nova Scotia and also in Louisiana where many Acadians ended up – as the Cajuns of bayou country.

Among the small waves of immigrants who followed were Scots, who found the highlands of Cape Breton every bit as lovely – and forbidding – as their own; Germans, whose accents may still be detected in Lunenburg; Blacks, from the slavery of the Caribbean to a life that was too often just as harsh and dreary in Halifax, and Loyalists, who flowed north following the American Revolution.

Halifax, now a city of 125,000 and the closest thing the Maritimes have to a Big Apple, was founded in 1749 by Lord Cornwallis to counterbalance the existence of the mighty French fortress of Louisbourg which one may still visit today on Cape Breton Island. Canada got its first schools, first mail deliveries and first newspaper in Halifax. And in 1848, Canada got responsible government here for the first time when the British-appointed governor of Nova Scotia grudgingly ceded some of his powers to the elected assembly.

With its magnificent, deep harbor Halifax has continued to be an important naval base and a fine all-year port. And it's the only place in the Maritimes that is actually sprouting skyscrapers. But, though most people include it on a trip to the Maritimes, it is not one of Canada's truly fascinating cities. In fact many Canadians from other parts of the country make no secret of their dislike of the place. Much of its unpopularity stems from World War II when many servicemen were either stationed, or shipped, through the city. It did everything but put out "no fun allowed here" signs and became known far and wide as "the city where you can't get a drink." The servicemen's animosity toward the place was so bitter that they did their best to wreck the city in the infamous Halifax Riots which began as part of the celebration of victory in Europe. Servicemen broke into liquor warehouses, looted stores, overturned police cars, drank in the streets (the cruelest blow of all) and put dozens of people in hospital.

Ironically, it marked the second time that Halifax, though never attacked by a foreign enemy, was cruelly treated by the vicissitudes of war. In 1917, the collision of two ships, one carrying munitions, in Halifax harbor touched off the greatest explosion to occur prior to World War II. Two thousand died as whole sections of the city were demolished. You can see a common grave where 249 unidentified victims were buried in Halifax's Fairview Cemetery. Nearby you'll see rows of markers from another great sea disaster, the sinking of the Titanic in 1912. The ship was closer to Newfoundland when it struck an iceberg but most of the victims were buried here.

But if some ex-Navy wag tells you "Halifax is worth five minutes of anyone's time, " you'll realize it's somewhat better than that.

WHAT TO SEE Aside from its great harbor, the city's most dominant feature is still a star-shaped fortress known as the **Citadel**. Begun in 1828 on the site of three previous forts, it is now a national historic park, containing a military museum, portions of the Nova Scotia provincial museum and an art gallery. Kids invariably love the place and the price is right, with both admission and guided tours offered free. (It's open daily 9 A.M. to 8 P.M., June 15 to Labor Day, slightly shorter hours in the off-season.)

The Citadel remains one of a glorious series of forts across Canada from which a shot was never fired in anger. But it has been used as a wartime detention center and as a jail; Russian revolutionary Leon Trotsky was held prisoner there in 1917. Beside the Citadel stands an 1803 clock, a lasting monument to King George III's son Edward, a punctual martinet who once ruled here as commander-in-chief of Nova Scotia.

A short walk down the hill from the Citadel is **Province House**, as fine a piece of Georgian architecture as you'll find in Canada and the oldest parliament building still in use in the country. Completed in 1818, Province House (bounded by Hollis, Prince, Granville and George Sts.) is open daily, except Sundays and holidays, 8:30 A.M. to 5 P.M. The only building in town that dates back to Halifax's beginnings is **St. Paul's Anglican Church** (Barrington and Duke Sts.). Its frame was shipped up from Boston in 1750 and erected on its present site.

Point Pleasant Park at the southern tip of the city is a tranquil, traffic-free place to wander if you are spending a few days in Halifax. It's one of the rare areas outside Scotland where you will find heather growing. Haligonians (as the natives call themselves) say sailors coming ashore here made a practice of shaking the stuffings out of their mattresses on this point to refill them with fresh grasses. Those stuffings contained heather seeds sturdy enough to take permanent hold. The round **Martello tower** you come across in the park is part of the city's never used defence system.

A Halifax curiosity is the **Chapel of Our Lady of Sorrows** in the cemetery at South and Park Sts. It was built in a single day in 1874 by 2,000 men. Altar carvings inside date to 1550.

What's new in Halifax is actually one of the oldest sections of the city, and it really is worth a visit. The section of the waterfront between Buckingham and Duke Sts. had its heyday during the Napoleonic Wars when privateers sailing from its wharfs made vast fortunes plundering French ships. (One of them, a swashbuckler-turned-banker named Enos Collins, was reputed to be the wealthiest man in British North America when he died in 1871.) Being the most ancient section on the city's magnificent harbor, it had become the junkiest and was slated to be torn down – you guessed it – to build a freeway. Then in 1964, preservation interests moved in, threw a roadblock into the freeway and presented plants to restore this section to its glory days. What has emerged is a thoroughly pleasant and romantic few blocks known as **Historic Properties**.

Crafts shops and boutiques fill former warehouses, a seafood restaurant overlooks the harbor, and a sailing schooner, a replica of the country's beloved Bluenose, waits down by the water to take you on summer tours of the harbor. The Bluenose was a working ship but it was also a racing champion of the Atlantic, regularly defeating New England vessels that came to claim her crown. You can see her in full flight on the back of a Canadian dime. When the Bluenose isn't waiting at the wharf, a regular cruise launch is. But if you want to get a less expensive peek at the harbor, which extends 16 miles inland from the sea, walk a few yards south and hop aboard the **Dartmouth ferry**.

It makes frequent crossings from Halifax to the more modern, though touristically uninteresting city of Dartmouth, on the other side. The ferry trip will cost you 25 cents.

Now you've finished with Halifax and the best of Nova Scotia lies ahead of you, all of it reachable over 5,700 miles of roads uncrowded even at the height of the summer season. The first thing to do is head for **Peggy's Cove**, just 27 miles southwest of the city over a new paved highway. Keep in mind as you drive there that you are about to see the perfect cliché of fishing villages, a place that has appeared on more calendars than the Queen. You'll recognize it immediately: Lobster traps stacked by a Fifth Avenue store window designer, buildings painted by the Group of Seven, expressions on the natives by Norman Rockwell, the whole thing put together by David Lean.

Yet, clichéd as it is, Peggy's Cove is actually one of nature's finest compositions. The sea is so violent here that fishing boats could not have found shelter except for an unexplained cut in the rocks that affords a tiny but snug harbor.

The houses that surround the cove where boats bob in the sunlight are in shades of matching pastels, and even the weatherbeaten fishing shacks are in good shape. The place is regarded as a national treasure and a commission guards against over-commercialization. In fact, the only bit we saw on our last visit was a seven-year-old in pigtails who had set up shop beside her house with a self-lettered sign saying "Sea Shells for Sale."

The only problem with Peggy's Cove is that it's just too perfect, too overexposed. There's no sense of discovery to it, none of the rewards of exploration that are the essence of a Maritimes adventure. Go and see it, then use it as a yardstick to the fishing villages you find for yourself. They won't be as quaint but they'll give you a better idea of what a Captains Courageous existence is all about. If you're the kind that wants to be led by the nose try one of the following:

Neil's Harbour, on the eastern tip of Cape Breton. It's all sagging wharfs and wind-scarred shacks. The homes of the 30 fishing families who eke out a living are scattered about the harbor, almost haphazardly. But you get the unmistakable impression that you've found the real thing here, a village where lobster fisherman pray for a "wind off" and find much of their own amusement in a remote corner of the world.

Lunenburg, an hour's drive southwest of Halifax, is world famous for the sailing ships it has built. The Bluenose came out of its shipyards, so did the Bounty that MGM used along with Marlon Brando in *Munity on the Bounty*. It has its own fishing fleet and a passel of homes which look as if they were painted yesterday.

Prospect is a tiny seaside hamlet even closer to Halifax than Peggy's Cove. "We've got everything Peggy's Cove has except the lighthouse," a native told us. Indeed it has.

Also take a look at **Arichat** and **Cheticamp** on Cape Breton – two French contenders, and **Little Harbour**, 50 miles east of Halifax. The latter is simply unforgettable when wrapped in fog or mist and it is one of several places along the coast where you can buy fresh lobster for a beachside boil during summer. The former two add an Acadian touch to your visit. **Arichat**, in the days of sail, sent ships out on two-year voyages around the world. Near **Cheticamp** you'll still find the old Acadian farmhouses with barns attached.

But our suggestion is that you head along any of the coastal roads until you spot a road leading down to the sea and simply follow it. The seaside hamlet

you discover on your own is the one you'll remember
most fondly. We guarantee it.

There are a couple of other requisites before you
can say you've "done" Nova Scotia. One is to drive
the **Cabot Trail**; the other is to visit **Louisbourg.**

The **Cabot Trail** is a 184-mile circle tour of the
Cape Breton highlands. It's a modern highway, but
still a roller-coaster of a road which clings to the
mountainside above an often angry sea. We'd driven
in bright sunlight and looked down on a sea of white
clouds which completely blotted out the waters below. The road takes you through the **Cape Breton
Highlands National Park**, one of the loveliest and
most rugged parks in North America, where chances
are excellent you'll spot some of the herds of white-
tailed deer that roam this whole area. Black bear, caribou, beaver, mink, even lynxes also call the park
home – but aren't nearly so easy to spot. There are
naturalist-led walks, seabird watching, and stunning
hiking trails with magnificent views.

The usual starting-off point for the Cabot Trail is
the resort town of **Baddeck**, which among other
things is the place where the great inventor Alexander Graham Bell made his summer home and where
he conducted many of his experiments in the pioneer
days of flight. From the town you can see the distant
purple hill where Bell lies buried and then visit what
is probably the best museum in the Maritimes, at
least in our books.

The **Alexander Graham Bell Musuem** contains
some 1,000 items dealing with the experiments which
Bell undertook in so many fields. For though he is
known to most of the world as the inventor of the
telephone, oldtimers around Baddeck will tell you he
was much more than that. At the turn of the century
his kites were a common sight flying over the bay; he
was a driving force behind the young group of pio-

neers who produced Canada's first manned flight at Baddeck in 1909.

In the museum you'll find many of the aeronautical experiments Bell conducted and the old, foot-pedal sewing machine which he used to transform Edison's plaything, called the phonograph, into a billion dollar recording industry. Edison had used tinfoil to record on, producing a scratchy, almost unintelligible sound. Bell, who as a teacher of the deaf knew about all there was to know about sound, was able to produce a much more suitable surface; and the record industry was on its way. His mind produced hydrofoils, systems for desalinating sea water, surgical probes, iron lungs, bullet detectors – and many of them can be seen here. On the way out, you'll find Bell's credo carved into a wall: "The inventor is a man who looks around upon the world and is not contented with things as they are. He wants to improve whatever he sees, he wants to benefit the world; he is haunted by an idea …." Admission to the Bell Museum is free.

Louisbourg is also on Cape Breton, 26 miles southeast of Sydney on Highway 22. Now connected to the rest of Nova Scotia by a causeway, Cape Breton is a mountainous and forested island settled after 1784 largely by Loyalists and Scots who thought they had discovered a New World edition of their highland homes. But it was French settlers who in 1713 began construction of **Fortress Louisbourg** as the mightiest military base in North America. Its construction was such a drain on the French treasury that Louis XV complained that he expected to wake up some morning and see it rising on the horizon of France. What he spent, however, was just a drop in the bucket compared with the cost of its reconstruction, a continuing multi-million dollar restoration of a magnitude found nowhere else in Canada – or in the rest of North America for that matter.

In a way, Louisbourg was one of the causes of the American Revolution. It was from here that the French preyed on New England shipping during wars between France and England. Then a daring raiding party of New Englanders seized the seemingly impregnable fortress, only to have it handed back to the French by a subsequent treaty. One can imagine the dissatisfaction this caused in Boston though Louisbourg was once again captured by the British in 1758 and demolished two years later. There it lay through more than two centuries, a remote and fogbound sheep pasture.

Reconstruction began in 1961, both as the country's major restoration project and as a plan to employ a large number of jobless coal miners whose plight had turned Cape Breton's economy into a disaster. They were retrained in 18th century stonecutting techniques, taught to hand-hew lumber and work in wrought iron, and then set to work restoring a fifth of the fortress, with a 1980 target date for completion. By 1969, the first phase of the reconstruction was completed when the 10-room Governor's Wing of the rebuilt Chateau St. Louis was opened to the public. The barracks of the King's Bastion, engineer's house and armorer's forge are all furnished in the period and with many of the mighty walls back in place. The fortress is open daily 9 A.M. to 8 P.M. from June 15 to Labor Day (check for the shorter hours in spring and fall) and closed Oct. 16 to May 15. Buses tour the sight from an adjoining visitor's center for a modest fee.

Other Nova Scotia stops you may enjoy include: **Annapolis Royal**, the capital of Nova Scotia from 1710 until the founding of Halifax. Seven miles from town you'll find a reconstruction of the first settlement in what is now Nova Scotia, **Port Royal Habitation**, Samuel de Champlain's ill-fated 1605 colony. This is a national historic site and admission is free. It's open 9 A.M. to 8 P.M. June 15 to Labor Day, check for shorter hours the rest of the year.

St. Ann's, if Scottish blood flows in your veins. Gaelic College there is the only one in North America. The campus can be visited Monday to Saturday from early July to mid-August. There's a highland festival in the first full week of August and a museum dedicated to highland pioneers and to Angus MacAskill, the 7-foot, 9-inch giant who was a legend throughout Nova Scotia.

Pictou, where a lobster carnival is held on the first weekend in July. The Micmac Museum, two miles east of town has Indian relics from the 17th century. Small admission.

Grand Pre, the principal site of the expulsion of the Acadians, mentioned previously. A national historic park contains a statue of Evangeline and a bust of Longfellow who told her story to the world.

HOW TO GET THERE Air Canada supplies frequent service to Halifax from major eastern Canadian cities and from Boston and New York. Eastern Provincial Airways supplies service to various Nova Scotia cities from other parts of the Maritimes and Montreal. Air Canada also supplies overseas service betweeen Halifax and London, England.

Most people, however, arrive by automobile, often aboard the car-carrying ferries that serve the province. Ferries from Portland and Bar Harbor, Maine, serve Yarmouth and ferries from Saint John, N.B., sail to Digby. Visitors arriving through Prince Edward Island can take a ferry from Wood Islands on P.E.I. to Caribou, N.S. Not all ferries run all year but summer service is frequent. The land route arrival point is along the Trans-Canada Highway across the narrow isthmus from New Brunswick. You enter the province near Amherst where a piper welcomes visitors during summer at the tourist information center.

GETTING AROUND There are 5,700 miles of paved roads, a third of them following the coast. No matter where you are in the province you're no more than 35 miles from the sea. The provincial government has outlined seven scenic routes, marked with signs and shown on provincial maps.

WHERE TO STAY The main concentration of large hotels is in the Halifax-Dartmouth metropolitan area. Best known is the aging but refurbished **Nova Scotian,** Hollis St., a Canadian National hotel, whose 316 rooms start at $28 single and $36 double. Personally, among the biggies, we prefer rival Canadian Pacific's ultra-modern **Chateau Halifax**, Scotia Square, from $32 single and $38 double. Other major hotels in the downtown area are the **Lord Nelson**, corner of South Park St., and Spring Garden Rd., and **Citadel Inn**, 1960 Brunswick St. The **Holiday Inn**, 99 Wyse Rd., across the harbor in Dartmouth has rates starting at $23 single, $27 double. Elsewhere the government-owned **Keltic Lodge** at Igonish Beach in Cape Breton is a very special place, situated on a cliff overlooking the sea. Daily rates, with meals, start at $45 single, $67 double. **The Pines**, also now owned by the province, exudes old-time charm at Digby, for rates starting at $43 single, $68 double (all meals included).

In most of the province you will need to depend on motels, guest houses and campgrounds for overnight stays though. There is an active farm vacation program for visitors who wish to book in with a rural family. You can get a list of farms taking guests by writing the Nova Scotia Department of Agriculture, Kentville, N.S.

Keep in mind that all kinds of accommodation are in short supply during summer. If you don't have reservations, start looking around early for a place to stay. An excellent chain of **Wandlyn Motor Inns** has properties in several parts of Nova Scotia with double rooms available from $22 up. Most motels, many of them family-run, cost slightly less than that. Tourist homes charge from $10 double. Camping fees at most provincial parks are $3 a day, with private campgrounds charging slightly higher. You can get a priced list to all Nova Scotia accommodation from the Department of Tourism, P.O. Box 130, Halifax, N.S.

WHERE TO EAT The pickings are a bit slim if you're in search of really memorable dining; there's nothing in the Maritimes to touch the best in Montreal, Quebec or Toronto. But we have no hesitation recommending **Fat Frank's**, 5411 Spring Garden Rd., as a top find in Halifax. We first met Fat Frank (Metzger) eight years ago when he was operating Fat Frank's Very Small Restaurant with only six tables in downtown Halifax. Each morning he went personally to shop for vegetables, each afternoon to shop for fish and meat. Now he runs a very big and very expensive restaurant – but he still takes that kind of care. His oyster bisque, house paté and baked brook trout get rave revues from most customers. Good, though expensive wine list.

The **Evangeline Room** of the Hotel Nova Scotian was once looked on as the best place to eat in Halifax. Some say it still is. Skip the usual hotel menu items and ask for the lobster or salmon. This is one place where they really are fresh.

Another Nova Scotia restaurant that has become famous, simply through word of mouth, is **Harris' Seafood Restaurant** in **Yarmouth**. Clara Harris, the founder, was the wife of a lobster fisherman who used to bring some of his customers home to dinner. They raved about the way she cooked seafood and one even insisted on backing her in a restaurant venture. Now people from Boston to Sydney stop there whenever they pass through Yarmouth. Prices are moderate.

We haven't had a chance to try the **Clipper Cay** in Halifax's waterfront Historic Properties (mentioned previously) but a Haligonian whose palate we trust says it's by far the best of the new restaurants in town.

WHERE TO SHOP Handicrafts, especially ship models, driftwood creations, handmade jewelry and hooked rugs are of high repute. Try any of the following for first-rate souvenirs. **Cooperative Artisanale de Cheticamp** – at Cheticamp, of course; the **Sea Chest Boutique** in Halifax, the many shops in Halifax's **Historic Properties** area; the **Apple Barrel** in Grand Pre.

NIGHTLIFE Major hotels in Halifax offer entertainment in their cocktail lounges. Harness racing is by far the biggest spectator sport with meets taking place in Truro, Halifax and Sydney from mid-May to the end of October. The **Neptune Theatre** in Halifax has a repertory company with a reputation that is the envy of theater groups in much larger cities. Otherwise, rest up for the next day's touring.

WHERE TO GET HELP WITH YOUR TRIP The Nova Scotia Department of Tourism, Travel Division, P.O. Box 130, Halifax, N.S. is the best source for maps, accommodation guides, hunting and fishing regulations and other specialized information pamphlets.

If your trip is going to take you to other parts of Canada, too, contact the Canadian Government Office of Tourism, 150 Kent St., Ottawa.

NEW BRUNSWICK

"The province of the Loyalists."

Half the travellers who come to New Brunswick on a typical summer day keep right on going. By nightfall, most of them are either ensconced beside one of the rolling sand beaches of Prince Edward Island or set to explore the rocky, lighthouse-dotted coast of Nova Scotia. Actually, New Brunswick offers these attractions, too. But to the casual observer this largest (at 28,280 square miles) of the Maritime provinces seems much more involved with its interior than with its 1,400 miles of seacoast. And, in fact, most New Brunswickers do make their livelihood from the forests that cover 80% of the province, the mines interspersed among the spruce and the rich farmlands that follow various river valleys. U.S. visitors will find this rugged province much more like Maine than its Maritimes neighbors.

But stop a day or two on a visit to eastern Canada and you will be rewarded. For New Brunswick offers a rich tourist mix. More than 100 covered "kissing bridges" still cross her many rivers, whitetail deer and black bear roam her woods and salmon still leap from her streams. The pace is slow, the culture rich and the history varied. The population of 620,000 is split more or less evenly between French and English – though even in totally French areas enough English is spoken to enable a visitor to get by without a language degree.

New Brunswick started out as a part of Acadia, the name the French gave the Maritimes after Champlain explored this region at the beginning of the 17th century. In 1604, he discovered the Saint John River and attempted a colony near what is now the New Brunswick-Maine border. Later Dutchmen from New Amsterdam and Puritans from Boston arrived but the French continued to dominate throughout the 17th century aided by the terms of treaties signed in Europe.

In the mid-18th century, the British wrested control of the Maritimes from France and in 1784 split Nova Scotia and New Brunswick into separate colonies to handle an influx of settlers from Britain and some 15,000 "Loyalists" from the American colonies. These people, who decided to stay loyal to the Crown after the American Revolution, were to dominate life in Saint John, New Brunswick's largest city, and in Fredericton, its capital. In 1849, Britain granted New Brunswick a fair degree of self-government and in 1867 it reluctantly joined the new Canadian confederation.

WEATHER REPORT Summer is definitely the best time for a visit. Days are generally in the low 70s (higher in interior towns and cities) and nights are usually cool enough for comfortable sleeping even without air conditioning. Don't forget – temperatures throughout Canada are now given in Celsius degrees. Zero is freezing point, 20 degrees C is room temperature and 30 C is a hot summer day. Expect rainy days any time of year.

WHAT TO SEE Our choice as the top spectacle in New Brunswick is the **Saint John River**, an idyllically beautiful stream flowing north to south for the whole length of the province. The marvellous thing about this river as far as the visitor is concerned is that the Trans-Canada Highway follows its banks for much of its journey. This section of "Main Street Canada" sometimes skirts a hill overlooking the river and sometimes runs right along its banks. Here and there you will find free car ferries which will take you across the river to follow the road on the opposite shore until you switch back on another ferry. Here, an oak leans into the river as if to drink; there, some cattle do the same thing. Mind you, the pulp industry which is so important to New Brunswick's economy has done its best to pollute the river but even that doesn't detract from its tranquil beauty.

At **Grand Falls**, you can stop to look at the 135-foot waterfall that gives the town its name. It can best be seen from a steel bridge that crosses the gorge itself. At **Hartland** you come on the world's longest covered bridge – 1,282 feet across the Saint John. The river also takes you to Fredericton and Saint John.

Fredericton vies with Victoria as the prettiest city in Canada. It's a small town with big league attractions, many of them endowments from Lord Beaverbrook, the British press baron who was a wartime confidant of Winston Churchill.

"The Beaver," as he was known in these parts, grew up in New Brunswick and always looked on it as his native heath. Along the banks of the Saint John in Fredericton you'll find his pride and joy, the **Beaverbrook Art Gallery**. It may just be the best small art gallery in Canada. The most awesome painting in the place is a 10 by 13½-foot Salvador Dali depicting St. James riding his horse into heaven. There are more than two dozen paintings by Cornelius Krieghoff (most famous of the Canadian primitives), the preliminary sketches for Graham Sutherland's controversial portrait of Churchill, and some water colors by Sir Winston himself. The gallery shows the

Beaver's preference for things English –
Gainsboroughs, Constables, Turners and Reynolds
all hold places of honor. Reynolds also painted the
portraits of King George II and Queen Charlotte
which hang in the plush assembly chamber of the
nearby legislative building. Across the road from the
gallery is another piece of Beaverbrook largesse, the
Playhouse theatre where you can take in productions
of Theatre New Brunswick throughout the year.
Within the same block is Fredericton's main hotel –
called the Lord Beaverbrook, naturally.

When you come out of the gallery, turn left and
take a stroll along the **Green**, which is what Fredericton calls its riverside park. This is a broad, lazy section of the Saint John where willows weep into the
river and elm-lined streets of frame, gabled mansions
run off in the opposite direction. Across from the
park is a gem of a church, **Christ Church Cathedral**, a
Gothic structure with a clock tower that predates Big
Ben in London. When Christ Church was consec-
rated in 1853 it was the first new cathedral established on British soil since the Norman Conquest.
What's more it's said to be haunted. Mrs. John Med-
ley, a nurse who was trained by Florence Nightingale
is said to roam the place in the togs of her trade –
though people who claim to have seen her can't say
whether or not she's carrying a lamp. Beaverbrook
also donated buildings to the **University of New
Brunswick** in Fredericton, as well as valuable papers
which include first editions by Dickens and H.G.
Wells. You can see these free Monday to Friday, 8:30
A.M. to 10 P.M. Beaverbrook, by the way, was made a
lifetime chancellor of this ancient (1785) place of
learning. He handed out honorary doctorates at will
and whim, including one to the late John Fitzgerald
Kennedy.

From Fredericton it's a 68-mile drive downriver to

the city of **Saint John**, one of the drabbest in Canada but one of the most historic. It was founded by United Empire Loyalists in 1783 and two years later it became Canada's first incorporated city. The area around **King Square**, the heart of the old town, grows on you despite the overall shabbiness of the city. Across from the square is an ancient burial ground with some of the stones dating back to the late 1700s and nearby is the **Old City Market**, which has been doing business daily at the same old stands for more than a century. It carries mainly fresh meat and vegetables but local Indians display hand-woven baskets and other handicrafts. The **New Brunswick Museum**, 277 Douglas St., is staid but houses a splendid collection of ship's models. (In summer it's open daily 10 A.M. to 9 P.M. Admission, 50 cents for adults, 25 cents for children and students).

The Reversing Falls, one of the phenomena caused by the 30-foot tides on the Bay of Fundy, is likely the city's most popular tourist attraction – but don't get the idea it's a showstopper. At low tide, the Saint John River flows down to the sea over a 15-foot rapids. But at high tide the water is forced back upstream in a whirling torrent. The falls are 2¼ miles southwest of the city center on Highway 1. There's a tourist bureau, with a viewing deck, beside the rapids.

There are a couple of other interesting creations of the Fundy tides, among the highest and most powerful in the world. At **Hopewell Cape**, near the mouth of the Petitcodiac River, the action of the tides has carved mushroom-like columns from the soft limestone – flower pots, they call them – with fir and balsam growing on top. At high tides they look like islands but at low tide you can descend the cliffs at the **Rocks Provincial Park** to look up and photograph these wierd creations. Watch the time when you're at the bottom. It's safe from two hours before low tide to two hours after – then the rapidly rising waters can be dangerous.

The other freak of nature produced by the tide occurs right in the city of **Moncton**, also on the **Petitcodiac River**. At low tide, the river becomes a mud flat clustered with sea gulls. Then the tide rushes up the river and, according to official description, turns the mud flat into "a roaring torrent of muddy waters." In fact that has happened only a few times in history. Usually that "roaring torrent" is an advancing ripple that doesn't even make the seabirds scatter. The whole thing gets our vote as the best-named tourist attraction in Canada – the **Tidal Bore**.

Bore Park, in the heart of Moncton, has a clock which tells you when this phenomenon will occur each day. The kids from town usually head for the park at the appointed hour too, not to look at the Bore but to watch the chins drop when tourists see what it's all about.

Just off the Trans-Canada at Moncton, **Magnetic Hill** is an optical illusion which has been fooling people for more than a century. You pull off onto Magnetic Hill road and drive to a white post at the foot of a hill. Then you put the car in neutral and release the brake – but don't take your hands off the steering wheel. You'll need that as the car seemingly rolls backwards up the hill. There's nothing magnetic about the hill, of course, just an illusion created by the contours of the surrounding countryside. Even the brook beside the road appears to run uphill. Not worth going too far out of your way to see – but certainly a notch above the Tidal Bore.

Fundy National Park, on the coast between Saint John and Moncton, is a prime Maritimes destination. Embracing 80 square miles of forested hills and valleys overlooking the Bay of Fundy, the park is crisscrossed by 58 miles of hiking trails, has a spectacular nine-hole golf course with the first tee on a 200-foot plateau overlooking the sea and much of the park, a riding stable, heated salt water pool, interior lakes and a wood filled with wildlife. Cliffs front much of the eight miles of coastline within the park, though there are beaches at **Herrin Cove** and **Point Wolfe**. But be forewarned: the bay's waters are frigid. Do your beachcombing along the seashore, your swimming in the heated pool or one of the lakes. The park also operates a summer school of arts and crafts.

Fishing in the park's lakes and streams is exceptional – you can even take the daily limit of 10 fish a day seriously. A fishing license is required, boat rentals are available on park lakes. Rental cottages, a motel and campgrounds are available in the park and there are clusters of cottages and motels at Alma on its eastern fringe. The park is open all year but busiest in the summer when holidayers show up from many parts of eastern Canada and the U.S. You can make inquiries about accommodation by writing to the Superintendent, Fundy National Park, Alma, N.B.

There are also 18 provincial parks in New Brunswick including the spectacular **Mactaquac**, built around the 60-mile-long headpond created on the Saint John River by a huge hydro dam. You won't find a prettier piece of riverside property this side of the Rhine and we would rate the 18-hole golf course at Mactaquac as the best in the province. There are two man-made beaches, sailboats and, alas, powerboats too. The restaurant in the park lodge serves some of the best seafood in New Brunswick. There are nearly 300 campsites available. One warning, the park is only 15 miles northwest of Fredericton and gets heavy local use. Arrive early in the morning if you're counting on a campsite.

Another national park is being developed on the

Northumberland Strait on the northeast coast of the province. **Kouchibouguac** is far from complete but there are some 150 campsites and facilities for boating and swimming. This will be a showstopper of a place when completed as the waters here are especially warm in summer – in the 70s most days.

Right now the warmest beaches are found around **Shediac** . . . also the best lobster. In July, this is the site of a seafood orgy, known as the **Shediac Lobster Festival**. By the way, when you're in this part of New Brunswick, you're in the heart of French-speaking Acadia. As in Quebec there has been an emerging awareness among people here of their French roots. Unfortunately, one direction this has taken is the scrawling of "En Francais" across English signs and "Arret" across stop signs. But don't let that worry you, the natives are friendly.

A quick and pleasant lesson in local history can be had by visiting **King's Landing**, 50 vintage buildings rebuilt into a community which might have existed between 1790 and 1870. Some hundred costumed characters show you around and there are oxcarts, a riverboat, oldtime gardens and a working sawmill with a 21-foot waterwheel to complete this step into the past. King's Landing is located 23 miles west of Fredericton on the Trans-Canada. Admission is $2.50 for adults, $1.25 for children. It's open daily, 10 A.M. to 7 P.M., May 29 – Sept. 12.

A similar historical village, depicting a French-speaking version of early life in the province is underway at **Caraquet** in the marshy lands of northern New Brunswick, the type of area into which some Acadians fled after the British expulsion.

The most popular seaside resort in the province is **St. Andrews**, a plushly preserved hamlet founded in 1784. Each year the same old families come back to rock on the porch of the rambling **Algonquin Hotel** and to feast on lobster dinners and wander amid buildings, most of which were erected before 1880 and 14 of which survive from the 1700s. Among the buildings of note are the white-framed Grenock Church, begun in 1822, and the handsome courthouse dating to 1840. The Bar Road lies under the ocean most of the time but at low tide you can use it to drive to nearby **Minister's Island**.

Close by are the **Fundy Isles**, the most famous of which is **Campobello**. This was the "beloved island" of Franklin Delano Roosevelt who spent his summers here from 1905 to 1921. His 34-room cottage is now a museum, the focal point of an international park. It was here that Roosevelt was stricken with infantile paralysis in 1921 – one of the interesting artifacts in the cottage is the makeshift stretcher used to carry him after he collapsed. Campobello can be reached by bridge from Lubec, Maine. **Grand Manan**, largest of the Fundy Isles, can be reached only by ferry from Blacks Harbor. This noted bird sanctuary, inhabited mostly by fishermen, is marked by dramatic seaside cliffs rising to 400 feet.

HOW TO GET THERE Air Canada serves New Brunswick with flights to Saint John, Moncton and Fredericton, from major cities in Eastern Canada. Eastern Provincial Airways supplies service from other points in the Maritimes and from Quebec City. Ferries from Prince Edward Island arrive at Cape Tormentine and from Digby, Nova Scotia, at Saint John.

But most people arrive by car, entering the province from Quebec at Edmundston and from neighboring Maine at several points but mainly through the Calais-St. Stephen border crossing.

WHERE TO STAY The Lord Beaverbrook Hotel in Fredericton, with 210 rooms and recently refurbished is the best-known hotel in the province, and a favourite with out-of-town members of the New Brunswick legislature. Singles start at $20, doubles at $24. We prefer the **Diplomat Hotel** on Woodstock Rd. or the **Wandlyn**, just off the Trans-Canada. They're less stuffy and both have good dining rooms. The latter offers doubles starting at $26 and the former doubles starting at $30. As in the case of Nova Scotia, the Wandlyn chain is found in several New Brunswick centers and is often a notch above the competition. In Saint John, the **Admiral Beatty**, under renovation after having fallen on bad times, in the heart of town; the **Holiday Inn**, Waterloo and Crown Sts., ($24 single, $29 double); **Wandlyn,** 609 Rothesay Ave., ($23 single, $28 double); and **Colonial Inn,** 175 City Rd., ($28 single, $30 double), are your best bet.

Moncton is a major accommodation center, with the **Hotel Beausejour**, 750 Main St. the top pick. Single rates for rooms, which are alternately done in Acadian and Loyalist decor, start at $28 doubles at $36. **The Algonquin** at St. Andrews is a prestige resort with prestige prices, starting at $49 single, with two meals included. Motel rates across the province start at about $15 and range up to $25. When renting a cabin for the night, make sure you inspect it first. Some were designed for rough-and-ready hunters only. Guest house accommodation is available just about everywhere and is a good budget bet in this part of Canada.

WHERE TO EAT We once asked a New Brunswick woman who had written a guide book where the best place to eat in Fredericton was. She replied: "There isn't a restaurant in town that you could describe as best. They're all fairly ordinary." But let's put that straight. The restaurants of New Brunswick aren't real bummers; it's just that they generally lack distinctive decor or exceptional fare. Portions on the other hand are usually large and the price usually right. Here are some we have tried and liked: **Cy's,** 170 Main St., in Moncton is a bustling seafood restaurant where oyster, clams, sole or scallops won't cost you an arm and a leg. The other Moncton choices, **Chez Jean Pierre** and the **Windjammer** in the Hotel Beausejour offer elegant surroundings, elegant prices and seafood that is about on a par with Cy's. **Marshland's Inn** at Sackville has a long tradition of hearty, homecooked meals. In Fredericton, the **Diplomat Hotel** on Woodstock Rd., serves up modestly priced Cantonese food and the **Wandlyn Motel** dining room is where Fredericton people take their guests.

WHERE TO SHOP At Mactaquac Provincial Park, the **Opus Craft Village**, has studios for glass blowing, leatherwork, pottery and candle making. The quality is exceptionally high and most creations are offered for sale. Handicrafts have a long tradition in New Brunswick, especially weaving, ship models, hooked rugs and ceramics. The **Craft House** in Fredericton has a good display as does the **Sea Captain's Loft** in St. Andrews. There's a good handicraft center in the **Admiral Beatty Hotel** in Saint John.

NIGHTLIFE Cocktail lounges with nightly entertainment are found only in the larger hotels. Harness racing is the biggest single item of night entertainment – at Saint John, Moncton and Fredericton.

WHERE TO GET HELP WITH YOUR TRIP   Tourism New Brunswick, P.O. Box 12345, Fredericton, N.B. will supply accommodation guides, a tour book, and free maps.

PRINCE EDWARD ISLAND

"It needs only the nightingale."
Explorer Jacques Cartier after a brief stop on the
island.

Within half an hour's drive of downtown Charlottetown, a visitor to Prince Edward Island can go dig-
ging for clams, swim in the warmest salt waters north
of the Carolinas, beachcomb amid sand dunes that
hide him from the world, or sit down to a plate of
strawberries picked just an hour before and smoth-
ered in thick, farm cream. No wonder this tiny island
province manages to attract half a million visitors
each summer. It's the closest Canada comes to having the ideal family playground.

Canadians realized this even before Columbus
sailed to the Americas. The Micmac Indians regularly made the nine-mile crossing from mainland
New Brunswick to cool off in summer. They called
the island Abegweit – "the home cradled on the
waves." Jacques Cartier claimed the 2,184-square-
mile island for France in 1534 and christened it Isle
St. Jean. After it was ceded to Britain, it was renamed
Prince Edward Island in honor of the man who was
to become Queen Victoria's father. Now just about
everyone calls it P.E.I.

They call it other things, of course. "The million-
acre potato patch," "the farm sandwiched between
two beaches," "Canada's biggest campground."
Mostly it's a gentle place, rolling farmland, rippling
brooks, tidy gabled houses, broad beaches lapped by
waters that stay in that much coveted 70s neighborhood most summer days. For the holidayer, P.E.I.

offers everything in an outdoor life except drama. No
rock-ribbed coves, no sheer cliffs, few violent seas.
Almost as green as Ireland itself – though with
patches of blood red soil sometimes showing through
– it is as pint-sized as Delaware – just 140 miles long
and from 4 to 40 miles wide. You are rarely more
than a 15-minute drive from Canada's best ocean
beaches. Some find the scenery bland and the people
overly conservative but just about everyone appreci-
ates the pace of life here – low gear all the way.

Someone's either a native born "Spud Islander" or
he's "from away." And if you're "from away" – no
matter where that happens to be – you are never
really accepted as a true islander – though you'll always be treated politely and get a friendly smile from
just about everyone. They tell the story of one old
spinster who spent 85 years guarding her sinful secret
from her neighbors – the fact that she wasn't born on
the island but brought there as a six-month-old baby.

Islanders have different favorites among the
beaches that almost continously circle P.E.I., but
most people "from away" make a beeline for **Prince
Edward Island National Park**, an eight-square mile
seaside playground that extends for 25 miles along
the north shore on the Gulf of St. Lawrence. Beautiful broad beaches, dunes patched with sea grasses,
red sandstone headlands dominate most of this shore.
Supervised beaches are found at **Cavendish**, **North
Rustico** (probably the most picturesque fishing village
on the island), **Brackley**, **Stanhope** and **Dalvay**. There
are more than 500 campsites in the national park and
dozens of private campgrounds and cottages on the
fringes. But keep in mind that this is eastern
Canada's most popular ocean playground. Some cottages are booked a year in advance and people jams
get bad enough to drive some vacationers to remoter
provincial parks or private campgrounds located far

from the national park – if "far" can be used to describe a location on this overgrown potato patch.

Charlottetown, on the south shore, is a medium-
sized town which serves as the island's capital city. It
has a large place in Canadian history for it was here,
in 1864, that delegates from the British North
American colonies met to plan the confederation that
led to the birth of Canada three years later. With typical conservatism and a mistrust of mainlanders
which remains even today, host P.E.I. balked at join-
ing confederation until 1873, six years after the
others. **Province House**, the stone Georgian building
where the 1864 conference was held, is a shrine that
every Canadian who comes to the island visits and
the chamber where the Fathers of Confederation met
is now a museum with the original table and chairs
still in place.

There is a 50th anniversary plaque on the wall
which says – perhaps on shakier grounds these days:
"Providence Being Their Guide, They Builded Better
Than They Knew."

Instead of putting up another plaque for the 100th
anniversary of the 1864 meeting, they built the $5.6
million **Confederation Centre**, almost in the shadow
of the room where the country's 34 founders met.

For much of the year, with fewer than 120,000 islanders to patronize it, the Confederation Centre often appears like a massive mausoleum – an ultra-
modern version of the pyramids – built to inter the
worthy fathers. But in summer the centre's theater
jumps as the site of the highly successful **Charlottetown Festival** in which a musical version of *Anne of
Green Gables* returns each year to play to packed
houses. Anne, though a storybook creation of P.E.I.'s
noted author, the late Lucy Maud Montgomery, is as
real in the minds and hearts of islanders as any true
life heroine. They love the little redhead with a pas-

sion that no one "from away" should challenge, even in jest.

WEATHER REPORT   P.E.I. shares much the same weather as the rest of the seaside areas of the Maritimes. Summer days are in the low 70s (20s C) and nights some 15 degrees cooler. On average, however, it does get more hours of summer sunshine than its sister provinces – about 245 hours in a typical July, for example.

WHAT TO SEE   **Province House** and the **Confederation Centre**, which contains a library and art gallery as well as a theater, are both worth a look. The drugstore across the street is Canada's oldest, dating from 1810, and nearby **Rogers Hardware** still stocks china chamber pots as it did way back then. Initial attempts are underway to turn the area into one of those nostalgic "old towns" where artists and craftsmen will ply their trades. But when we last looked, these efforts had met with only modest success.

St. Dunstan's Basilica, with its intricate rose window and three slender spires, and **St. Peter's Anglican Cathedral**, with its fine murals, are two of the nicer churches in the Maritimes. Outside Charlottetown, plastic playlands, car museums, wax museums and fairylands have sprung up to entertain the crowds of summer. Most are worth bothering with only when the children have driven you to the breaking point or the rains have driven you from your tent.

But we think you'll like **Woodleigh Replicas** at **Burlington**, a short hop from the north shore beaches. It's a family-built garden of famous buildings from Dunvegan Castle to the Tower of London and Anne Hathaway's Cottage, all built to painstaking scale from original plans. Admission is $1.50 for adults, children under 12 free. Open daily except Sundays. **The farm home**, which may or may not have been the setting Lucy Maud Montgomery had in mind when she wrote *Anne of Green Gables* is furnished in traditional island style, from its green gables on down. It's located near Cavendish in the national park right beside the park's lush golf course. Admission is free and there are guides to show you around. You can get a pamphlet outlining lesser, paid and unpaid, attractions from the Tourist Information Division, P.O. Box 940, Charlottetown, P.E.I.

HOW TO GET THERE Air Canada and Eastern Provincial Airways both fly to the island from major eastern cities. But most people arrive on the car ferries which make frequent crossings in summer. Canadian National ferries sail to the island from Cape Tormentine, N.B., arriving at Borden. A second service runs between Caribou, N.S., and Woods Islands, P.E.I. The Trans-Canada Highway crosses the island between the two ferry ports and there are 1,800 miles of eminently driveable roads, criss-crossing the island.

WHERE TO STAY When islanders talk about "the hotel," they're invariably referring to the **Hotel Charlottetown**, Kent and Pownal Sts., the closest thing available to a big city hostelry and a comfortable, old place at that. Rates for a double start at $28. Other centrally located Charlottetown digs include: the **Inn On The Hill**, 150 Euston St., from $24; **MacLaughlan's Motel**, 238 Grafton St., from $20, and the **Kirkwood Motor Hotel**, 455 University Ave., from $28. **Dalvay-by-the-Sea** at Dalvay Beach is the island's most elegant resort, housed in a turn-of-the-century mansion. Rates, including meals, start at $44. Family-run motels are found along the Trans-Canada and clustered around Summerside, the second "city."

Many island farms now accept guests, for as little as $8 per couple, with lower rates for children. Most of these are located within a few miles of a beach. You can get a list from the tourist information office (see above).

By the way, because it is so compact, P.E.I. runs the best government tourist service available in Canada. Tourist officials have their own radio system to keep visitors up-to-date on available accommodation and there is a highly successful Dial-the-Island reservation service which has been running for many years. On your way, in neighbouring New Brunswick or Nova Scotia, just dial the toll-free number, 1-800-565-7421, and they'll find you a place to stay.

WHERE TO EAT   We think the lobster church suppers at **New Glasgow** and **St. Ann** held every evening during summer, are the best seafood value available on the island. For about $8 you get a full-course meal – lobster, home-grown vegetables, homemade pies – the works. Formal dining isn't generally memorable, but **Minnie's,** 130 St. Peter's Rd., Charlottetown, as unpretentious as its name would suggest, dishes up marvellous scampi and sole – if you can eat anything else after the chowder. A good meal with wine won't cost more than $14 to $16, high for the island but moderate for what you get. The **Canton Cafe,** 73 Queen St., used to be the only restaurant worth mentioning in Charlottetown and it's still good. The dining room at the **Hotel Charlottetown** is modestly priced and more than acceptable. **Lobster Shanty North** at **Montague** is also good.

WHERE TO SHOP   The P.E.I. Craftsmen's Council has a Charlottetown outlet known as the **Island Crafts Shop**, 31 Queen St. Quilts, pottery, woodcarving and ship's models are offered. You can get a list of people producing handicrafts for sale from the tourist information office (see below).

WHERE TO GET HELP WITH YOUR TRIP   Write to the Tourist Information Division, P.O. Box 940, Charlottetown, P.E.I. for maps, accommodation guides, fishing and hunting regulations and other specialized information.

QUEBEC

"Quebec is the most interesting thing by much that I have seen on this continent ..."

Matthew Arnold, 1884.

And so, for many, it remains. It has been a special place for English-speaking tourists for generations because its French language and heritage, make Quebec something like a foreign country. But at the same time, a foreign country in which you feel secure. English is understood and spoken, the familiar products are in the stores, the same news is on television and radio. It's like both going away and staying home at the same time.

Today there's a dramatic new dimension. Or rather, a heightening of an old, long-muted one. While you stand among the reminders of the past, the heirlooms of Quebec's nearly four centuries of European settlement, history is being made again, in ways that may reshape or destroy Canada or, indeed, change North America.

Many Quebeckers, who feel they and their ancestors have been uncomfortable and out of place in the Canadian confederation, want independence from the rest of Canada. In November, 1976, a provincial government was elected which is pledged to the separation of Quebec from Canada. Federalists, in and outside Quebec, are fighting just as hard to convince French-speaking Quebeckers that their future, and that of Canada, lies in continued union.

It is an exciting drama being played out in the narrow streets of old Quebec City, against the backdrop of the Parliament buildings in Ottawa, in the quaint villages of the Gaspé, in the bustling metropolitan offices of Montreal.

The battle for the minds and emotions of Quebeckers is being waged more than 200 years after Britain's Wolfe slipped with his soldiers up the heights at Quebec to defeat Montcalm on the Plains of Abraham, and make the British the possessors of this continent. France formally ceded away its claims in 1763, four years after that battle.

And it's going on just a little over a century since the U.S. Civil War, in which Americans worked out, in blood and combat, the future course of their union.

The battle in Quebec is non-violent and don't let it keep you away. Indeed, the attempt of Quebeckers, particularly the young, to become "masters in our own house," inside or outside of confederation, has made the province an even more interesting place to visit.

The province retains its grace and its courtesy to visitors. But what has happened in the last few years is a cultural flowering and an increase in self-confidence.

French-speaking Quebec is not really France, nor quite American, nor Canadian in the same sense as the other provinces. It is, simply, Quebec. It has drawn from the others. But it has its own culture, its own music and poets and writers, its own ways – and vibrant those ways are.

If you have a conception of Quebec as a little bit of France, populated by lovable artisans turning out wood carvings in quaint villages, modify it. There are craftsmen who turn out magnificent carvings and ceramics and fabrics, and there are quaint villages, and they are among the charms of the province.

But consider these facts: Quebec is Canada's biggest province, with 594,860 square miles. You could put France in it, and the United Kingdom, and Texas, and still have room for part of New England. But 75% of that vast area is uninhabited, and 80% of Quebec's 6.5 million residents live in cities. More than 80% of them are French-Canadians, and the province has the flair and liveliness that goes with the Gallic heritage. Quebec is fun.

Language is a major source of controversy. English and French are the official languages of Canada. French-speaking Canadians, led by the provincial government, are making French the primary language in Quebec. Language rights are important to them; many Francophones see English as the symbol of the way in which, they feel, English-speaking imperialists held them subject, especially in the marketplace.

However, most Quebeckers, including the most ardent separatists, are fluent in English as well. Quebeckers are hospitable. They enjoy having guests. An obvious visitor virtually never encounters discourtesy or hostility because he has difficulties with the French language.

Quebec is history. Reminders of the past are everywhere. In cobblestone streets. In the walls of old Quebec. On the long strips of farms which run down to the St. Lawrence River, laid out so each farm has its own narrow bit of waterfront. In the baronial Anglo mansions of Westmount and country estates in the Eastern Townships.

Quebec has the lovely patina of age. New France (the original name of the province) was first visited by a white man, as far as we know, in 1534, when Jacques Cartier stepped ashore on the Gaspé Peninsula in the Gulf of St. Lawrence and claimed the entire territory for the King of France. Canada's first vehicular highway was opened in 1734 on the north

shore of the St. Lawrence. Today a four-lane highway, the Trans-Canada, runs the 170 miles from
Montreal to Quebec City on the south shore. If you
can, skip it and stay on Highway 2 on the north
shore, tracing the original route through villages centuries old. You will also see the grandeur of nature in
Quebec, the barren places, the wooded hills, the lakes
and rivers and mountains.

Quebec has dignity, and sophistication. Its restaurants in Quebec City and Montreal are unsurpassed
in North America, ranging from high French cuisine
to hearty peasant fare, from escargots to thick pea
soup. It is gay with Gallic laughter, and yet its singers
and poets can tear away at your heart.

A new society, where the priest no longer rules the
village, and youth sees the Church as often irrelevant,
Quebec has thousands of beautiful old churches as
part of its heritage. Quebec is age and youth, back-
woods and urbane, sophisticated and rugged, delicate
and boisterous, filled with intensity and old-world
civility.

Enjoy.

MONTREAL

"Some Canadians pray that when Gabriel blows his bugle, they'll go to Heaven. Others prefer Montreal."

Include us in ... but let's admit that if we do get our way, one old saying had better be wrong. We'll have to find a way to take it with us. Money, that is. Take plenty along to Montreal. There are, it is true, many ways to cut corners on your spending in Canada's most glamorous city. But if you are going to cut loose anywhere, here is the place. You can aways buy a Big Mac at home. But there is no Chez Bardet carre d'agneau (rack of lamb) in Medicine Hat, and the Beaver Club doesn't deliver its Malpeque oysters to Peoria.

Montreal is Canada's largest and most joyous city. More than half its 3 million people are French-speaking, which makes Montreal the biggest French-speaking city in the world outside of Paris.

Certain qualities symbolize many Canadian cities: Toronto is money, Fredericton is propriety and graciousness, Vancouver is youth and breathtaking scenery. But Montreal is just about everything. Montreal is sexy and domesticated, hard-working but torn by labor problems, stingy and spendthrift. It is high fashion and graciousness and old money and young trends and swinging discos, laughter and a Gallic shrug at petty annoyances. It is Canada's first metropolis and history is in the air around you; it is hills and river, mansions and slums, high cuisine and bourgeois food and the best delicatessens in Canada.

An island filled with trees, on the ground it is silver-grey from the local stone used in its buildings, from the air a verdant green. Once a city with a decaying center, known as Canada's vice capital, it still has swinging night clubs. But in the summer, like workaholic housewives, civic workers hang plants from light posts, plant 15,000 trees along streets, keep downtown roads and sidewalks swept startlingly clean of litter.

Montreal has problems. Taxes are high and reform politicians say the city administration has allowed the plumbing to go bad and dry rot to set in at the foundations, while polishing up the parlor for the world to come in to the 1976 Olympics and other attractions. But in the Montreal the tourist sees, it is virtually impossible to hunt up a bad meal or a homely girl.

We think of a woman who lives across the street from Olympic Stadium. For five years she had endured construction noises and dust as the stadium was built, eating into the park across from her once-quiet little street. Then hundreds of thousands of people milled about during the 1976 Olympics. She thought it was great. "We have the whole world out there on our doorstep." That's a Montreal attitude.

A word for Montreal is big-league. Within the last two decades, it has: Opened one of the most modern subway systems in the world, the Metro, where rubber-tired cars glide silently at 50 miles an hour and people come to admire the muraled, artistically designed stations; conducted a World's Fair, the 1967 Expo which celebrated Canada's hundredth anniversary and which left as a legacy a permanent playground, Man and His World, which draws 3 million visitors a year; held the 1976 Olympics, the only Canadian city ever to host the summer games, again leaving the legacy of a 70,000-seat stadium and other magnificent, if obscenely costly, facilities; and opened the Place des Arts, one of North America's most compelling centers of concerts, dance and the other arts.

And, of course, in the sporting scene Montreal has the Canadiens, most successful of all National Hockey League teams; the Expos, first major league baseball team in Canada; the Alouettes, perennial contenders in the Canadian Football League; and major league harness racing at two tracks.

The French fact, the English presence: they dominate Montreal's history, its atmosphere, its way of life. Explorer Jacques Cartier was the first white man known to have come upon the wooded island in the St. Lawrence, with its Indian settlement called Hochelaga. That was in 1535. The name Montreal comes from Mount Royal, the mountain which dominates the island.

It was 107 years later that French philanthropists sent Paul de Chomedey, the Sieur de Maisonneuve – a name given to one of the city's main streets today – and 50 other colonists to establish an outpost of Christianity and save the heathen Iroquois. Religion doesn't matter as much in Montreal as it once did, but churches do. Religious buildings are among present-day historical treasures.

For more than two centuries after Cartier's arrival, Montreal was French. Some of the most romantic names in North American history came by: de la Salle, who settled Chicago; Cadillac, who founded Detroit; du Luth and Le Moyne.

But European wars spread to North America and in 1763 Great Britain took over all of what had been French Canada. During the American Revolution, Continental Army troops occupied Montreal for several months. Benjamin Franklin set up a printing press there and tried vainly to persuade Canadians to join the American cause; you can still visit the Chateau de Ramazay, where Franklin stayed and where General Benedict Arnold slept.

The Americans departed, and other tides of immigrants came: fur merchants, railroad builders (one of whom, born in a Wisconsin city, was knighted by the queen and is known as the peer who made Milwaukee famous), Victorian financiers and businessmen who built their mansions in places like Westmount and their warehouses downtown.

There were Irish laborers, and English and Scottish merchants, Jews driven from Europe, immigrants and refugees from many lands, and of course the majority, deeply rooted in and proud of their French heritage. They all made Montreal Canada's first truly cosmopolitan city.

Between the world wars, Montreal revelled, or wallowed, in another reputation. While its downtown decayed, the city gained a name for being wide open to the vices: gambling, prostitution, rackets. It was a natural center for bootleggers during prohibition.

Even after World War II, the city was struggling. But in 1954 a gang-busting prosecutor named Jean Drapeau came along to be elected mayor. For more than two decades since, he has led the city, working seven days a week, autocratic, austere, yet a dreamer.

During his time as mayor came the subway, Expo, the Place des Arts, the Olympics, downtown development such as the giant office and shopping complexes of Place Ville Marie and Place Desjardins, new hotels, a new skyline, the renovation of Old Montreal.

During the Olympics in 1976, the controversial games which had brought harsh criticism of spending and administration, the people of Drapeau's city cheered him. He said the city needed a breathing spell before pushing on to any new large projects. But everyone in Canada continued to wonder, what will

Drapeau do next? Whatever it is, it will be spectacular.

GETTING THERE Montreal is a transportation center and always has been, from its very beginnings when Canada's first peoples settled here. Modern voyageurs just use different craft, which doesn't mean you can't get here by boat. You can. Also by a score of airlines, rail, a half-dozen superhighways, bus or whatever. The city is headquarters for both the Canadian National and Canadian Pacific Railways, for Air Canada, and for the International Air Transport Association. It is an hour's direct flight from either New York city or Toronto, five hours by expressway to Toronto by car or nine hours to Detroit. It is on the Trans-Canada Highway to west and east. If you come from Toronto, the high speed Turbo or Rapido passenger trains are excellent; they offer a faster passage than by motor, comfort and good service.

If you fly in, get a flight that goes to Dorval Airport if you can, rather than the mammoth new Mirabel facility. Dorval is a 25-minute drive from downtown, Mirabel takes an hour. Comparable fares to downtown by airport bus and taxi are $3.25 and $11 from Dorval, $5 and $30 from Mirabel. The federal government, which operates Canada's airports, tries vigorously to make people love Mirabel. Not many people do.

GETTING AROUND It is remarkably easy to find your way in Montreal. Streets are laid out on a grid: main arteries run roughly north-south and east-west. Many are one-way. Numerous fine highways and expressways lead in and out of the city.

Street numbers run east and west from St. Laurent

Blvd., and north from the river. However, the real
center of the city for tourist action is the intersection
of Peel and St. Catherine Sts.

You'll find major hotels, night clubs, restaurants,
shopping, within a few blocks in each direction. To
the east are Olympic Park, Old Montreal and largely
Francophone residential areas. To the west are the
Forum, fashionable shopping malls and the mansions
of Westmount. To the north is Mount Royal.

Driving is no problem, once you let your nerves
settle. Montreal motorists are quick on both the gas
and the horn. Rush hour should be avoided. Cau-
tions: Quebec law compels use of seat belts by drivers
and passengers, under threat of fine; right turns
against red lights, which are legal in Ontario, are not
allowed here.

As a tourist in Montreal, use your car as little as
possible. If you are staying in the outskirts, it's a good
idea to park at the big publicly-owned lots at the ends
of the subway line, at Henri Bourassa station in the
north end or at Longeuil on the south shore, and use
public transit. There are 1,000 spaces at Henri Bourassa, for instance, at $1.50 a day.

Downtown, you'll pay $4 or more for the day at an
off-street parking lot. Short-term parkers are hit hard,
as much as 85 cents for each of the first two half-
hours.

Subway, or Metro as it is called in Montreal, is easily the best way of getting around. Montreal is proud
of its subway and keeps it sparkling clean. Charges
are laid if people are caught smoking in the station.
Metro trains are rubber-tired and quiet; they whip
along at 50 miles an hour. Subway stations, individu-
ally designed with murals, tapestries, special stone or
brickwork, are themselves tourist attractions.

There are two main lines and a spur line which
goes to **Man and His World** and on across the St.

Lawrence to Longueuil. Most of the tourist's world lies right on the subway lines: **Olympic Park**, the **Forum, Place des Arts, Old Montreal**, the Greenwich Village-like section of **St. Denis St.**, Montreal's famous miles of underground shopping malls and major hotels. Fares are 50 cents cash or 13 tickets for $5. This includes free transfer to bus lines covering Greater Montreal.

Taxicabs are plentiful and cab drivers are generally friendly and polite. During normal traffic it should cost you about $11 to get from Dorval airport to Peel and St. Catherine (it's $3.25 on airport buses), and a bit over $4 to get from downtown to Olympic Stadium. Be wary of rush hour. Cabs then take three times as long as the subway and meters tick rapidly along while you sit stalled in traffic.

Walking is an essential part of visiting Montreal. The city's streets are litter-free and they are also safe. Street violence is virtually unknown in the areas where tourists go. Montrealers are friendly and helpful to visitors.

But one essential word of caution. When you are on foot, there is only one way to approach a Montreal intersection and that is very carefully. The green light is supposed to give you the right of way. But don't count on it. Drivers are kinder than they used to be. They are turning soft. Some give the pedestrian a sporting chance. And some don't even aim at walkers. But again, don't count on it.

WEATHER In summer, bring shorts. In winter, wear boots. Montreal weather is like that of the northeastern United States, only more so. In July and August, the temperature can get up into the 90s Fahrenheit. (Don't expect to hear it described that way;

Canada has gone metric and measures temperatures in Celsius).

In winter, Montreal is one of the snowiest cities on earth. It gets more than 110 inches of snow each year, largely in February. Sometimes it seems to fall all at once. You'll probably see more fur coats in Montreal than in any other city you've been in. Even the men wear them. Some Montrealers become like moles in winter once they get downtown. They work indoors, eat, drink and shop underground.

LANGUAGE   Language is a hot issue in Canada, particularly in Quebec. In Quebec, a majority of the population is French Canadian. French is an official language of Canada and under the law is supposed to have equal status with English.

Many French-speaking Canadians are aggrieved by the failure of many English-speaking Canadians, who work and live in Quebec, to speak the language of the majority. English-speaking Quebeckers, in turn, feel threatened by this attitude and government policy which implements it. Caught in the middle are immigrants, many of whom tend towards English as the language of most of Canada.

Although there are many abrasions over language in the work-a-day world of Quebec, tourists needn't worry if they don't speak French. Montrealers seems to have a sixth sense for knowing who is a visitor, even if he doesn't wear odd shirts or talk in funny accents. Virtually all French-speaking Montrealers are fluently bilingual and even those who are most militant on the language question will converse in English with visitors.

It is both polite and useful, however, to make an effort to use some common French words and phrases, even if only to say *bonjour* (hello), *merci*, (thank

you) or *pardon* (excuse me). It's safer, too – if the sign
says *arret*, you'd better stop. Generally, street signs
give the message in both languages.

You will learn a few words quickly from their use
on signs or store fronts. Some samples are *defense de
fumer* (no smoking), *ouvert* (open) and *fermé* (closed),
libre (free) and *occupé* (occupied), *caisse* (cash or
cashier), *auberge* (inn), *coiffeur* (hairdresser), *magasin*
(shop), *supermarché* (supermarket), *église* (church).
Sens unique means one-way on a street sign; *defense
de stationnement* means no parking.

Whether you know French or not, listening to it in
Montreal is fun. Quebec French is filled with idioms
and words that wouldn't be recognized in Paris. And
more and more there is Franglais, the term given to
the incursion of English words with French pronunci-
ations. You are likely to hear words like hot dog, or
parking, or hamburger, in sentences otherwise
French.

Catch swear words on the street if you can. Most in
French are adapted from religious practices or objects. So you may hear a motorist fervently scream
"Tabernak!" (tabernacle) at a benighted pedestrian
who had the nerve to step out on a green light.

WHAT TO SEE There are two special vantage
points from which to see Montreal as a whole. From
Westmount Lookout there is a spectacular view of the
silver-grey of stone and the green of trees. Take a
stroll in the bird sanctuary. The summit is directly accessible by car via the Camillien-Houde parkway. It's
a short run then up the Côte-des-Neiges, a main
street, to Parc Mont-Royal. The road winding
through the park takes you up **Mont Royal**, where
you can park near the top and walk the last bit to the
Cross of Christ, highest point in the city. In **Mount**

Royal Park you can see art exhibitions at a stone farmhouse dating from 1858, or watch children sail model boats on Beaver Lake.

On the north slope of Westmount Mountain is **Saint Joseph's Oratory**, 3800 Queen Mary Rd., main goal of religious pilgrims in Montreal. About 2 million persons a year, many seeking cures for various ailments, come to this edifice founded half a century ago by Brother André, a humble lay brother. Near the Oratory is a major wax museum with scenes from Christian and Quebec history.

Newest attraction in Montreal is **Olympic Park**, in the east end. The 70,000-capacity stadium, magnificent swimming facilities and spectacular velodrome (designed for bicycle racing) are a few minutes from downtown by subway. Use either Pie IX or Viau stations. It's best to see them when in use and both the National Baseball League Expos and the Canadian Football League Alouettes use the stadium. During the summer there are guided tours, for $2.50 a person.

Every tourist must go to **Old Montreal**, the marvellously restored section which occupies the same area as the original fortified town. It is small and you can, and should, walk through all its narrow streets. Here you will visit museums, boutiques, antique shops, art centers and, if you are wise, some of the best restaurants in Montreal. Go by subway to Place d'Armes station.

A good place to start is at **Place Jacques-Cartier**, almost in the shadow of city hall. You may sit at a sidewalk cafe to get your bearings and imagine you are in Paris. But be warned, you may pay $1 for a cola, $2.25 for a Scotch, $2.70 for a hamburger, $1.20 for a lemonade.

There is history in the air among the cobblestone streets: horse-drawn carriages, strolling musicians and hanging baskets of flowers. **Notre Dame**, the main thoroughfare, was laid out in 1672 and **St. Paul**, at the foot of Place Jacques-Cartier, is Montreal's oldest street. It was once just a path through the woods.

For your strolls through Old Montreal, pick up one of the several excellent detailed guides which are available, like *Smith's Montreal*, by Desmond Smith. But here are a few of the things you will see:

Two of Montreal's most beautiful churches – **Notre-Dame Church**, on Notre Dame St. E. built in 1829, which can seat 5,000 people and hold 2,000 standees as well; and the sailor's church, **Notre-Dame de Bonsecours**, 400 Rue St. Paul, oldest (1772) still standing in Montreal. It has a museum and from the tower you can get an excellent view of town and river.

The first monument to **Lord Nelson** erected anywhere in the world, stands at the head of Place Jacques-Cartier across from City Hall.

Chateau de Ramezay, 290 Notre Dame St. E., begun in 1705 by Claude de Ramezay, eleventh governor of Montreal, residence of governors – both French and English – and headquarters for military men, is now a museum. Tues. – Sat., 10 A.M. to 4:30 P.M., Sunday afternoons, adults $1, ages 6 - 14, 25 cents. The **Del Vecchio** house nearby, where there is a collection of silverplate and the traditional arms of the Royal Canadian Mounted Police. **Place Royale**, oldest public square in Montreal, dating from 1676, where fruit and vegetables were sold and where the gallows stood when hanging was common.

In Old Montreal you will find street vendors of art, and you will drink and eat at tables next to young artists and writers. However, if it's not enough like Greenwich Village for you, try **St. Denis St.** and **Prince Arthur St.** at St. Louis Square. You get there by taking the subway to Sherbrooke station and walking west.

Again you will find young people, writers and artists, boutiques and several fine restaurants (one of our favourites is **La Picholette**, 1731 St. Denis St.), and cheap, clean rooming houses and small hotels. The atmosphere is very French.

A major tourist treat since 1967, when the world came to Montreal's Expo, is **Man and His World** on Ile Sainte-Helene. Millions of people each year visit this permanent playground and cultural center. On Ile Sainte-Helene and adjacent islands – easily reachable by subway or road – you can also see the marvelous **Montreal Aquarium**, (adults 75 cents, children 50 cents) the **Museum of Contemporary Art** (free), a multilingual theater at **La Poudriere**, an old powder magazine, and the **Military and Maritime Museum**, which features drills in costume during summer (10 A.M. to 5 P.M. daily in summer, adults 50 cents, children 25 cents). The city operates the **Helene de Champlain restaurant**, a gorgeous dining room in a picturesque mansion, one of the best eating places in Montreal.

Place des Arts, the magnificent city-built center for music and arts, (guided tours Tues. and Thurs. afternoons, adults 50 cents, children 25 cents) is at the subway station named for it. Just across St. Catherine St. is Montreal's newest office-hotel-shopping-dining center, **Place Desjardins**, a startling multi-tower structure. Drop in to window shop and enjoy the noontime concerts in the lower mall.

The Forum, one of the world's great hockey arenas, is also used for concerts and other entertainments. It is at the Atwater subway station.

Perhaps it properly belongs under a "shopping" heading, but don't forget Montreal's **indoor-underground city**. If you want to (and in winter this might seem a good idea) you can spend your whole time in Montreal without venturing out into the weather. You can stay at a hotel, shop in boutiques, dine in luxury, drink in cheery surroundings at the top of towers or underground, go to a hockey match or a baseball game, without going out. The major centers are at **Place Ville Marie**, the vast complex which started Montreal's downtown redevelopment in 1962, **Place Bonaventure**, **Place Victoria**, and two big shopping centers at the Atwater subway station.

WHERE TO STAY Like any large city, Montreal has hotels running the gamut from luxurious and expensive to cheap and dumpy. All your familiar chain hotels are present. We will name just a few hotels, giving the lowest rates for single and double rooms.

The **Queen Elizabeth,** 900 Dorchester Blvd. W., ($41, $51) biggest (1200 units) and most popular, is a bustling spot above the subway and the Canadian National station. It has enough dining rooms and coffee shops to serve a small town, including two of the city's best, the **Beaver Club** and **Salle Bonaventure**, both in the very expensive bracket.

Less commercial, but classy and classic, is the venerable but elegant **Ritz Carlton**, 1228 Sherbrooke St. W. ($47, $57). It is out of the range of the ordinary tourist. Other first-rate downtown hotels include **Chateau Champlain** at Lagauchetiere and Peel Sts. ($50, $60), **Hotel Bonaventure**, 1 Place Bonaventure ($52, $64), and the Hyatt Regency, or, in Montreal, **Le Regence Hyatt**, 777 University Ave., ($39.50, $52.50), brand new and plush. All have every facility from health clubs to supper clubs and all are more suited to upper echelon expense-account travelling than to family touring. Another in this bracket, the **Meridien Hotel**, 4 Complexe Desjardins, ($43, $53), is under shared ownership of Air France and the Quebec government. It is especially convenient: across the street from the Place des Arts, and at a subway stop.

All Montreal hotels of any repute are what we call expensive. For example, two of the better bargains still are the **Sheraton Mount Royal**, 1455 Peel St., ($25, $36), and the **Windsor Hotel**, 1170 Peel St. ($32, $38). Both are elderly and were at one time the city's two best hotels, except for the Ritz Carlton. The Mount Royal is still large, with 1011 units, has been tastefully refurbished and has a warm and comfortable feeling. The Windsor is now a relatively small hotel but retains a touch of elegance.

Downtown or close, and including many with lower rates, recommended hotels include, the **Auberge Richelieu**, 505 Sherbrooke St. E., ($33, $44); the **Chateau Versailles Hotel**, 1659 Sherbrooke St. W., ($20, $28); **Constellation Hotel**, 3407 Peel St. ($34, $44); **Hotel De La Salle**, 1240 Drummond St., ($24, $28); **Holiday Inn-Downtown**, 420 Sherbrooke St. W. ($36, $42); **Place Howard Johnson**, 425 Sherbrooke St. E. ($33, $40); **Ramada Inn-Downtown**, 1005 Guy St. ($30, $38); and **Seaway Motor Inn**, 1155 Guy St. ($20, $30). Even this is not a complete list, of course.

There are dozens of other hotels in the suburbs and at the city's approaches. They include more Holiday Inns and other chain representatives, too many to list. Generally, the outlying hotels have lower rates. For instance, the **Holiday Inn Chateaubriand**, ($28, $34) five miles northwest at 6500 Côte de Liesse Rd., is a large hostelry, with 280 units.

However, you can be charged as much as downtown. At the **Dorval Aeroport Hilton**, 12505 Côte de Liesse Rd., near the airport, singles and doubles start at $40 and $48.

WHERE TO EAT Almost anywhere . . . in Montreal, this is literally true. No other city in Canada has the quality, quantity and variety of food offered by Montreal's 5,000 restaurants. French cooking is of course the mainstay of the fine restaurants, both haute cuisine and the hearty French-Canadian habitant style. But most other national cookery styles are represented, too.

Dining in style in Montreal is not cheap. At almost any fine restaurant, a couple will pay from a minimum of $40 to $50 or more. Wine mark-ups are high. One of us paid $9 at one restaurant for a bottle of the *house wine.* And on another occasion, at a suburban seafood restaurant, the proverbial back-breaking straw was a 25-cent charge for soda water tacked on top of a $2.25 charge for a single Canadian whiskey.

There are some short cuts. Most restaurants offer a fixed price luncheon, so you can sample fine dining rooms for half the price of evening dinner. At lunch, too, most restaurants offer wine by the carafe; many will not at dinner.

Reservations are essential at most top-grade restaurants, and the establishments rigorously honor them. Make sure you keep them.

If, like many tourists, you hoard eating money for a good bust-out every couple of days, don't neglect the pubs and brasseries for thrifty meals in-between. Numerous establishments which are primarily beer-drinking spots serve good, hearty food cheaply. And the atmosphere is fun.

Chez Bardet, 591 Henri Bourassa Blvd., is the choice of many connoisseurs as Montreal's number one restaurant. Drive or take the subway; the restaurant is just across the street from Henri Bourassa station, the Metro's northern terminus. This is where anybody who is anybody takes a guest who is anybody when he's on an expense account. It's elegant.

It's expensive. Unless you go with the cheapest table d'hote, it will cost you $60 a couple or so for dinner and wine.

There are literally scores of other first-class dining rooms. Many are in downtown hotels, like the excellent **Beaver Club** at the Queen Elizabeth Hotel. Try the **Ritz Carlton** for gracious living. One could eat every night in Old Montreal, at **Le Fadeau,** 423 St. Claude, or **Le St. Amable**, at **Gibby's,** 298 Youville Sq. or **Guinguette Les Trois,** 273 St. Paul E., all excellent, all in the $40 to $60 range. Also in Old Montreal, we love the hearty habitant fare at **Les Filles du Roy,** 415 St. Paul E. and, on 211 Notre Dame W., seafood at **Delmo's**. Go at lunchtime, when businessmen fill two long bars in the outer room.

Fun places for tourists to eat don't always fit gourmet requirements, of course. Here are a few places, most of which don't make anybody's "best" lists, which we like for various reasons, usually price:

Helene de Champlain, on St. Helen's Island, is one place where tourists can have fun and gourmets are comfortable. It's run by the city and its wine prices are reasonable. It's a gorgeous old building with splendid views of the island in the middle of the St. Lawrence river. You should get reservations and a couple can dine for about $40, with wine.

The Old Spaghetti Warehouse at 29 St. Paul St. in Old Montreal is cheap and the food is unexciting. But the place is warm, cheerful and pleasantly decorated. Two people can eat heartily here for under $10.

Also in Old Montreal, the **Auberge St. Gabriel**, on St. Gabriel St., at the site of an old trading post, is touristy as the dickens. There's a life-sized horse in the lobby, pulling a buggy. Montrealers may tell you the food isn't great and they may be right. But why be ashamed of being a tourist? It's fun.

There's both atmosphere and good food at the

Club des Moustaches, 2070 Mountain St. You walk in through a scruffy-looking beer parlour to a back room that looks like a Paris bistro. The day's specialty is written on a slate, the waiter writes your order on the table. Food – tripes, kidneys, beef bourguignon and so forth – is tasty. You and your friend can get out for $20 or so. **Le Paris,** at 1812 St. Catherine St. W., is a neat, pleasant place with good food and satisfied regulars. Try it for lunch.

There are a number of good Chinese restaurants ranging in price up to expensive **Ruby Foo's,** 7815 Decarie Blvd., where you may spend $40 a couple on Chinese food and a drink or two. One we like is the extremely reasonable **Jasmine,** 62 Lagauchetiere W., a block south of Dorchester. Looks like nothing at all from the outside or the inside. Service is friendly and helpful; food inexpensive. Dining alone, one of us had beautiful pickerel, another dish or two, and got out for $7. Unlicensed, though.

A special event is the re-enactment of a 1691 feast at **Le Festin du Gouverneur,** the former powder room of the Old Fort on St. Helen's Island. Buy your tickets in advance at any Ticket Reservation Service outlet, for $14.95 per person. Without napkins or forks, you will eat things like Cornish hen, vegetable soup, corn and other food as it might hve been served in 1691. The diners become part of an entertainment put on by the singing waiters and waitresses.

Montreal smoked meats are famous throughout Canada. The three delicatessens (for the works, dill pickles, sauerkraut, pastrami, cream cheese, etc. etc.) we like best in order, are **Schwartz's,** 3895 St. Laurent Blvd., **Ben's,** 990 Maisonneuve Blvd. W., and **Dunn's,** 892 St. Catherine St. W. **Curly Joe's Steak Houses,** at several locations, usually please the kids. **Pepe's** on Peel St. just below St. Catherine's serves Italian food and the **Hunter's Horn**, almost next door, is fun for pub food and Irish singing.

NIGHTLIFE Montreal used to be famous throughout North America for its raucous and wide-open nightlife. Things are a bit quieter today, but there is still plenty doing, from quiet drinking in subdued lounges to swinging discos.

The center for concerts, plays and dance is the **Place des Arts** already mentioned, with its own subway stop and a drive-in box office off Maisonneuve Blvd.

Night clubs in hotels like the **Bonaventure** and the **Chateau Champlain**, feature leggy chorus girls and floor shows presented with high style and prices to match. You can easily go through $80 and up a couple.

Many tourists prefer to wander in summer through Old Montreal, sit in sidewalk cafes, watch the passing parade of humanity and listen to street musicians.

Discos are in style, but this industry is so trendy the ins and the outs change frequently. Among the most popular at time of writing were the **Rally Club**, 1423 Crescent St., nearby **Gaby's**, 1472 Crescent St., and **Le Tube**, 1498 Stanley St. Old Montreal is crowded with discos and one of the most popular is **La Nuit Magique,** 22 St. Paul E. Expect to pay about $2 and up for a drink.

SHOPPING Montreal has always been a city of high fashion. You will find many exclusive shops on **Sherbrooke St.** and in the underground shopping centers along the subway: **Place Ville Marie, Place Bonaventure, Les Terrasses** and **Alexis Nihon Plaza.** Cashmere, fine woolens, china and perfumes are among the imported items traditionally featured in Montreal stores.

The large department stores, **Eaton's, Simpson's, The Bay**, and **Ogilvy's,** are strung along St. Catherine St. downtown and clustered in huge suburban plazas. **Birk's** is the name recognized throughout Canada for jewelry and china.

For native French-Canadian and Eskimo and Indian carvings, drawings, rugs and other crafts, be sure to visit the **Canadian Handicraft Guild**, 2025 Peel St., and the **Quebec Handicraft Centre**, 1450 St. Denis St. There are many small shops in Old Montreal as well, which specialize in work by Quebec artisans and artists.

INFORMATION For detailed information about Montreal, its attractions and prices, write: Montreal Municipal Tourist Bureau, 155 Notre Dame East, Montreal, Quebec H2Y 1C6.

QUEBEC CITY

*"If Montreal is the heart of French Canada,
Quebec city is its soul."*

You lean out the window of a small hotel in the heart
of Quebec city and wonder if somehow during the
night you haven't been magically swept across the
seas. Below you in the street a man in a beret is am-
bling along with a frenchstick tucked under his arm
like a folded newspaper. Across the way, the proprietor of another small hotel is sweeping his sidewalk,
paying no attention whatever to the bony nag and
tourist carriage rattling on by. You stare up at the
chimney-potted skyline, then down at the tilted band-
box of a café where you mixed wine, escargot and
French music last night. And you realize that here,
within an easy day's drive of New York or Toronto,
you have discovered a city like no other in North
America.

Yes, this capital of French Canada is something
special, far and away the most European city on the
continent, a city that might just as well be found
along the Breton coast or in a distant corner of Paris.
The only walled city in Canada, it even has its own
mighty chateau, a pseudo-Gothic hotel that has dominated the city's skyline since before the turn of the
century. Yet, in this town where you can sit down to
a meal in a restaurant housed in a 300-year-old cottage, the Chateau Frontenac must be regarded as a
johnny-come-lately.

Although there are now 440,000 people living in
the Quebec urban area, no city in the world is better

suited to being explored on foot – though one should be forewarned that streets go in only two directions, uphill and down. It matters little that everything seems to be built of the same, ancient grey stone; it still comes out as an architectural symphony of narrow, winding streets that gives your spirits a lift, as if you were strolling in Paris or Prague.

Moreover, the area you have come to see is extremely compact, covering only a few hundred acres. It's made up of the section of **Upper Town** enclosed by the ancient walls and the **Lower Town** section directly below it, running down to the banks of the mighty St. Lawrence River. For this is a split-level city, part of it dramatically situated atop a 200-foot-high cliff; the rest just above river level. It's a magnificent setting, perfectly ordained for the city which once held the key to the continent, from which explorers discovered the Mississippi, opened up the west and gave the world its new frontiers.

It's very French. Nearly 95% of the populace are Francophones. But don't let that worry you. English is spoken as a second, if somewhat grudging language, by much of the population and the natives are among the most hospitable in Canada.

But before we start looking around, let's take a peek back in time.

The search for a passage to India, as in the case of so many other New World discoveries, led to the first sighting of Quebec by Europeans. Frenchman Jacques Cartier, sailing from the port of St. Malo in 1534, planted a cross on the rocky shores of the Gaspé peninsula and claimed all the land beyond in the name of the King of France (the fact that much of this forested world was inhabited by Hurons, Iroquois, Algonquins and other "red men" wasn't considered worth noting). Cartier then sailed up the St. Lawrence as far as Montreal, looking for that elusive passage to the wealth of the Orient, and then reluctantly turned for home. Winter forced him and his men to take shelter at an Indian village, called Stadacona, which was at a narrowing of the river known as "Kebec" in the native language.

And so Quebec remained for three-quarters of a century before another great French explorer, Samuel de Champlain, founded the first permanent settlement in 1608, building his "Abitation" below the cliffs of Cape Diamond. He and the Jesuit missionaries used this rough-hewn capital of New France as a base for exploration and conversion of the Indians of the interior, much as the romantic "runners of the woods" and merchants did during the following centuries when the fur trade paid the bills.

All this changed dramatically in 1759 when the centuries-old quarrel between France and England for North America came down to one big battle. It was fought in just 20 minutes on the Plains of Abraham, which still lie today just outside the walls of the city. The British, under the youthful command of General Wolfe, crept up the cliffs under the cover of darkness and at dawn's early light stood in a thin, menacing, red line ready to do battle with French General Montcalm's defenders of the city. Whether due to the element of surprise or the months' long bombardment which had levelled much of Quebec, the British scored a decisive victory and five days later the city capitulated. Both Wolfe and Montcalm were fatally injured on the field of battle and today you can visit a simple monument in the Governor's Garden dedicated to both. Inscribed in Latin are the words: "Valour gave them a common death, history a common fame, posterity a common monument."

This battle was something more than an historic turning point. It still looms large among the seeds of discord that have given rise to a separatist zeal among

many French Canadians. School children growing up
in English sections of the country were taught to regard Wolfe as the "conquering hero" who had come
to plant the British flag on "Canada's fair domain,"
as though it were there for the taking. Only French-
Canadian children could see he was also an invader
who defeated not only the French but also native-
born Canadians, whose families had inhabited Quebec for a century and a half. Nonetheless, the British
did make a wise move a few years later when they
passed the Quebec Act of 1774. It guaranteed the
Quebec people the right to their own language, laws
and religion and helped keep them loyal to Britain
when the American colonists rebelled a year later.

In fact, when the Revolutionary Army attacked
Quebec city with two forces (one commanded by
Benedict Arnold) a year later, the French joined the
British in beating them off. This left Quebec city to
grow up in a unique way – still the proud capital of
New France, still filled with old-world charm, gallic
flair and the kind of hospitality you won't find else-
where on the continent. So let's take a look at it.

WEATHER   All you have to know about Quebec
city is that it's situated in the heart of one of
Canada's prime ski areas to understand the winters
can be – and usually are – snowy and cold. In December, January and February, temperatures rarely
rise above the freezing mark. Summer weather is especially fine and warm, a few degrees cooler than
Montreal's, both by night and day.

HOW TO GET THERE   Most visitors arrive by car,
usually along the Trans-Canada Highway (Highway
20 in Quebec). The drive from Montreal takes about

three hours, considerably longer if you take the more leisurely Highways 2 and 3 along either shore of the St. Lawrence. The Trans-Canada also gets you to Quebec city quickly from neighboring New Brunswick. Air service is good and frequent via Air Canada from the rest of the country, Quebecair from the rest of the province, or Bar Harbor Airlines from Boston. Train and bus service is frequent, especially from Montreal.

GETTING AROUND   This is a highly walkable city, especially the ancient Upper and Lower Towns that you have come to see. There are also caleches (horse and buggies) and open-air buses available at the central Place d'Armes – the little square beside the Chateau Frontenac Hotel.

We recommend walking. To do that best get a copy of the "Walking Tour of Old Quebec." It's available free from the Tourist and Convention Department of the Quebec Urban Community at 60 Rue d'Auteuil, just inside the St. Louis Gate, one of the entrances through the wall that surrounds the old section of Upper Town. The booklet describes the historical shrines in minutest detail and, with the use of an accompanying map, leads you easily between them.

Use of your car isn't recommended within the old city. Streets are narrow, plunge suddenly, and offer few parking places. Seat belts are mandatory and right turns on a red light aren't permitted.

Cruises on the St. Lawrence are available through **Quebec Waterways Sightseeing Tours,** 10 Dalhousie St. ($4.50 to $10 for adults, half fare for children 12 and under, depending on which cruise you take). You can see life on the river much more cheaply by hopping aboard the ferry to Levis (which faces Quebec across the river). The ferry dock is within sight of Place Royale in Lower Town.

One special note on getting about that any visitor to this split-level city will appreciate. There's an elevator (*ascenseur*) which, for 25 cents, takes you up and down the cliff. You'll find its entrance on Dufferin Terrace right beside the Chateau Frontenac Hotel. Find Sous le Fort street in Lower Town for the ride back up.

WHAT TO SEE As we mentioned before, if you want to see the city in depth, there's no better guide than the "Walking Tour of Old Quebec." If there's one problem with it, it's that it includes much that the average tourist may consider trivial. Pick one up anyway, even if you are more interested in a shorthand view. When you come out of the Tourist and Convention office on d'Auteuil street, turn right, and right again along Rue St. Louis and you'll reach the wall of the old city at St. Louis Gate. Walk through the portal and take a look at the walls that surround the city. Outside the walls you'll notice the skyscraper trappings of any modern city, the highrise hotels peering over the walls of the old city. Inside, all is frozen in time. Now, walk back through into another century.

You are on Rue St. Louis. Keep walking away from the gate and you'll reach the **Chateau Frontenac,** the castle of a hotel which dominates the city like a chateau-fortress from feudal days. Actually it's one of the new boys in town, completed in 1892 by Canadian Pacific, the pioneering Canadian railway company which is big in hotels and just about anything else that makes money. Beside the hotel, along the cliff is an 80-foot-wide boardwalk known as the **Dufferin Terrace** which affords a splendid view of the river and the city of Levis on the south shore. If you walk west along the boardwalk, you come to an extension known as the **Promenade des Gouverneurs** which takes you below the outside walls of the **Citadel**, a star-shaped fortress built by the British on the site of earlier French fortifications. Keep going and the path will take you right out onto the **Plains of Abraham** where the battle that shaped the future of Canada was fought.

Walk east on the Terrace and you'll come to a handsome statue of Champlain, hat in hand, looking proudly out on his city. In the adjoining square, **Place d'Armes**, you'll find caleches awaiting you. Always agree on the price before hopping aboard. Whether you are going to sightsee by caleche or on foot, here are the places you should see:

Place Royale, in Lower Town, just below the cliffs and the Chateau. This is the site of Champlain's original "Abitation." In fact if you look at the roadway just outside Notre Dame des Victoires Church, you'll see patches in the asphalt where archeologists recently dug to find traces of the original foundations of his fortress. More than $20 million has been spent in restoring Place Royale to its 17th and 18th century splendor, when it was home to the wealthy merchants who ruled New France.

Notre Dame des Victoires, the focal point of the restoration, was built in 1688 in gratitude for several victories over the British. It was all but destroyed by Wolfe's guns and later rebuilt with the altar in the shape of a fortress. A fully rigged model ship hangs from its rafters. Near the church, the **Chevalier House** is perhaps best restored and fitted out with marvellous furniture from early Quebec. In **Charest House** you'll see an English cannonball from 1759 imbedded in the original wall.

Place Royal is the site of some of the best restaurants and watering holes in the city, often set in cave-like cellars, candlelit and delightful. Before heading back up the elevator to Upper Town, go down to the ferry dock for a brief river trip that will show you the city from its most dramatic side.

Battlefield Park: This 220 acre piece of greenery – or whitery for the five months of winter – encompasses the Plains of Abraham where the famed battle took place. Tablets mark the course of the battle. You get to the park by driving out the St. Louis Gate and following the wide and handsome Grande-Allee or by walking along the Promenade des Gouverneurs. Inside the park, the **Quebec Museum** with its art and antique furniture collection and display of historical documents is worth a short visit.

A more interesting museum is contained in the **Ursuline Convent**, 12 Donnacona St. The convent, founded in 1639, has been a school for girls for most of its history. General Montcalm's remains were buried in the convent's chapel. The museum houses 17th century items, including a bread oven and clothes, implements and furniture of the times.

The Citadel, is another of those glorious Canadian forts from which a shot has never been fired in anger. However, this one is built on the site of French defences which saw plenty of action. Constructed between 1820 and 1832, it cost the British some $7 million, a vast fortune then, which demonstrated their suspicions of those Americans just to the south. Star-shaped and tied in with the overall wall system of Upper Town, the Citadel is comprised of some 25 buildings, tunnels and parade grounds. It was here that Roosevelt and Churchill met for their Quebec Conference during World War II. Mid-June to mid-September there is a ceremonial changing of the guards at 10 A.M. In summer, the Citadel's museum is open from 9 A.M. to 7 P.M., shorter hours the rest of the year. Admission is 75 cents for adults, 25 cents for children under 17. Admission includes a guided tour.

The Musée du Fort, at 10 Rue Ste. Anne, opposite the Chateau, presents a sound and light diorama which outlines the events of the Battle of Quebec and the five other sieges of the city. It's not great but for people interested in the events of 1759, it's worth the admission price: $1.50 for adults, $1 for university students, 75 cents for others. Alternate French and English versions are given, so it's worth checking ahead for starting times. A wax museum a few doors along St. Anne is worth a stop in a bad rainstorm.

You get a real Left Bank feeling as you walk into the tiny laneway called **Rue du Tresor**, off Place d'Armes. It's lined from one end to the other with the paintings of "starving artists" hung up for sale. They used to show them surreptitiously and run when the police came. Now they pay for a space and business, if not all the artwork, is good. From $3 up.

The **Basilica of Notre Dame**, at the corner of Baude and Fabrique, and the **Anglican Cathedral of the Holy Trinity**, Des Jardins St., both have lavishly ornate interiors. The French Renaissance **Parliament Buildings**, home of the National Assembly, as Quebec calls its provincial legislature, are just outside the St. Louis Gate and worth at least a picture. Guided tours are offered free in summer from 8:30 A.M. to 4:30 P.M. Debates inside are usually animated and conducted in French.

Just outside the city are several prime attractions. Best known is the **Basilica of Ste. Anne de Beaupré**, 18 miles northeast of the city. More than 2 million pilgrims a year come to this famous shrine, many of them still seeking miraculous cures, such as those recorded by the hundreds who have left their crutches behind. On the way to the shrine you can take in **Montmorency Falls** at 274 feet, higher than Niagara, but much less impressive. Also on the way to Ste. Anne is the bridge link with **Ile d'Orleans**, a farming and summer home island which has maintained its habitant charm.

WHERE TO STAY   Quebec city offers the visitor a wider choice of accommodation than any major tourist city on the continent. You can come here and live in the grand style or opt for a Left Bank existence in family hotels of a type you simply can't find in other Canadian or U.S. cities.

Most of the small hotels in Quebec are officially classified as tourist homes, though some offer rooms with a private bathroom attached. Mostly, you can expect a small, sparsely furnished room with a shared bathroom down the hall – like the small, family-run hotels of Europe. There are nearly 50 of these establishments within the walls of Old Quebec. And the price is still right as one of us discovered last year when he arrived without reservations and booked into the **Manoir LaSalle** on Rue Ste. Ursule. The tab for the night came to just about the same as the taxi ride from the airport – $8.60.

Some tourist homes charge much less and although they invariably offer a clean bed, staying in them involves a kind of Russian roulette daring, largely because of the city's popularity with young travellers. If you're lucky, the other people sharing the same floor as you are a couple of octogenarians. If not, they'll likely turn out to be a barbershop quartet or four college kids celebrating their 18th birthday or the fact that they've been able to borrow ID cards showing that they're old enough to drink.

These tourist homes almost never offer meals of any kind – but that's no great source of concern. If they're within the walls of the old city, they're never more than a five minute walk from a good place to eat. Among tourist homes we've tried, we give highest marks to **Manoir LaSalle**, 18 Rue Ste. Ursule. **La Maison Demers**, 68 Ste. Ursule, is fine for the young crowd. **Au Vieux Foyer,** 71 Rue St. Louis, and **Le Gite de la Place d'Armes,** 24 Rue St. Anne, are both good and central.

A hotel building boom during the past decade has given Quebec more than its share of luxury hotels. But in our books, none of them rates with the **Chateau Frontenac**. It had gone steadily downhill since the days when it welcomed Churchill, Roosevelt and various members of the Royal Family. Then Canadian Pacific decided to spend $10 million on its grant dowager, to return her to her glory days. They've done just that. It's in the $30 plus single, $40 plus double category. Also in that price range are the new **Hilton**, 3 Place Quebec; **Loew Concorde**, 1225 Place Montcalm; **Auberge des Gouverneurs**, 690 Boulevard St. Cyrille East; and the downtown **Holiday Inn**, 395 Rue de la Couronne. All are located just outside the walls of the old city. A notch down in price are the **Clarendon Chateau Laurier**, 695 Grand-Allee, and the **Auberge Fleur de Lys**, 115 Rue Ste. Anne, a motor inn right in the heart of the old city. A large motel row is located at **Ste. Foy** on the western outskirts of the city.

WHERE TO EAT   Dining out here is intimate but surprisingly sophisticated. It goes without saying that all the big hotels have large and expensive dining rooms. We strongly suggest that you largely ignore them and get out into the city to try such spots as: **La Traite du Roy**, 25¼ Notre Dame in Place Royale, where the paté is almost as memorable as the duck in orange sauce; **Aux Anciens Canadiens**, 34 Rue St.

Louis, in a house which celebrated its 300th birthday in 1975 and still serves superb French-Canadian fare – pea soup, meat pies, a tasty pork meat spread and custard with maple syrup. **The Café de la Paix**, just around the corner at 44 Desjardins, specializes in mussels and scampi, while **Le Bonaparte**, 680 Grande-Allee E., serves skewers of beef and kidney in a fine old house of Empire-style decor. Veal cutlets and stewed rabbit are the specialties at **Le Rabelais**, 2 Petit Champlain, just off Place Royale. Of the hotel restaurants the **Café Canadien** in the Chateau Frontenac is highly regarded by Quebeckers while **Le Toit de Quebec** in the Hilton offers a view from the 23rd floor, a high-class buffet and prices to match both elevations.

Expect to pay about 20% less for a good meal than you would in Montreal or Toronto but don't forget that most restaurants have good wine cellars, a thing which can easily put a meal in the $20 a person and up bracket.

If you are budgeting, try the brasseries where you can get a beer and meal in the $3 to $5 price range. **Le Gaulois**, 65 Baude, presents live entertainment, grilled meats and pizzas while the **Ciderie d'Youville**, barn-sized and mirrored, offers skewered meat and authentic Quebec cider at 866 St. Jean.

Remember that even well-regarded French restaurants can be very small here. Always phone ahead for reservations. Don't worry about the language problem in restaurants. Quebec survives largely on tourist dollars and every restaurant has someone on duty who speaks English. Menus usually have English translations.

You can get a list of restaurants in various price categories from the Tourist and Convention Department, 60 Rue d'Auteuil, Quebec 4. Also a list of hotels and tourist houses.

NIGHTLIFE   Much more limited than in Montreal. After all there are fewer than 200,000 people in the city proper, just 440,000 in the metropolitan area. Intimate piano bars, discos in ancient cellars with walls thick enough to seal in the sound – they're the thing in Quebec. **La Traite du Roy**, 25¼ Notre Dame in Place Royale is the best known discotheque while the **Bastille**, nestled in the thick walls of the Citadel at 47 St. Genevieve is a piano bar with a steady following. The **Chateau** usually offers a quartet, quiet enough so that you can hear yourself talk.

SHOPPING   Quebec is every bit as fashion conscious as Montreal and has an array of boutiques that belies its size. **Rue St. Jean** in Upper Town is cheek by jowl with boutiques and the new **Place Quebec** indoor shopping center, attached to the Hilton Hotel, is loaded with shops for those who are loaded with money. **Rue Ste. Anne** has a sprinkling of less pretentious boutiques. For arts and crafts shopping head for **Place Royale** in Lower Town or for the **Centrale d'Artisanat du Quebec**, a non-profit organization that offers wood carvings, jewelry, fur goods, pottery and other artifacts of Quebec craftsmen. The main store is in Montreal but there's a satellite shop in **Place Laurier** in suburban Ste. Foy. Place Laurier is worth taking in anyway. It claims to be the largest shopping center in Canada.

SPECIAL EVENTS   The **Quebec Winter Carnival** is the true Mardi Gras of the north and Canada's biggest winter event. Held for two weeks early in February, it manages to bring the city out of its annual icebox with truly spectacular parades, fireworks, bonfires, hockey tournaments, a whole street of ice sculptures, ski races and an ice canoe race across the treacherous St. Lawrence. Participants stay fortified against the weather with warm parkas and hollow, plastic canes filled with a mixture of red wine and spirits which they call "caribou." The Carnival is presided over by a seven-foot animated and talking snowman known as Bonhomme Carnival. It's a time of rare abandon and no place for a member of the Women's Christian Temperance Union. Annually it means $1 million in extra business to the Quebec Liquor Corporation.

WHERE TO GET HELP WITH YOUR TRIP The Tourist and Convention Department, 60 Rue d'Auteuil, Quebec 4, is a good source for maps, accommodation and restaurant guides. Once you reach town, its staff will also try to help you find accommodation if you come without confirmed reservations – a mistake in summer or at carnival time.

If you plan to visit other parts of Canada, too, contact the Canadian Government Office of Tourism, 150 Kent St., Ottawa, Ontario K1A 0H6.

WHAT ELSE TO SEE IN QUEBEC

When you have seen Montreal and Quebec city, there's still an area roughly the size of Alaska left to explore. For Quebec is Canada's largest province, sprawling across 594,860 miles of forests, lakes and low-slung mountains which are believed to be the world's oldest. But don't let the vastness scare you. Most of what you'll want to see is located along the mighty St. Lawrence River, within a few hundred miles of the U.S. border. Even in these easily reached portions of the province, a visitor can get his fill of primitive forests, picturesque seashores, timeless villages and lush river valleys. Here's a look at the highlights:

THE LAURENTIANS The Laurentian mountains actually cover almost nine-tenths of Quebec but when people say "the Laurentians" they're usually referring to the all-year resort area that lies from 40 to 80 miles north of Montreal. Though Mont Tremblant, the highest peak in the Laurentians, is only 3,150 feet, this is one of North America's prime skiing areas with no fewer than 150 resorts in a 35-square-mile radius. There are fun villages such as St. Savveur, Ste. Agathe, Val Morin and St. Jouite, with luxury lodges, family-run hotels, inexpensive pensions and even a winter trailer park where you can spend the night for as little as $5.50. This is a place for all seasons. Its hills, some of them floodlit at night, many of them equipped with snow-making machines, are busy from December to April. Its lakes and mountains pack in summer escapees and in autumn it puts on one of the most spectacular color foliage shows to be seen anywhere in the world. Its tradition for fine cuisine and lively night entertainment is unmatched by any ski area on this side of the Atlantic – it's no secret that several Montreal hotels have tried without success to lure away chefs from Laurentian resorts. There are 32 ski centers, a host of ski schools and 25 chair lifts. One-week ski packages range in price from about $140 to $330. Plush resorts charge a couple anywhere from $50 to $80 a day (with two or three meals included). Plushest and priciest is the **Mont Tremblant Lodge,** right at the foot of the Laurentians' main peak. Other top-line resorts include: **Gray Rocks, Le Chantecler, the Alpine Inn, Auberge Yvan Coutu.** We like **Chateau Beauvallon** at Mont Tremblant where a room for two with two meals a day costs under $40. There are dozens of motels and pensions scattered among these ancient hills.

THE GASPE   It's as remote as the Laurentians are handy but nonetheless something very special for any Quebec visitor. A peninsula jutting out into the Gulf of St. Lawrence, the Gaspé was settled by Breton fishermen who were able to preserve their ancient ways almost completely until early in this century because their rockbound home could be reached only by boat. Today a paved highway gets you to Gaspé and skirts the coast where classic fishing villages cling to the shore beneath gigantic cliffs. The scenery is especially awesome between St. Flavie and Percé where a huge pierced rock sticks out of the sea like a temple of nature. From Percé be sure to take the boat trip out to **Bonaventure Island**, one of the top bird sanctuaries in the whole country. Rocky ledges house more kinds of birds than most people have seen in their entire lives. The boat stops at the island so you can climb a trail to the top of the cliffs and look down into the nesting areas. The trip takes about 1½ hours and costs $4 for adults, $2 for children.

Percé has the widest selection of motels and restaurants on the peninsula, with rates for a double ranging from $25 to $40. At Gaspé town you'll find the granite cross which commemorates the 1534 landing of explorer Jacques Cartier. Nearby is one of the Gaspé's newest attractions, **Forillon National Park,** the first to be developed in Quebec by the federal government. It's far from complete but offers deep-sea fishing, swimming, nature trails and campsites. One thing about the Gaspé – you don't just happen on it. It's at least a two-day round trip from Riviére-du-Loup, the jumping off point, and should take three or four days for proper appreciation of its old-world charm – fishermen mending their nets, roadside shrines and two-century-old Norman buildings.

ST. JEAN-PORT-JOLI   People whittle while they work in this village on the south shore of the St. Lawrence River. It's the wood-carving capital of Canada and the place which is mostly responsible for Quebec's renown in this art form. You can visit the **studio of the Bourgault brothers,** the Michelangelos of wood-carving, and of other carvers – some of whom employ whole shops filled with apprentices specializing in, say, a left leg or right nostril. Yes, the assembly line has even come to wood-carving. You can see some of the best Bourgault pieces in the lobby and restaurant of the **Auberge du Faubourg.** You get a wider selection of the carvings in St. Jean Craft shops – but don't expect a price break. This village, founded in 1721, is an hour's drive east of Quebec city on the way to the Maritimes or the Gaspé.

EASTERN TOWNSHIPS   This corner of the province, just north of the Vermont border, is another prime ski area. Sherbrooke and Granby, which has a zoo that captivates children, are the principal cities. Mont Orford has topnotch slopes and a fine lodge, the **Auberge Cheribourg.**

TROIS-RIVIERES   (Three Rivers) Most people travel the south shore Trans-Canada route between Montreal and Quebec city. But if you take the more leisurely north shore route make sure you stop briefly at this second-oldest French city in North America, dating to 1634. Sieur de La Verendrye left from here to discover the Rocky Mountains and the older section of the city still contains buildings that were constructed around that time. Take a look at the fine **De Tonnancour mansion**, dating from 1690.

Also worth a stop are **Mont St. Anne**, northeast of Quebec city, a ski area with fine cross-country trails and the longest ski runs in eastern Canada; **St. Felicien,** site of an exceptional zoo with 1,000 specimens of birds, amphibians, invertebrates and mammals; **Gatineau Park,** just north of Ottawa and Hull, where 25 miles of roads wind through a rocky area forested by 60 types of trees and countless wildflowers; the **Saguenay River,** cut between immense cliffs which can best be seen on Soviet cruise ships sailing out of Montreal in summer along the St. Lawrence and Saguenay.

PROVINCIAL PARKS   Quebec also has vast provincial parks which cover an area equal to that of Massachusetts, Rhode Island and Connecticut. Several are well off the beaten track, almost the exclusive preserve of canoeists and fishermen. **La Verendrye,**

for example, offers 1,500 square miles of waterways. This largest of Quebec parks (5,250 square miles) is just north of the Laurentian resort area.

WHERE TO EAT   Few eating establishments in the rest of Quebec match those in Montreal or the capital. But that doesn't mean they aren't first-rate by other standards. The poached salmon at **La Sapiniere at Val David** in the Laurentians is as outstanding as its wine cellar (expensive); the **Chateau Blanc at Bonaventure** on the Gaspé peninsula is a topnotch seafood house and the comfortable old dining room of the **Hotel Chicoutimi** in that rough-and-ready city of the same name is a great place to try habitant dishes.

WHERE TO STAY   Mostly you have to depend on motel accommodation once you leave Quebec's big cities. Count on paying between $20 and $35 for a double in summer, depending on how early you stop to look and how short rooms are in the area of your search. One out-of-the-way place worth mentioning is the **Chateau Montebello** on Highway 148, some 80 miles west of Montreal and 40 miles east of Ottawa. Once the most exclusive of Quebec private clubs, it has been turned into a distinctive resort that's open all year. The fireplace alone is the size of some cottages. Count on paying between $72 and $83 for a double with two meals a day.

WHERE TO GET HELP WITH YOUR TRIP   Information centers are located near the borders on main highways from Ontario, the Maritimes and U.S. points. You can write ahead for maps, accommodation guides and the like to the Department of Tourism, Fish and Game, Parliament Buildings, Quebec City, P.Q. If your trip is to take you to other parts of Canada too, contact the Canadian Government Office of Tourism, 150 Kent St., Ottawa.

ONTARIO

*"We are all immigrants to this place (Canada)
even if we were born here: the country is too big
for anyone to inhabit completely ..."*
                    novelist Margaret Atwood

Toronto and Ottawa are Ontario's two biggest drawing cards. But if you don't go outside them, you are
short-changing yourself.

Outside those two big cities are world-famous Niagara Falls, thousands of lakes and streams, bass tail-
walking against a Georgian Bay sunset, beaches and
camping and hunting and snowmobiling, Grand Prix
auto racing and a symphony orchestra (Hamilton's)
that plays at the mills for steel workers on their lunch
hour.

There is Shakespeare at one of the world's great
drama festivals, and George Bernard Shaw in a
lovely Georgian town, country harness racing against
a background of fiery autumn leaves and summer
dances in big old halls at resort beaches.

You can eat escargots in a restaurant in Collingwood, a ship-building town, or drink imported wines
at Haileybury, which started as a mining camp, hunt
moose or ski or visit Alexander Graham Bell's house
at Brantford.

It is a big and varied and spacious place, nearly
twice as big as Texas but with only a few more people
than New York City. At its widest and longest places,
you can travel for 1,000 miles and still be in Ontario,
from the border cities which are further south than
Chicago, to a town on James Bay where Eskimos live.

You can dance to disco music in a resort town. Or sit on a lonely shore by a quiet lake and dream.

One great charm of Ontario is its seasons, distinct and individual, from 80 degree days in summer to arctic temperatures in winter. Travel the seasons: maple sugar festivals in spring, fall fairs with their competitions for livestock and preserves and vegetables, blossoms in the grape and orchard country of Niagara in spring; fall colors as the leaves change in autumn and set every woodlot ablaze, winter carnivals in northern cities.

No matter where you stay in Ontario, you'll appreciate the fact that the provincial government recently suspended, until 1980, a 7% tax which normally was added to all hotel and motel bills. Well-stocked with hotel and motel rooms, Ontario also provides camping in four national parks, 122 provincial parks and many privately-owned camp and trailer sites. The more than 20,000 provincial park campsites are $3.50 per night, $4 with electricity. Vehicle entry is $1.50 per day but a seasonal permit costs $15 and is good at all provincial parks.

For specific details on camping, fishing and hunting, events and attractions, boating, tours and other areas of interest, write to Ontario Travel, Queen's Park, Toronto, Ontario, Canada M7A 2E5. The government provides excellent booklets, even to such specialized interests as a guide to country inns. Two essential ones are *The Traveller's Encylopedia,* a concise guide to all parts of the province, and the annual *Guide to Accommodations,* listing facilities and rates.

If you are coming to Ontario from the U.S., don't worry about feeling out of place. You'll see much the same television, Big Macs, Kentucky Fried Chicken, Fords, Chevrolets and Plymouths, as you do at home.

Do, learn a little about the metric system — temperatures are given in Celsius, speed limits in kilometers per hour – a kilometer is five-eighths of a mile. Buckle up your seat belt. That's the law, punishable by a $28 fine. Make sure your tires don't have studs; they are banned.

Change your American money at the bank. Any restaurant or retailer will take U.S. money, but your best rate is at the bank or a currency dealer. Bring the same weight of clothing that you would need for the same season in Ohio, Massachusetts or other northern states.

OTTAWA

*"... I would like to say how much I appreciate,
and how proud I feel of, the request that the
Hog's Back Falls, near Ottawa, should be called
Prince of Wales Falls."* – the Duke of Windsor, in
1919, when he was Prince of Wales.

There's always been a lot of Hog's Back Falls in the
Ottawa most Canadians think of: small town, provincial, perhaps a nice place to live but unexciting to visit. Ottawa's restaurants are still uninspired, to put it
kindly. There isn't much to do after dinner but sleep.
The Chateau Laurier Hotel has great distinction but
other major hotels are more attuned to the fellow on
a government or business expense account than to a
chap with vacation pay.

But there's some good news. Things have changed
a bit recently. Ottawa does have some beautiful
things to see and the best of them are *free*. A visit to
Canada's capital is one of the better tourist bargains
in eastern Canada. And keep in mind that Ottawa is
close to other places of interest. You can easily see
most of Ottawa in a day and go on for the night: to
Montreal, only a 90-minute drive away; to Kingston
or the Thousand Islands area, to the hills and lakes
across the Ottawa river in Quebec, or to eastern Ontario cottage country.

Or, if you prefer, you can take two or three leisurely days and see some of Ottawa's hidden treasures.

Along with the natural beauty of Ottawa, the
flowers, parks, and rivers that delight the eye, you'll

also experience the tug at the heart that comes from discovering the historical references of a proud country, and the drama of today's turbulent politics.

Ottawa became the nation's capital in a typically Canadian fashion: it was a compromise between the interests of Upper and Lower Canada. If the capital had been situated in either Montreal or Toronto – the other two potential sites – the excluded section of the country would have been jealous. Ottawa was in neither Upper nor Lower Canada, and therefore offended nobody. The small, modest city possessed other advantages as well. It did not have Montreal's volatile population – the citizens there had burned down temporarily erected government buildings. Ottawa was also easily accessible by water from Montreal and Toronto, and had good railroad connections with the rest of the country. Its position far in the interior of Canada meant that it would draw some of the population away from the highly populated frontier area. And its distance from the American border, in case of war, also added to its attraction from a military point of view. Stores and troops could be sent to Ottawa from Kingston or Quebec without exposure on the St. Lawrence to the American frontier. There was also a commercial consideration in Ottawa's favor – if the capital was situated there it would increase traffic on the Rideau Canal. (The Canal had just recently been built and was not making a profit due to lack of river traffic.)

But one could sometimes wish that Queen Victoria had chosen a place with better weather than the lively little logging center known at the time as Bytown. No place in Canada feels colder than the bridge across the Rideau Canal on a February evening, nor any place muggier on an August afternoon.

For many decades, Ottawa seemed a drowsy little place. The unflappable, efficient mandarins kept the civil service running quietly and other countries sent their superannuated diplomats to Ottawa to sleep away their declining years. The community had a small town feeling about it that made it seem even smaller than it actually was. As recently as a generation ago, Prime Minister Louis St. Laurent, known to Canadians as "Uncle Louie," daily walked the two blocks between his apartment and his office on Parliament Hill. Once the Royal Canadian Mounted Police apologetically questioned a man they'd seen following Uncle Louie for three days. He turned out to be a Time Magazine correspondent preparing a cover story. Cabinet ministers drove themselves around town, or walked. Others dropped into Chinese restaurants, for after-midnight snacks.

Today they ride in chauffeured cars. Security is tighter. But there are still traces of the old informality. Ottawa now has 300,000 residents but in many ways it's still a small town.

You can look at the prime minister's official residence at 24 Sussex Dr., but there are no public tours of it, as there are of the White House in Washington. You can often visit the gardens and grounds of the governor general's residence nearby. You may rub shoulders on the Sparks St. mall with the famous; or listen to young people playing folk songs. And, most days of most weeks, you can follow the dramatic cut and thrust of politics from the galleries of the House of Commons.

The best time of year to visit Ottawa is in May, preferably the last two weeks. May is spring flower time. There are 600,000 daffodils, 500,000 crocuses and three million tulips, originally a gift from the Netherlands for Canada's help in World War II. The Dutch royal family stayed in Ottawa during the war, and Canadian troops helped liberate Dutch towns.

May is also a month for school trips. The thousands of youngsters crowd things a bit but they also add to the emotion you'll feel about the nation's heritage.

WHAT TO SEE **The Hill**, as you'll find yourself calling Parliament Hill, in the manner of Ottawa residents, will be the focal point of your visit. Broad lawns march down from the three Gothic buildings which house Parliament and its offices. They look much alike, but the Centre Block, seat of the Commons, the Senate and the 291-foot Peace Tower, is 50 years younger than the East and West blocks. The Centre Block was rebuilt after a disastrous fire in 1916.

During the summer, free tours of the **Centre Block** and the **Peace Tower** are conducted from 9 A.M. to 9 P.M. The young guides are friendly and articulate. Expect a line-up – 15,000 people a day turn up to see the chambers from which they are governed.

The Peace Tower is dedicated to the 66,000 Canadians who died in World War I and a Book of Remembrance contains their names. A page is turned each day. The tower carillon has 53 bells, and recitals are given regularly.

From mid-June to Labor Day, the best show in town is the **Changing of the Guard**, each day at 10 A.M. on the lawns in front of the Parliament buildings. For 45 minutes, the Governor-General's Footguards or the Canadian Grenadier Guards, march in scarlet tunics and black bearskins. Around the Hill are the scarlet dress uniforms of the Royal Canadian Mounted Police, or Mounties.

Question period in the **House of Commons** is at 2 to 3 P.M. Monday through Thursday, 11 A.M. to noon on Friday. There is always a line-up for the lively, daily question period, so get there early. After question period, the leading parliamentarians usually disappear to other meetings or office work and the droning speeches begin. You can't take cameras or tape recorders into the gallery. But you can take notes; a long-standing prohibition against note-taking in the public galleries was removed in 1976.

The **Senate chamber**, with its deep red motif, is as handsome as the green House of Commons. But it's nowhere nearly as important in the political scheme of things. However, many Senators are leaders in their professions and you may occasionally hear a good speech in the Senate or in one of its committees.

Much of what you want to see in Ottawa is within walking distance of the Hill. The **Sparks St. mall**, three blocks of a main shopping street which has been closed to cars and trucks, is a block away. Here are stores, restaurants, plants, music, exhibitions of art and people – for this is prime people-watching territory. Everyone walks there, many of them pretty young civil servants. It's one of the best girl-watching spots in Canada.

Also within easy walking distance of the Hill:

Just to the east, the **Rideau canal**. It's one end of a 100-mile waterway linking Kingston on Lake Ontario, with the Ottawa river, just behind the Parliament buildings. The canal was built in 1826-32 under the supervision of Colonel John By, for whom Bytown was named. A boat trip is a pleasant way to spend a couple of hours for a few dollars. You don't have to look for the boatmen, they'll pester you if you go to the bridge over the canal, by the Chateau Laurier.

On either side of the canal are motor parkways and bicycle paths. They are among the works of the National Capital Commission which has made Ottawa one of the world's loveliest capitals.

Overlooking the canal is the **National Arts Centre**, at Confederation Square, a $46 million complex with three superb theaters, two restaurants and several terraces. You can have lunch and a drink there in an outdoor garden by the canal, or take a conducted tour, at noon or 3 P.M.

The **Chateau Laurier**, across the street from the Arts Centre, is one of Canada's fine hotels, a mainstay of the Canadian National chain. Its turrets and green roofing make it look like a fairy land castle.

The **National War Memorial** stands in the traffic circle in front of the Arts Centre. The nearby **National Gallery of Canada** has an extensive collection of traditional art (Rubens, Reynolds, Gainsborough), modern painting and sculpture (Picasso) and Canadian works. There's a fine sampling of the Canadian **Group of Seven,** at one time castigated for their radical approach to art, now revered for their influence on Canadian art. Impress your companions by making knowledgeable remarks about Fred Varley's distinctive purple tones. There are also striking works by Paul Kane, who painted the native peoples, and Cornelius Krieghoff, who portrayed pioneer life. The **market,** two blocks east of the Chateau Laurier, one block north of Rideau Street, is one of Ontario's most bustling farmer's markets. Flowers, food, fish and great fun.

Also just a walk away are the **Canadian War Museum,** 330-350 Sussex Dr., with a collection which includes Hermann Goering's armored car; the **Supreme Court of Canada**, just west of Parliament Hill at Kent and Wellington Sts., the dazzling new all-glass **Bank of Canada headquarters** at Bank and Wellington Sts. and the **National Library** and **Public Archives,** on Wellington St. across from the Garden of the Provinces. All have free admission.

If you have a car, take a drive out Sussex Dr. Soon after you leave downtown, you'll see the striking new Ottawa **City Hall**, a spacious building on Green Island, to your right. Exhibitions, ranging from art to cookery, are held frequently in the lobby. You'll pass the opulent chateau which is the **French embassy** before you come to the **residence of the prime minister** at **24 Sussex Drive**. It is not open to the public.

Almost across the road is **Rideau Hall,** residence of the governor-general, the Queen's representative. Write ahead well in advance or phone to ask if you can go in and stroll through the grounds where diplomatic garden parties are held. It's often permitted. Government House, Ottawa, phone (613) 749-5933.

You could also drive through **Rockcliffe,** a wholly residential municipality, with big and gracious homes housing the powerful politicians and diplomats.

One of Ottawa's top shows is the **National Aeronautical Collection** at Rockcliffe Airport, which includes 80 aircraft from before World War I up to the present. It's free, 9 A.M. to 9 P.M., closed Mondays.

There are thousands of acres of parkland and picnic area in the capital area, both in Ottawa and across the river in Quebec. Hull, the Quebec City across the river, is undistinguished. But nearby there is skiing in the Gatineaus, fishing, swimming and boating in summer. In winter, you can skate for miles in Ottawa itself along the frozen canal, which is cleared and patrolled by the National Capital Commission. You can often see dignified bureaucrats and businessmen skating to work, briefcases in hand.

Other things to see if you have time:

The National Museum of Science and Technology, at 1867 St. Laurent Blvd., has steam engines you can climb aboard, a luxurious private railway car, 26 vintage automobiles, a button you can press to set off a non-nuclear bomb. Admission free, daily 9 A.M. to 9 P.M. except closed Mondays from mid-September to mid-May.

The National Museums of Man and Natural

Sciences are housed together at McLeod and Metcalfe Sts. in a building that served as a temporary parliament after the 1916 fire. They have dinosaurs, stone age tools, an astronaut's suit and the country's finest collection of Canadian Indian art. Admission free. Tuesday- Sunday 10 A.M. to 6 P.M.

The National Postal Museum at Heron St. and Riverside Dr. is a philatelic paradise with displays dating back to 3,000 B.C. Free, 9 A.M. to 5 P.M. Tues.-Sat., Sunday noon to 5 P.M.

Laurier House, 335 Laurier Ave. E., was home to two of Canada's greatest prime ministers, Wilfrid Laurier and Mackenzie King. Historical memorabilia crowd its 20 rooms. Free, Tues.-Sat. 10 A.M. to 5 P.M., Sundays 2 to 5 P.M. Closed Monday.

At **Major's Hill Park**, behind the Parliament buildings, the noonday gun is fired at noon, except on Sundays when it goes off at 10 A.M.

The Canadian Mint. See money being made. But you must write ahead or phone for an appointment. 320 Sussex Dr., phone 992-2348. It's closed on holidays.

Royal Canadian Mounted Police barracks, at Rockcliffe, is open to the public from 9 to 11 A.M. and from 1 to 3 P.M. on weekdays. The kids love it.

Dominion Arboretum and Botanic Garden has 65 landscaped acres of hardy trees and shrubs, overlooking the Rideau Canal, on highway 16 at the southern approach to the city. The 1,300-acre **Central Canada Experimental Farms** opens its animal barns to the public daily except weekends. Free, Monday-Friday 8.30 A.M. to 4.30 P.M.

WHERE TO STAY   The **Chateau Laurier**, opposite Confederation Square ($30-$38) is the pre-eminent hotel. It's old, majestic, yet comfortable and homey.

Other main hotels are concentrated within a few blocks. They include the **Carleton Towers**, 150 Albert St., ($43.50-$49.50), **Holiday Inn Centre**, 100 Kent St., ($39-$41) and **Holiday Inn Downtown**, 350 Dalhousie St., ($30-$33.50), **Inn of the Provinces**, 350 Sparks St., ($36-$42), **Skyline**, 101 Lyons St., ($34-$40). **The Lord Elgin**, 100 Elgin St., ($21.50-$24.50) used to be Ottawa's second-best hotel. It is no longer but it's convenient, just two blocks from Parliament Hill, but instead of second-best we found it second-rate. The rates cited are for lowest standard singles and doubles.

Several apartment-hotels offer daily rates and kitchen facilities. We have enjoyed the **Berkeley Savoy** ($20-$24), 10 walking minutes from the Hill, at 140 Slater St. Many units are 2-3 rooms; kitchens are $2 extra.

Just a few minutes drive from downtown are many good motels. A few of the best include, with rates for two: **Embassy West**, 1400 Carling Ave. $25; **Macies Ottawan**, 1274 Carling Ave., $25-$30; **Sheraton El Mirador**, 480 Metcalfe St., $36; **Talisman**, 1376 Carling Ave., $41.75; **Town and Country**, 1476 Richmond Rd. $22.

If you go to Ottawa en famille, as most tourists do, why not try the rooms at **Ottawa University**? The university rents them from mid-May through June, and mid-August to early September. Spartan, clean and cheap. Special rates for students. Write Pavillon Tabaret, Ottawa University, 5 McDougall St., Ottawa.

WHERE TO EAT Somewhere else. That's what many Ottawa residents will tell you. The capital is not famed as a gourmet's paradise. Some embassies serve good food, but few tourists get to table there. Most Ottawa movers and shakers entertain at home.

If you know a member of parliament well enough to snag an invitation, the two best places in town for good meals at reasonable prices are the **Parliamentary Restaurant,** on the top floor of the Centre Block, and the **West Block Cafeteria.** They're heavily subsidized. If you get in you'll see politicians and newsmen and bureaucrats, and they guard their privileges. One of the most impassioned speeches we ever heard in the hallowed Commons was the Horatio-at-the-bridge attempt by a Toronto MP to prevent the price of parliamentary coffee being raised from a dime.

Generally the busiest and perhaps the most consistent restaurants in town are at the major hotels. Most venerable and still number one is the **Canadian Grill** downstairs at the **Chateau Laurier Hotel.** Cabinet ministers, civil service mandarins, lobbyists, dine there. There's schmaltzy music for dancing but not many people do. It's in the $40-$50 a couple range.

Like every other city, Ottawa has its share of trendy dining rooms, seafood places with nets and lobster traps, Japanese rooms with knives flashing. If you want something different and don't mind spending a little money, go across the river to Hull for fairly classy French cuisine at any of half a dozen spots. Try **Café Louis IX** in Hull if money's no concern.

For most tourists, it is. Particularly in a city like Ottawa, which draws families. Here are some restaurants we like and which a couple can usually escape from with both arms and legs and a bill of under $20, if you go easy on the drinks.

The National Arts Centre serves a fine luncheon buffet for about $5. **Nate's,** 320 Rideau St., is a delicatessen serving food of a quality rare outside of Montreal or Toronto.

Our favourite Italian restaurant is **La Roma,** 673

Somerset W. Handier downtown are the **Del Rio,** 217
Rideau St., and the **Bel-Air,** 123 Queen St. **Monte
Blanco,** 1268 Wellington St., serves Latin-American
food. The Ottawa version of the **Old Spaghetti
Factory** (six of its spaghetti dinners are under $3
each) is at 126 York St. Try **Chalet Suisse,** 1386 Base-
line Rd., for fondues. All the above restaurants are licensed.

A Chinese lady insists the **Emerald Garden,** 501 Rideau St., is as good as you'll get in Ottawa. An old
favorite is the **Canton Inn,** at 205 Albert St., in the
heart of downtown, and the **Pine Tree Village,** at 354
Elgin St., is popular.

Al's Steak House, 327 Elgin St., is representative of
Ottawa's many steak restaurants (New York cut, sir-
loin, $8.50). We like the **Carriage House,** 171 Bank
St., for seafood, though it is pricey (lobster cocktail
$4.30, rainbow trout $9.45).

In an old house five minutes walk from downtown
is the charming **La Seigneurie,** 140 Bay St. Each time
we visited it was quiet, uncrowded – and the Spanish
and French food was inviting, from the delectable
gazpacho on.

NIGHTLIFE As we said earlier, Ottawa is a great
place to sleep. Ottawans get around quite a bit but
the tradition is to visit each other. You won't get into
the round of political and bureaucratic cocktail parties, teas and garden parties. Many people will tell
you you're lucky.

However, there is live entertainment in most of the
hotels and a number of discotheques have sprung up.
Check the **National Arts Centre.** Ottawa has a festival
of cultural events through the summer. Many are excellent. The **Ottawa Little Theatre** is a resident group
which has produced some solid professional actors

for Canada's theater scene. Ottawa's entertainment scene, however, is most notable for the stars who came from there and shine elsewhere: Paul Anka and Rich Little. The **Central Canada Exhibition** in late summer is a sizeable fair.

Ottawa has the perennial eastern champion or contender in professional football, the **Ottawa Roughriders. Rideau Carleton** harness racing track has a first-rate dining room and fair horses; **Connaught Park** across the river in Aylmer, Que., is noisy and fun; in contrast to Ontario tracks you can buy beer or booze at stalls and wander around with it.

For late-night snacks, the restaurant off the lobby in the **Skyline Hotel** is as good as anywhere. The food is edible and the place is open 24 hours a day.

For details on Ottawa attractions and for maps, write Canada's Capital Visitors and Convention Bureau, 251 Laurier Ave. W., Ottawa.

TORONTO

"The last great city not yet devastated by progress."

Marshall McLuhan.

There is something about Toronto that immediately strikes visitors from some other large cities: nobody switches downtown off at 5 P.M., when the offices close. People stay down in the evening, or come down from the suburbs, to dine, drink, play. They are not afraid in lonely parking lots, or in quiet downtown streets. At dawn in winter, you will often see a shapely girl ice-skating alone on the rink at city hall square, in the heart of downtown, or a woman walking along the boardwalk at the eastern beaches.

For years Toronto residents boasted there wasn't a street in town they'd fear to walk alone at night. That is no longer so. As the city grows, so does the crime rate – a bit. Still, it is basically a city at peace. And a city which enjoys itself. Not long ago, a Detroit journalist wondered out loud why Toronto's murder rate was only five per cent that of his own city. He found the answer himself: ". . . everyone appears to be enjoying life too much to take someone else's."

More than 8 million people a year visit Toronto from outside Ontario and many of the visitors remark upon the city's friendliness. The signs in the parks say "Please Walk *on* the Grass." Visitors also notice that Toronto people actually like their police constables (as officers are called in a lingering bit of British heritage).

Its 2.8 million residents make Metro Toronto – a

federation of the core city, Toronto, and five boroughs – the second largest city in Canada, after Montreal. But in communications, entertainment and wealth it is Canada's first city. It is also the headquarters for the country's business and finance centers.

Toronto is cosmopolitan, an ethnic mosaic. Every second person in Metro was born outside Canada. Forty per cent are non-Wasp, largely southern European, with large spicy dashes of the Caribbean. Toronto has nearly as many Italians as Venice, almost as many Germans as Bonn – and the restaurants and other folkways to go with them.

It is a city of surprises and nobody is more surprised at the lively dame Toronto has become than the long-time residents who remember the quiet lady, some say the stodgy prude, she used to be. The surprises start from the moment you sight Toronto. You see a magnificent high-rise skyline just off the waterfront. (Toronto is a major port, on Lake Ontario, just 70 road miles from Niagara Falls, 90 from Buffalo.)

The CN Tower, tallest, free-standing structure in the world, stands like a needle – near four of the tallest office building complexes in the British Commonwealth. One reaches 72 stories up. Another is sheathed in glimmering gold-bronze. All four were put up by banks.

Go closer. Stand atop the tower. You will see that Toronto is also a city of trees, and ravines, and parks, and homes, a city of neighborhoods.

Drive through the neighborhoods and you will see something of the city's Victorian heritage and Toronto's effort to retain it. But when you arrive at the Ontario Science Centre, or Ontario Place (a playground built on man-made islands in Lake Ontario), you find modern magic. You play tick-tack-toe with a computer and see not just the latest, but the future, in film techniques.

As we have mentioned before, you will see that Toronto's downtown is alive. People of all income ranges still live in the city's core, or on the fringe of the inner city. They provide a basic population to support Metro's 4,000 restaurants, more than 30 live theaters, 161 night clubs and taverns, and big league sports.

For generations, Toronto was the place other Canadians called "Hogtown," caricatured as a smug, hypocritical monster sitting there draining the wealth of the hinterland. It was also a place of blue laws and thin lips. Eager customers stood in line-ups around the block, night after night outside the first post-prohibition cocktail lounges finally permitted by an Ontario premier in 1948 – but the affronted voters in his Toronto constituency turfed him out in favor of a prohibitionist nonentity. John Dos Passos wrote a friend that Toronto was "a beastly place." Allan Lamport, a mayor with a gift for malapropisms, who led the fight against blue laws and obtained approval for sports on Sunday, mused: "Nobody should visit Toronto for the first time." Like Philadelphia, Toronto was the butt of vaudeville jokes. W.C. Fields told a Buffalo audience: "I passed through Toronto one Sunday. It was closed." His listeners howled their recognition.

Toronto has always been a law-abiding city. But it's only in the last 20 years that visitors have accused the place of being fun. The city is in danger of being embarrassed by the praise it received from visiting journalists and municipal experts. *Fortune* magazine, which says Toronto used to be just a "tedious provincial capital," called it "the world's newest great city." *National Geographic* said that in many ways Toronto "resembles the New York city of half a century ago," the magnetic metropolis, drawing the talented and ambitious, warm and friendly.

The change came or coincided with a flood of immigration starting in the early 1950s. Until then, Toronto was Wasp country, with a minority of Roman Catholics, largely Irish, and a small but influential and creative Jewish community.

In the last two decades, nearly 300,000 Italians have settled in Toronto and its environs. Then came more than 100,000 each of Greeks and Portuguese, and large numbers of central and northern Europeans: Germans, Poles, Hungarians, Czechs, Ukrainians. In the 1970s the Caribbean and the Indian subcontinent have provided the largest number of immigrants to the city.

As the immigrants settled into the city, Torontonians noticed strange things. There were odd languages in the subway. Contrary to law, some of these folk drank wine in public at their picnics and kicked soccer balls around – and the sky didn't fall. Quaint little restaurants opened and served exotic sauces and dishes that were hard to pronounce.

Perhaps Toronto's happiest time these days is a 9-day summer festival called Caravan, in which about 60 different ethnic groups show off their crafts and cultures and cuisines.

As the population grew, new buildings had to be erected. For a while, Toronto was "Boom Town," or "Hustle City," as *Time* magazine once called it.

One building in particular stirred the city, and led development. Plans were chosen from those submitted in a world-wide competition among architects and Toronto built a new city hall. Facing each other like parentheses, or clam shells, the two curved buildings of the new city hall did not enrapture all of Toronto's citizens.

A Toronto newspaper ran a front-page, main headline based on fears an engineer had expressed about the building. If a gust of wind caught between those curved buildings, the wind could be spun around and around and come out at the top like a tornado, he said. "New City Hall May Spawn Tornadoes," the newspaper trumpeted.

No tornadoes were generated. But the striking new buildings, and the square in front, where office workers could lunch in the sun in summer, or skate in winter, did spawn a new spirit in Toronto's downtown.

But it was still hard to make out exactly where "Boom Town Metro," as the Toronto Star labelled it, was going. Irish playwright Brendan Behan reckoned Toronto would "be a fine town when it is finished."

Suddenly, the frantic race for the sky slowed. Toronto's politicians and its people seemed to wonder all at once if it wasn't time to catch a breath. The provincial government said a long-planned expressway couldn't be built. City council put restrictions on downtown building. Steps were taken to protect neighborhoods. Coincidentally some people who had moved to the suburbs started moving back to downtown. Homes were renovated. A client class for downtown facilities moved in.

Outsiders say it has worked. *Harper's* magazine called Toronto "an exception to the world's endless nightmare procession of malfunctioning cities." *Fortune* says the city is "remarkably liveable" and told its high-salaried readers: "As a tourist attraction, Toronto passes a simple test that most U.S. cities flunk. Your wife might beg to accompany you there on business."

If she does, she'll find a place that has room for a full range of lifestyles: high fashion and high cuisine, concerts in the parks, Caribbean carnivals, bagpipe festivals and benches provided on the main street in the financial district where you can sit and watch the passing parade.

With each year, the Indian word Toronto, meaning "place of meeting," takes on more significance.

PROBLEMS IN PARADISE Another useful Indian word around Toronto would be wampum. The city's main tourist problem is the high cost of living. It is a high-price area – for residents and visitors alike. Take a look at the real estate ads while you are there. The average price of a new, but ordinary, three-bedroom home is in the neighborhood of $60,000 – a pretty plush neighborhood indeed. Those tall, narrow, old high-gabled Victorian brick houses you'll pass in the whitepainters' neighborhoods downtown go for $100,000 and often much more.

Your own hotel and restaurant bills will be an education, too. In 1977, the cheapest standard double rooms in the 25 downtown hotels and guest houses listed by the Convention and Tourist Bureau of Metropolitan Toronto averaged $32.60. And that's including a couple of real cheapies.

There have been hopeful signs in the last two or three years. After two summers of high vacancy rates, hotels started to show signs of bending a bit towards the customer. Most installed special weekend rates. One of the truly luxurious hostelries set aside 25% of its rooms at a special $29 price. Several new budget-priced downtown hotels opened.

Be prepared to pay $2 or more for drinks in many bars and restaurants. In a luxury hotel like the Harbor Castle on the lakefront you will pay nearly as much for a Dubonnet as you would for a whole bottle of the stuff at the liquor store.

It's accepted that dinner with a drink and a bottle of wine will set you back $35 or more a couple – in most restaurants of any repute. And at quite a few without any.

Off-Broadway style theaters – which means most live theater in Toronto – are quite reasonable. The O'Keefe Centre and the truly grand old Royal Alexandra, both of which bring in New York and London touring productions, generally charge a couple of dollars less than you'd pay on Broadway.

Toronto is a great sports city, with knowledgable fans. It is a pleasure to sit in Maple Leaf Gardens and hear the reaction of discriminating hockey fans, who cheer good plays by opposing teams almost as much as those by the home town Maple Leafs.

But inflation has hit ticket prices. In 1977, prices for National League Hockey games ranged from $4 to $12 a ticket. (If you just want to see fast hockey, watch the juniors on Sunday afternoon, at $1 to $3 tops; they're the big leaguers of a year or two from now.) Baseball is cheaper, but Toronto's brand new Blue Jays charged the most in the majors, with a top of $6.50.

Adding to the cost problem is availability. Maple Leaf hockey tickets have been sold out to season subscribers before the schedule starts every year for a generation. Rights to season tickets are handed down in families. You can get tickets from scalpers but they range up to $50 a ticket and more for big games. The best tickets for Argonaut football games are also generally sold out in advance.

A similar problem exists with the "in" restaurants. On weekends, make sure you get your reservations in advance. Many of the best restaurants are small. As in other cities, it is a good idea to do much of your sampling at lunch time, when prices are as little as half those charged at dinner. Even then, at the fashionable restaurants, wait until 1:30 P.M. or so, when the worst of the noon crush is ended.

WHERE IT IS AND SOME OTHER STUFF Metro Toronto is on Lake Ontario, just 32 miles as the marathon swimmer goes, from upper New York state. On a clear day from the top of a downtown skyscraper you can see Rochester, if that's your bag. By air it is 557 miles from New York City, 296 miles from Cleveland and 531 miles from Chicago.

It is reached by two super-highways: the Queen Elizabeth Way, Canada's first expressway, from Niagara Falls and the Buffalo area; and Highway 401, formally called the Macdonald-Cartier Highway, from west (Detroit) and east (Montreal). Both are multi-lane, limited access. Some years ago two ladies crossing from Buffalo asked a Canadian customs officer the best way to Toronto. "Take the Queen Elizabeth," he said. One turned to her friend and said "Oh dear, I don't think we want to go by ship, do we?"

Driving is easy in Ontario and in Toronto. The city is laid out on a grid system, following the squared off surveys for settlement. Most streets run east-west and north-south.

U.S. drivers should watch for three driving patterns: 1) You can pass on the right and many American drivers find it unnerving when Canadians do. 2) You can make a right turn at a red stoplight after coming to a full stop and giving pedestrians the right of way. Toronto drivers don't use their horns much but they will if they are stuck behind someone who dallies on a right turn. 3) Driver and passengers must wear seat belts under pain of a $28 fine.

Toronto uses one-way streets in many residential areas in the city's core. But only a few main downtown streets, notably Adelaide and Richmond, are one-way.

Metro Toronto is a gateway to summer cottage country. It is 60 miles from the beginning of the widespread holiday areas with their thousands of lakes. With nine yacht clubs and public marinas, it is a major center for pleasure boating as well as a major port on the St. Lawrence Seaway.

Besides the lake, Toronto's center is bounded on west and east by the Humber and Don rivers. They were the reason for the Indians meeting here in the first place. Because of pollution, you can't do much with them, although the Don, scene of the classic nature tales of Ernest Thompson Seton, is cleaner than it used to be.

It was on this river that a demonstration of Toronto delicacy at its finest occurred. During a royal visit, Queen Elizabeth's schedule called for her to walk a foot bridge across the Don. At a carefully calculated moment, city workers dumped several thousand dollars' worth of perfumed cleanser into the river so it would arrive at the same moment as the Queen, and prevent the royal nostrils from being offended by the river's usual odor. The flushing of the river occurred as scheduled. Some said the perfume smelled worse than the river. Her Majesty didn't comment.

Toronto is further south than some parts of the United States and its weather is like that of northern U.S. cities. It gets much less snow than Buffalo. Winters are not so much cold as clammy; summers are hot. January temperatures average minus 4.4 Celcius, 24° F. July averages 21.8° C. or 71.2° F. Still, every year there are stories of Americans crossing the border in summer with skis strapped to their cars, headed for Toronto. Don't. Bellboys might laugh at you.

If you come in winter, wear boots or have a protective solution put on your shoes. Toronto uses unadulterated salt after snowfalls to clear its streets, and lays it on thick. It ruins leather. It rots cars, too, so make

sure your car is thoroughly washed, including a rinse
of the underside, after a Toronto winter visit.

For information on accommodation, attractions,
and so on, write the Convention and Tourist Bureau
of Metropolitan Toronto, Eaton Centre Galleria,
Suite 110, 220 Yonge St., Toronto M5B 2H1.

LANGUAGE, YOU KNOW? For U.S. residents,
Toronto is a foreign city and yet it isn't, really. Television, radio, newspapers, commercial products, ad-
vertising, are basically the same as south of the border. You may find French useful in a good French
restaurant, and you will hear half a dozen languages
and a score of accents on one subway trip, but English is the language of Toronto.

The city sometimes tried to be more English than
the English. That's no longer true. But some vestiges
remain. Canadians say "leftenant" but there are only
"leftenants" in the armed services, not in the police
force. Z is still "Zed" most of the time but a lot of
people say "Zee." Don't be confused by a cross line
on the leg of a 7, as 7; you'll see it frequently. It's
British style.

There is a Toronto English, spoken by natives or
long-term residents. If you hear frequent references
to "a boot," it's not a foot fetish; the speaker probably means "about." "Eh" as used by Torontonians
can mean anything from "I didn't make out what you
said, please repeat," to a request for agreement, to
simply "that's the end of the sentence." Eh?

THE PAST The Indians were here first. They
landed at Toronto on their way up the Humber River, en route from Lake Ontario to Lake Huron. They
called Toronto the Carrying Place. The French, led

by the explorer LaSalle, followed and established a fort and trading post. It was burned to prevent English occupation when the French withdrew to Montreal in 1759, during the Seven Years' War. Toronto and the rest of French North America were ceded to Britain in the Treaty of Paris in 1763.

In 1793 the town of York was laid out on the site of Toronto. The first governor, John Graves Simcoe, changed the name to honor the Duke of York, son of King George III. It became Toronto again in 1834. Simcoe eventually became a lieutenant-general but was never a nobleman, in spite of the mistakenly-named Lord Simcoe Hotel in Toronto.

The most colorful part of York's early history was its part in the burning of Washington during the War of 1812. In 1813, American troops occupied York and burned the legislature building and the archives. In reprisal, the British burned Washington.

Other than skirmishes during the short-lived 1837 Rebellion, when a few reformers in Ontario and Quebec rose up against rule by the Family Compact, the oligarchy which today we'd call the Establishment, Toronto's history has been mostly social and commercial. How many other cities would include in an official summary of its historical highlights items such as "1881, street arc lights first demonstrated?"

Names which loom large in Toronto history, memorialized not only in their commercial enterprises but in the public institutions they funded, are Eaton (department stores) and Massey (farm implements). The business of Toronto was business.

It still is, to a great extent. But the change in this century can be seen in such things as the career of Vincent Massey as governor general and patron of the arts, his brother Raymond as actor (Abraham Lincoln and scores of other roles) and an Eaton as an international racing driver.

Toronto has done well in the professions, science, medicine (insulin, the saver of diabetics, was discovered here) and in the arts. The Group of Seven, the most famous Canadian school of painters, was centered here; the Art Gallery of Ontario has the largest collection of Henry Moore sculptures in the world.

Actors and writers, who used to flee to more receptive fields, stick around longer. Toronto is an international film-making center now. Residents became, if not blasé, at least accustomed, to seeing Richard Burton at the next table in a downtown restaurant or Liv Ullman in Trader Vic's.

THE NATIVES ARE FRIENDLY   Some of the best things about Toronto are its neighborhoods. They are many; they are varied. And it costs little to window-shop on the way the people live.

Curiously, downtown Toronto is itself a friendly village in the summertime. A tourist's most essential stop is at **the square in front of city hall.** In summer, there is a pool and fountains – in winter, ice-skating. Office workers bring their lunches and take the sun on benches in front of the clam-shaped city hall.

South on Bay St. are the huge office complexes. There is free, live, noon-time **music** on the courts of both the **Toronto-Dominion Centre** – the big, black blocks at the southwest corner of King and Bay – and silvery **Commerce Court**, on the east side of Bay St. The TD grounds have grass; the Commerce Court, cement – but it has more benches, a pool, and a sidewalk café beside the platform where the musicians play.

When you're at the Commerce Court, make sure you walk through **Commerce Court North**, the old 32-storey Bank of Commerce headquarters which used to be the British commonwealth's tallest building.

Now it is dwarfed by its neighbours, but many still think it is Toronto's most beautiful office building, inside and out.

Canada's tallest building now is **First Canadian Place**, whose 72 stories thrust up from King St., just north of the TD Centre. Visit its quiet downstairs galleries where beautiful objects are on display. Outside, sit and watch the people. Our favorite bench is on King St. just west of Yonge, in front of Montreal Trust, just east of Commerce Court.

In communities easily reached from downtown, you can watch different peoples and cultures; shop and eat exotically. Old time Torontonians love **the Beach**. It's almost a village to itself in the east end, by the waterfront. The main drag is an eight or ten block stretch of Queen St. east of Woodbine Ave. It's a 15-minute streetcar ride from downtown, or a 10-minute drive. Queen St. at the Beach has gone artsy-craftsy, with antique shops, paintings and health food markets.

Visitors love **Griffiths**, 2086 Queen St. E., a German-style delicatessen. Go on through to a crowded, dimly-lit dining room, all wood and old things, for light lunches and dinners. Or get fish and chips at $1.25 an order at **Nova Fish Store**, 2209 Queen St. E., one of the best samples left of a dying cuisine for which Toronto once was famous.

You might enjoy taking your chips and eating them as you stroll in **Kew Beach park** or along the boardwalk at the lake. The beach is, logically, the Beach's main attraction. It's a magically warm, nostalgic place on a July evening.

Take a walk on **St. Clair Ave. W. in the Dufferin St.** area and you might think you are in Rome. Bustling, hustling, noisy – you may not hear a word of English. Buy a cone of Italian ice cream and amble. Or stop for a meal at someplace like **San Marco**, 1231 St.

Clair Ave. W. (scampi in garlic and butter, $7.75), or the **Sidewalk Restaurant and Tavern**, 1662 Dufferin St. (especially for veal).

Bloor St. west of Spadina is also European, with a bit more stress on central Europe. Take the subway to Bathurst St. and walk a block west, to stare at **Honest Ed's** and his **Markham Village**. Honest Ed Mirvish made his millions by running Toronto's first big discount store. It is a circus, with brassy signs and slogans, pushy patrons and genuine bargains. He put some of his money into refurbishing Markham St., which now has tony places and chic art galleries.

When your ears have been assaulted sufficiently at Honest Ed's, walk in either direction along Bloor St. It's hectic. Clothing racks and produce counters crowd the sidewalk. There are many good places to eat or drink. One likeable spot is **L'Europe**, 469 Bloor St. W., a homey Hungarian restaurant with roast suckling pig and gypsy musicians. The food is filling and reasonable (two can eat and drink well for $20), and its even cheaper in L'Europe's **Blue Cellar Room**, where students congregate to drink beer. Or drink some beer at nearby **Brunswick House**, 481 Bloor St. W., a loud and lively beer parlor where poets read and amateurs sing.

If you prefer a Greek atmosphere, go the other direction east on the Bloor St. subway, get off at Pape Ave., and explore both east and west on the Danforth. You'll find several fine Greek restaurants, such as **Hellenic Place**, 124 Danforth Ave. ($15 for two). Or try one of the better pizzas in town at **Centaurus Restaurant and Pizza House**, 707 Danforth Ave.

Toronto's **Chinatown** is rivalled in Canada only by Vancouver's. Toronto's is centered on Dundas St., west from Bay St, and in recent years, downtown rebuilding has forced Chinatown to spread west as far as Spadina.

Don't just go there to eat, although there are literally dozens of fine Chinese restaurants. Window
shop. Talk to people like Jean Lumb. She's a sort of
unofficial mayoress and is usually at her **Kwong-Chow**
tavern, upstairs at 126 Elizabeth St. at the corner of
Dundas St. W. It's one of the community's most popular eating spots. Plush, palatial dining rooms have
been built recently in Chinatown. But some of the
best food is served in unpretentious tiny places like
Shanghai, 334 Spadina Ave. Try the Shanghai
shrimp.

From Chinatown, it is only a short distance to one
of Toronto's most colorful neighborhoods. The
Kensington Market is a polyglot paradise of fish
stores, kosher butchers and sidewalk sales. There are
live quail in cages on the sidewalk, and delicatessens
with 20 kinds of salami. And a dozen different languages. It's shrill and noisome and fun, especially on
Saturday morning.

The Kensington Market is made up of half a dozen
blocks centered on **Augusta and Baldwin Aves.** Take
Dundas St. W. just past Spadina and go north on Augusta. The market was once totally Jewish. Portuguese are now in the majority but there are many
other ethnic strains: Jewish, Jamaican, Italian,
Greek. Among several first-rate Portuguese restaurants in the market, we like the comfortable **Lisbon**
Plate, 184 Augusta Ave., where two people can dine
well for $20. Try the sampler plate of squid and other
seafood called "Lisbon Revolution."

For a look at how the restorers are bringing back
old neighborhoods, visit north **Cabbagetown.** That
was the name given a downtown area settled originally by Anglo-Saxon workmen, most of whom grew
vegetables in their front yards. Go north on
Parliament St. to **Wellesley** or **Carlton Sts.** and turn
east. Wander through the side streets where skinny,

tall old Victorian houses, neglected for generations, are being gutted and restored.

There are many good restaurants in the area: You might try **Bumpkin's** a plain spot with no liquor license but fine food, 557 Parliament St. Two people can dine well for $10. One warning: the place is so cheap and the food so good, there is often a line-up to get in. It's open for dinner only, from 5:30 P.M. Or **Parkes**, 226 Carlton St., a Victorian house converted into an elegant restaurant, $25 or so for two.

An effort has been made to restore old York, just east of the city's downtown core. On Saturday morning, go to the **St. Lawrence Farmer's Market**, behind the cleaned-up and renovated **St. Lawrence Hall**, at King St. E. and Jarvis St., once Toronto's city hall. On Saturday mornings in summer and fall, the farmer's market is thronged with people shopping for fresh meat and produce. Tourists can buy leather goods and other crafts, homemade preserves, maple syrup and maple sugar. **The Old Fish Market**, at 12 Market St., a popular nearby seafood restaurant in an old warehouse, serves delicious chowder for Saturday breakfast or brunch.

Whether or not you eat there, be sure to visit its neighbor, at 20 Market St., the **Rare Wine and Spirits store** of the Liquor Control Board of Ontario. It is made of sandblasted brick, wooden beams, antiques and flagstone floors. Its reason for being, of course, is an intriguing variety of rare potables ranging up to a magnum of 1966 red Chateau Latour at $108.30. There are many reasonably priced vintages as well.

WHERE TO SHOP As in any suburban shopping mall of consequence, Toronto's downtown shopping is anchored by big department stores. Busiest area is

from Richmond St. to Dundas St., on Yonge St. –
three long city blocks.

A sight to see, as well as a place to shop, is the
mammoth **Eaton Centre**, opened early in 1977 after
many years of planning and political controversy.
Eaton's is a household name in Canada; the
country's first really national, department store firm.
For years it dominated the field but since World War
II it has been slipping in competition with younger,
nimbler merchandisers. In a daring toss of the dice,
Eaton's closed three downtown stores to build its new
eight floors of shopping, at Dundas and Yonge. Cou-
pled with it is a galleria of hundreds of other stores.
From outside, it looks like a greenhouse; inside, it is
spacious and bright.

Meanwhile, **Simpson's**, Eaton's main competitor,
remains in its elegant old store at Yonge and Queen,
making a virtue of age. It plans to renovate but also
to hold on to its gracious, dignified yet lively atmosphere. Both Eaton's and Simpsons rank among the
great department stores of the world.

For several blocks above Dundas, Yonge St. is raucous, in places sleazy and tawdry, speckled with blue
movies and game arcades. But a few more blocks
again to the north is the city's second main shopping
area, which many say is the best place in the city to
shop for quality and high-style. It is priced to match.
This is the area centered on **Bloor between Yonge and
Avenue Rd.**, a short subway ride from downtown.

The corner of Yonge and Bloor is anchored by the
large **Hudson Bay Co.** department store, main rival to
Simpsons and Eaton's. Along Bloor St. and in the underground malls are dress shops with couturier origi-
nals, elegant fur stores, and boutiques carrying imported goods from all over the world. On Bloor St.
west of Bay is the **Colonnade**, a ritzy mall with prices
to match the chic.

At Bay or Avenue Rd., walk north a block from
Bloor and roam through **Yorkville**, generations ago a
separate village, for a time a rundown neighborhood,
then Toronto's bohemian center, now one of the
city's most elegant collections of specialty shops and
eating places.

As you wander through the city, you will find unusual shops in strange places. If you like candy, stop at
1283 Gerrard St., at Greenwood Ave., in a neighborhood that can kindly be called nondescript. For more
than 60 years the Clayton family has been making
and selling real homemade candies, including awesome chocolate sculptures. It's open daily to 9 P.M. except Saturday, when it closes at 5:30 P.M.

And for dreamers, there's **Grand Touring
Automobiles**, 183 Front St. E., which stocks Rolls
Royces at up to $92,000, Aston-Martins, Saabs and
BMWs.

WHAT TO SEE   Toronto's main tourist attractions
are mostly of recent origin. But there are many links
with the past. In a day, you can make a simulated
moon landing, walk in a fort build in 1793, peer
down secret passages in a fantastic giant castle, and
listen to a free symphony concert under the stars.

Some attractions, like the annual Canadian National Exhibition, or the polyglot Kensington market,
are listed under other sections of this chapter.

Prices and hours in the following list of specific attractions are subject to change. Many are closed or
observe different hours on various holidays. A visitor
should phone first if he intends to go to one of them
on a holiday.

You'll see Toronto's newest trademark from miles
away as you approach the city. It's the gleaming red
and blue and grey-white $40 million needle on the

waterfront, the **CN Tower**, the world's tallest free-standing structure at 1,815 feet, five inches. (CN is short for Canadian National, the government-owned railway and communications company). Its worka-day role is to serve broadcasting stations as a trans-mission center. But it is open daily for visitors ($3.75 adult, $1.50 children under 12). Glassed-in exterior elevators whisk visitors to observation platforms at 1,120, and 1,500 feet, and to a luxury revolving res-taurant at 1,150 feet, where the charge is $30-$50 for dinner for two with wine. On a clear night, you can see Rochester's lights 171 miles away.

Buildings are important to Toronto. The structure itself is half the fun at four of the city's most compel-ling tourist draws: **City Hall, Ontario Science Centre, Ontario Place** and **Casa Loma**.

The facing curved towers have been standing at Queen and Bay Sts. since 1965 but Torontonians still call it the **New City Hall**. (The old city hall across the street is worth a gander, too, since it's been cleaned up: solid, grand, dignified, it's used mostly for the courts.) City hall was designed by Finnish architect Viljo Revell in a world-wide competition. There are free tours from 10:15 A.M. to 5:15 P.M. Outside, sit for awhile in the sun in Nathan Phillips Square, named for the mayor who pushed the project through. It's one of the town's best places for people-watching. Buy popcorn or hot chestnuts. Chat with a mounted policeman. Stroke the smooth curves of Henry Moore's controversial sculpture "The Archer."

The **Ontario Science Centre** is an enchanting place where they think you learn best about things by working them yourself. You can play tic-tac-toe with a computer, be a conductor for an electrical current which literally makes your hair stand up, simulate a moon landing, or manipulate mechanical hands. There are more than 550 exhibits in the three connected buildings sprawling over a hillside site. There are also movies, adequate fast-foods service, a fair licensed resturant, and an outdoor beer garden. The center is 8 miles from downtown, at 770 Don Mills Rd. (corner of Eglinton Ave. E.). Go by subway to Eglinton station and take the Eglinton East bus, or to Pape station and take the Don Mills bus. Open daily 10 A.M. to 6 P.M. Adults $1.50, students 75 cents, children 25 cents, senior citizens 50 cents, $3.50 for a family.

The provincial government put three man-made islands in Lake Ontario just off the Canadian National Exhibition Grounds and called it **Ontario Place**. It is 96 acres of magic on a summer evening. Cinesphere Theatre shows breathtaking films on a screen six stories high. Free entertainment ranging from rock groups to the Toronto Symphony Orchestra is presented evenings at the **Forum**, an outdoor amphitheater with room for more than 8,000 people. It's so popular though that you have to get there early to make sure of a seat. Kids love the two-acre **Children's Village**. There are 9 snack bars and 12 licensed ethnic restaurants (8 with entertainment), picnic spots, boat tours, strolling musicians, a marina, and a World War II destroyer. Open daily from May 21 to Labor Day 10:30 A.M., to 1 A.M. except for a 10 P.M. closing on Sundays. Open weekends from Labor Day to the second weekend in October. Adults $2, youths 13-17 $1, children $1 or 50 cents if accompanied by a parent. Drive six miles from city center on Lake Shore Blvd. W., or take a Dufferin bus or Bathurst streetcar.

Casa Loma was built by financier Sir Henry Pellatt in 1914 for over $3 million. It is a fantastic 98-room palace that looms on its 6-acre site at the top of a hill like a medieval castle out of an illustrator's imagination. It has a secret staircase, hidden passages and a tunnel to a stable made out of mahogany and marble.

The free-spending millionaire, who raised and equipped a regiment of soldiers for World War I, finally fell on hard times and his dream castle went to the city for taxes. Open daily from 10 A.M. to 4 P.M. year round, to 6 P.M. in summer. 1 Austin Terrace, at Davenport Rd. and Spadina Rd., 1.5 miles from downtown. Adults $2, students 13-18 $1, children and senior citizens 50 cents.

The **Royal Ontario Museum** is Canada's biggest. It has one of the finest collections of Chinese art and artifacts in the world. The ROM has 5 million items in its collection, including dinosaur skeletons, armor and weapons, ores and minerals. At the corner of Bloor St. W. and University Ave., it has its own subway stop, Museum, on the University line, or get off at St. George on the Bloor-Danforth line. It's only a block or two from Bloor's fashionable shopping. Open daily 10 A.M. to 6 P.M., until 9 P.M. on Sundays and Tuesdays in July and August. Adults $1, children, students and senior citizens 50 cents, family rate $2. Children under 12 must be accompanied.

Next door to the museum is **McLaughlin Planetarium**, where you recline in special seats for the afternoon and evening shows. Closed Mondays. Adults $1, students and senior citizens 75 cents, children under 6 not admitted to the theatre.

The **Art Gallery of Ontario** has the largest collection of sculptures and other works by Henry Moore in the world. The 300 Moore pieces are included in the total collection of 6,000 works which also provides a comprehensive look at Canadian painting and a solid collection of old masters. There is a cafeteria and a licensed French restaurant. Closed Mondays. Open 10 A.M. to 5 P.M. Tuesday, Friday, Saturday, 10 A.M. to 10 P.M. Wednesdays and Thursdays, noon to 5 P.M. Sundays and holidays. Adults $1, students 50 cents, children under 12 accompanied by an adult admitted free. Admission includes entrance to the **Grange**, Toronto's oldest surviving brick house, dating back to 1817, now fully restored to show life as it was for the upper middle classes in the mid-1830s. The Art Gallery is on Dundas St. between McCaul and Beverly Sts., a short walk west of the St. Patrick subway station on the University Ave. subway.

There is no admission charge at the **McMichael Canadian Collection**, in the village of Kleinburg, about 35 miles northwest of downtown Toronto. In 30 gallery rooms, in a building constructed from hand-hewn timbers and native stone, there are 900 works by the Group of Seven and other Canadian artists like Emily Carr and Clarence Gagnon. From the gallery, there is a breath-taking view of woods and valley. Open afternoons, closed Mondays. The view is spectacular, the food ordinary, in a moderately-priced, pine-paneled dining room. A pleasant place to take afternoon tea.

For generations, **Toronto's zoo** was a small collection jammed into cages on a tiny site virtually downtown. Several years ago Toronto opened one of the world's most modern zoos in a rural suburban setting of rolling hills and valleys. Instead of rows of cages, there is a 710-acre landscape of pavilions and animals roaming in spacious near-freedom. The zoo divides the world into six areas and puts animals among their native trees, flowers and vines. There's a slow-moving train around the grounds if you get tired of walking and in winter, people ski through the zoo grounds. Open year round, 10 A.M. to 7 P.M. in summer. In summer, there are two restaurants and three snack bars. Take exit 61A from Highway 401, about 15 miles northeast of downtown Toronto. Adults $3, youths and senior citizens, $1.50, parking $1.

Fort York is a military museum in the old fort established by governor John Graves Simcoe in 1793.

Once the lake lapped near the base of the fort, but because of the gradual filling in and development of the waterfront it is now more than a quarter-mile from the shore. American troops sacked the fort during the war of 1812. Scarlet-clad guardsmen re-enact military life in the old town with parades and battle drills. Open year-round, in summer from 9:30 A.M. to 5 P.M. daily. In winter, opening hour on Sunday is 12 noon. Enter off Fleet St, between Bathurst and Strachan Aves. Bathurst street car. Adults $1, children and senior citizens 25 cents, family rate $2.50.

Near Fort York is the **Marine Museum of Upper Canada**, in Exhibition Place. It's located in one-time army officers' quarters built in 1841. Exhibits, including a complete steam tug, tell the story of shipping and waterways from the canoe to the cargo ship of today. Open year round, 9:30 A.M. to 5 P.M., except Sundays when it is open from noon to 5 P.M.. A treat on Sundays is English tea from 1:30 P.M. to 4 P.M. in the Ship Inn. Adults 50 cents, children 25 cents.

Other bits of history to view are three houses restored and furnished in the styles of more than a century ago: **Colborne Lodge**, in the south end of High Park; **Gibson House**, illustrating life in a farm house, at 5172 Yonge St., 2 miles north of Highway 401; and **Mackenzie House**, the downtown home of Toronto's first mayor, at 82 Bond St., two blocks east of Yonge St. just south of Dundas St. E. All are open year round from 9:30 A.M. to 5 P.M., Sundays noon to 5 P.M. and admission to each is adults 50 cents, children 25 cents.

The best depiction of life in early days is at **Black Creek Pioneer Village**. Its 30 buildings show lifestyles between 1793 and 1867, including the progress of a rural family from first shanty to substantial house. Skilled workers dressed in period costumes make brooms, spin, cook, print, farm, and so on as their predecessors did. They're articulate and friendly. Open from March to January, from 10 A.M. until 6 P.M. in summer, 9:30 A.M. to late afternoon in most of the rest of the year. Adults $2.50, children 75 cents, Monday to Friday family rate $5, senior citizens $1. There is an excellent licensed restaurant with period decor and costumed waitresses.

Toronto Island is actually three islands, formed a century ago when the sandy connection to them was washed away. There are now a 612-acre playground with a small zoo, a children's park, a farm, barnyard animals, bicycling, pony rides, kiddie rides, swimming, boating, snack bars, a light plane airport. A pleasant 75-cent ferry ride at the foot of Bay St. gets you there. **High Park**, at Bloor St. W. and Parkside Dr., (High Park subway station), is the closest thing Toronto has to New York's Central Park. It has fishing, gardens, nature trails, a miniature zoo, duck ponds, boat delivery, picnic areas and an excellent restaurant.

Other highlights among Metro's more than 100 parks: **James Gardens**, 27 acres of formal gardens; **Edwards Gardens**, 35 acres of rolling lawns, trees, streams; **Sunnybrook Park**, public stable and bridle path; **Allan Gardens**, indoor and outdoor botanical displays in the city's core. Call city or Metro parks departments, 367-7251 and 367-8186, for more details on locations and activities, including free concerts and dances almost nightly in summer.

Some more free things:

Craven Foundation Automobile Museum, 760 Lawrence Ave. W., 68 vintage cars from 1901 to 1933. Open all year, 9:30 A.M. weekdays, 10 A.M. Sundays and holidays, to 4 P.M.

Hockey Hall of Fame, Exhibition Place on C.N.E. grounds. All year, 10:30 A.M. to 4:30 P.M. Artifacts of Canada's national game.

Toronto Stock Exchange, 234 Bay St. From a gallery overlooking the floor where 70% of the dollar value of all share trading in Canada is handled, you can watch the action and hear it described by a recording. These days it isn't very exciting but it is free and quick.

Harbourfront is a year round congerie of arts, crafts, movies, dancing, variety shows, and concerts in a federally-financed attempt to change the waterfront into a park. It's free. Current events are listed in newspaper ads or call 369-4951 to check what's on.

THE SPORTING LIFE Toronto has big league teams (Babe Ruth hit his first professional home run here). But they haven't been very good in recent years. The storied Maple Leafs, members of the National Hockey League for half a century, last won the Stanley Cup in 1967; the fabled football Argonauts last won the Grey Cup in 1952; the American League Blue Jays are an expansion baseball team which only began playing in the city in 1977. Still, fans support them and the best tickets are hard to get.

Metro Toronto is also big league in horse-racing. The best stakes horses in North America come to harness racing's **Grand Circuit week** in July at Greenwood track. Thoroughbred jockeys Sandy Hawley and Ron Turcotte, international favorites, sharpened their skills in Ontario; the great Secretariat won the last race of his career at elegant Woodbine. The Queen's Plate for three-year-olds, Canada's premier race, is North America's oldest continuously run stakes race. It is held at Woodbine in late June.

Hockey is Toronto's game. More than 100,000 area youngsters play in organized leagues. Fans are knowledgable. Maple Leaf Gardens' 16,000 seats are always sold out. In spite of sporadic police crackdowns, scalpers abound on Carlton St. outside the gardens, particularly in the subway station. Most exciting visiting teams are Montreal, Philadelphia, Buffalo, Boston, New York Islanders. Ticket prices: $4 to $12 per seat.

If you simply want to see fast hockey, try the Junior **A Marlboros**. They play Sunday afternoons at the Gardens. They are the 17- to 20-year-olds who are being groomed for the major league. Tickets: $1 to $3. Or ask someone for directions to any rink where Metro Toronto Hockey League games are played. Any evening or all day Saturday and Sunday, for 60 cents you can see dedicated kids from 8 to 16 years old. The quality of play will surprise you. Look for games in AA category.

Football is played by Argonauts at Exhibition Stadium. Pre-season games start in July, regular season in August. It ends in November. Tickets: $4 to $12.

College football is sparsely attended. The University of Toronto team is usually a power. It plays at midtown Varsity Stadium, a beautiful place to be in early fall, on Bloor St. just west of University Ave. Take the Yonge-University subway to St. George station.

Baseball got off to a good start when Toronto set a record for season tickets sold by an expansion club. Play starts at Exhibition Stadium in early April, usually too chilly for baseball, and ends at the beginning of October. Tickets: $2 to $6.50.

Horses race year-round. Thoroughbreds run at Greenwood Raceway, virtually downtown, or Woodbine, one of the continent's most impressive tracks, from March to November. Take the Queen St. E. streetcar to Greenwood. Drive or take special race buses to Woodbine, on highway 27 north of highway 401, in Metro's northwest end. It's $15 or so by cab from downtown. Night harness racing is conducted at Greenwood or at Mohawk, an hour's drive west of Toronto just off highway 401.

There is Sunday racing at Woodbine and Mohawk but not at Greenwood. For a special treat, lunch or dine at the track. The food is nothing to cheer about, drinks are pricey but it is a sybaritic feeling to sit overlooking the finish line while friendly messengers take bets at your table. Admission for both thoroughbred and standardbred racing is $2 grandstand, $4 clubhouse (Mohawk has no clubhouse).

Golf is a major sport. There are more than 100 golf courses in and around Metro Toronto. Many are open to non-members. But avoid weekend play unless you are very patient. On Saturdays and Sundays, your best time to avoid crowds is in mid-afternoon. The two most challenging municipal courses are Don Valley, on Yonge St. just south of highway 401, and the Lakeview course on Dixie Rd., a mile south of the Queen Elizabeth Way, west of Toronto. Fees range upwards from $4.50 for adults at all times at Don Valley, lowest rate around.

Other sports events include horse shows at the Canadian National Exhibition in August and the Royal Winter Fair in November, including international grand prix jumping; the Toronto Star indoor games, a major stop on the North American track and field circuit, in February; and the Rothman professional tennis tournament, which draws international champions in February.

CALENDAR OF SPECIAL STUFF Toronto has a crowded calendar of annual special events around which you can plan visits.

The **Canadian National Exhibition** is the world's largest annual fair, drawing more than 3 million visitors in its three-week run. The **Royal Agricultural**

Winter Fair is the largest exhibition of its kind in Canada.

But the most joyous fête and biggest success story is **Caravan**, a nine-day wonder every June. More than 50 ethnic communities show off their cultures, crafts, arts and foods in cabarets set up in clubs, schools, churches and community halls across Metro. Each is named for a different city, from Amsterdam to Zagreb. You can see, or dance, the flamenco in Madrid, the hopak in the Ukraine, a jig in St. John's, Newfoundland, eat Melton Mowbray pie and drink pale ale in London, sip vin rouge in Paris, sing Ein Prosit in Berlin and Waltzing Matilda in Sydney and waltz to an oom-pah-pah band in Vienna.

Passports which admit you to all pavilions cost $5 ($4 if you get them in advance). Special bus routes run directly from pavilion to pavilion. Some people go every one of the nine days and evenings in late June. Caravan started in 1969 with 29 pavilions which drew 600,000 visits. Number of visits now is up to 2 million a year. The concept is expanding to take in some professional arts groups like the Canadian Opera Company.

For up-to-date information or to order passports in advance, write Caravan, 263 Adelaide St. W., Toronto M5H 1Y2, phone (416) 868-0466.

Several of the most popular pavilions are: Kiev (folklore), Odessa (musical theatre), Vienna (polkas, waltzes, schnitzels), Tokyo (delicate water painting, displays of martial arts, sampler servings of tempura and teriyaki) and Prague (dancing under the stars on an outdoor floor in a park setting, Czech beer).

The **Canadian National Exhibition** is an institution in Toronto. It is both supported and mired by mostalgia. Critics call it stale and outdated; aficionados value its tradition. It's a sprawling, noisy melange; many people grumble but still go year after year. Its midway is vast (figure on about $20 with a couple of lively kids). There are sports (baseball, snooker, water-skiing, bowling and others); livestock and crops competitions; a first-rate horse show; an art gallery; free musical programs; a nightly variety show, and many other attractions.

Among our favorites: the fragrant and colorful horticultural exhibition. Lumberjack competitions. The travel pavilion operated by the southern United States where recording stars put on free country and western concerts. The Ontario government's exhibit of fish and wild life. On everybody's "must" list is the Pure Foods Building, filled with the most enticing smells. Visitors used to lunch free on samples here. There are few free samples now but some exhibitors serve hot dogs and other light lunches at loss-leader prices. You can buy cheeses and smoked meats, candy and imported preserves, most fast foods and delicatessen specialties, at special sale prices.

Warnings: Wear comfortable shoes, Exhibition Park is mostly pavement. Dress lightly; the "Ex" comes in Toronto's hottest days, the last three weeks of August. If you decide to eat at the "Ex," caveat emptor and check out the dining room you choose carefully. Some, like Stoodleigh's, at the Grandstand, are experienced in coping with the temporary flood of eaters. Some have done a pitiful job, however. Even the best is no gourmet paradise.

Some events on the annual calendar:

FEBRUARY: National Ballet of Canada spring season, O'Keefe Centre.

Rothman's International Tennis Tournament, Coliseum, Exhibition Place.

MARCH: Canadian National Sportsmen's Show, Coliseum, Exhibition Place. Canada's largest sports show.

APRIL: National Home Show, Coliseum.

JUNE: Caravan.

Mariposa Folk Festival, on Toronto Island features three days of recording stars in outdoor concerts in the park.

JULY: International Picnic, spaghetti, beauty contest, dancing, Toronto Island.

AUGUST: Canadian National Exhibition.

SEPTEMBER: National Air Show, aerobatics, military aircraft, etc., in conjunction with last several days of C.N.E.

Canadian Opera Company at O'Keefe Centre.

NOVEMBER: Royal Agricultural Winter Fair, nine days and 27 acres of championship livestock, food displays, flower show, livestock auctions and the Royal Horse Show. Plutocrats and plebs come to the Grand Prix team competition, a main event on the international circuit.

EATING OUT   Not long ago, you could count the good places to eat in Toronto without taking off more than one shoe. Now you can dine at a different spot every night and you'd need nearly 10 years to sample them all.

Toronto's 4,000 restaurants range over dozens of ethnic cuisines, from the utilitarian fast food spot, to Saigon Village with its vermicelli noodles with shrimps. Name your choice: the spicy Romanian sausage mititei, or pirogi, or crepes or scampi or strawberry Romanoff, prosciutto or duck feet in oyster sauce, squid and schnitzel and paella and tempura or haggis . . . .

A complete listing is impossible. We'll name a few of the very glossy dining rooms but generally we will try to mention a number of places of special interest to dollar-watching tourists, and some that we have personally enjoyed.

A warning. Prices are not low. Dinner bills of $35 and $50 for two have come to be considered reasonable. Don't forget there is a 10% tax on meals over $6. It soon adds up. So do stratospheric prices for drinks. Don't be embarrassed to check the drink menu first.

When we give rough price estimates, we are talking about dinner for two, with a drink or two and a bottle of reasonably priced wine. Lunch, of course, is much less expensive and a good way to sample well-known restaurants. In restaurants other than the fast-service chains, reservations are advisable and sometimes requisite. It's best to lunch at 1:15 P.M. or later; crowds thin out then.

The ubiquitous McDonald's and other familiar chain restaurants are in plentiful supply. **Scott's**, the local Kentucky Fried Chicken outlets, are mostly take-outs. For a different flavor in chain-cooked chicken, you might try **Swiss Chalet**, which has its own piquant sauce. **Frank Vettere's** pizza and pasta restaurants offer quite tasty and inexpensive spaghetti (99 cents special on Wednesdays). A relatively new and Toronto-based chain is **L'il Porky's Brick House**, at 21 Yorkville Ave., a volume place with seating for 400 which specializes in spare ribs but has a Sunday brunch at $3.95 for adults and $1.50 for children.

If money's not paramount – you've got it to splurge once anyhow and you want a memory – and talk turns to the best of the best, **Winston's**, 104 Adelaide Ave. W. ($50 up), is always mentioned. Lush, plush, impeccable, with seven chefs from Europe and a 16,000 bottle wine cellar, its continental cuisine is policed by owner John Arena, who raises some of the ingredients on his own farm. Others in the special category include **Le Chateauneuf**, at the Harbour Castel Hotel on the waterfront ($55 and up), with specialties like "scampi in love," **Westbury Hotel dining room**, 475 Yonge St. ($40 up), with seductive

Brome Lake duck, **The Pinnacle**, 43rd floor showcase of the Sheraton Centre Hotel, 123 Queen St. W., ($50 up), with specialties like entrecôte marchand de vin.

Also the Hyatt Regency's **Truffles**, 21 Avenue Rd., high luxury with Dover Sole a la Truffles at $13.75; the Prince Hotel's **Le Continental**, 900 York Mills Rd., the elegant restaurants in the **Three Small Rooms** at the Windsor Arms Hotel, 22 St. Thomas St. near Bloor and Bay. Out at the airport hotel strip, **La Residence**, at the Cara Inn, 6257 Airport Rd., where you might try the trout stuffed with shellfish, is recommended. They're all in that same $50 or more category.

If you want to go dining and dancing, or to watch a floor show, the flagship is the **Imperial Room**, at the Royal York Hotel, which gets the headliners on the North American night club circuit. The **Beverley Hills Motor Hotel**, 1677 Wilson Ave., just north of Highway 401, also brings in name club acts. Other dining rooms with dancing include **Cafe of the Redwoods**, Sheraton Centre Hotel, **Odyssey** at the Hyatt Regency, and one of the most elegant of all, **Cafe de l'Auberge**, at the Inn on the Park, 1100 Elginton Ave. E., just up the Don Valley Parkway from downtown to the Eglinton exit. These all will set you back $40 or $50 at a minimum for a couple, on up to $80 or $90.

There are many fine French-style resturants. A brief sampling might include **Le Provencal**, 23 St. Thomas St., ($40), established and consistent; **Troy's**, 31 Marlborough Ave., ($35), which has only 26 seats, marvellous rabbit in wine sauce and a loyal bunch of regulars; **Lhardy's**, 634 Church St., ($40), another fixed price menu of excellence. A lovely spot for lunch is **Le Casse Croute**, 2 Bloor St. W., ($15), bright in green and white, offering a score of fillings for its crepes. Try the fruits de mer: lobster, shrimps, scallions, chicken and mushrooms in brandied cheese.

Italian restaurants range through all price brackets up to $45 for **La Scala**, 1121 Bay St. below Bloor a four-star spot. Lunch at **Florentine Court**, 97 Church St., can be had for $5 or $6, per person, compared to an evening table of $35 and up per couple. Up where the Italians hang out, on St. Clair and Eglinton, you might try the **Sidewalk Restaurant**, 1662 Dufferin St., below St. Clair Ave. W., ($20), or **Monte Carlo**, noisy and fun at 1028 Eglinton Ave. W., ($25), or **San Marco**, 1231 St. Clair Ave. W., ($30), whose specialties include broiled scampis. Way up north at 890 Wilson Ave., just above Highway 401, is **Mastro's Tavern**, where both Prime Minister Pierre Trudeau and Aldo Moro, former prime minister of Italy, have dined. Owner Livio Camarra has built up one of the most varied cellars of Italian wines in North America, more than 45 reds and 20 whites, plus a number of French wines.

Greek restaurants offer informality – most are glad to have you visit the kitchen and pick up the pot lids to see just what you wish to order – and reasonable prices. Some of the best are on Danforth Ave. between Broadview and Pape Aves., along the subway line. Try **Dionysos**, 500 Danforth Ave., ($10), or **Ellas**, 702 Pape, right across from the Pape subway station, ($20). The neighborhoods don't look like much. The food is dandy.

Toronto was late in getting good seafood restaurants. Some say the first, the **Moorings,** 404 Yonge St., ($40), is still the best. Some others prefer **The Mermaid**, 724 Bay St., ($40), which is so popular there are often line-ups at lunch time. The **Whaler's Wharf**, at 144 Front St. W., ($45), just about a block from the Royal York Hotel, offers a dimly lit, seafaring atmosphere and some exotic things like She-Crab

Soup. The fish is always fresh, the chowders always tasty. Our own special favorite is the tiny **Round Window**, upstairs at 729 Danforth Ave., ($25), where the Greek owner cooks the fish with tender, loving care and his family waits on table.

For something different, you might try a floating restaurant. **Captain John's**, is a well-established restaurant on a boat moored at the foot of Yonge St., ($35). A newer venture is the **Mark Twain Show Boat**, in Port Credit harbor, 15 miles from downtown, out the Queen Elizabeth Way and south at Highway 10. It's an 1896 Mississippi riverboat which was a restaurant in Chicago for years, then was brought over by three Yugoslav immigrants who spent $750,000 to renovate her and dress her up in red velvet.

Chinatown offers a dazzling array of dining rooms and reasonable prices. Some of the best food is provided in tiny spots with formica-topped tables. Many have no liquor license, like the **Shanghai**, 334 Spadina Ave., (about $10 for two), where the Shrimp Shanghai has to be tasted to be believed. The **Peking**, 257 College St., ($10), isn't licensed, either, but Woo Jen Chi started cooking when he was 15 in Taiwan. Some say unlicensed **Yung Lok Gardens**, 394 Spadina Ave., ($10), has the best hot and sour soup in town.

In recent years, a number of fancy and relatively expensive Chinese eateries have opened. But a favorite among many people who have visited Toronto is **Lichee Gardens**, 118 Elizabeth St., ($25), one of the first of Chinatown's classier restaurants. Many people say **Sai Woo**, 130 Dundas St. W., ($25), is the best in town. Could be. One of the best reputations is possessed by **China House**, 925 Eglinton Ave. W., ($20-$25), which is miles from Chinatown. Give Alex, the boss, a day or two's notice and he'll draw up a menu for a Chinese feast for you and your guests at $11 or $12 a head that will knock your salivary glands out.

Top of the line for Japanese food is **Katsura**, at the Prince Hotel, 900 York Mills Rd. in Don Mills. It's costly. **Tanaka of Tokyo**, 1180 Bay St. at Bloor ($30), has a colorful act with waiters with flashing knives, chopping the food at your table. More restful are **Nikko Garden**, 460 Dundas St. W., ($20), **Taste of Japan**, 103 Yonge St., ($20), both downtown; and **Fuji**, 769 Yonge St., ($30), and **Furusato Inn**, 102 Avenue Rd., ($15), both near Bloor St.; **Michi**, 459 Church St., ($25), is popular, peaceful and offers a fixed price dinner, such as Sakura, which includes both beef teriyaki and shrimp tempura.

Among the best steak houses are **Barberian's**, 7 Elm St., ($35); **Carman's Club**, 26 Alexander St., ($40), where the premises are crowded and the steaks are garlicky; and **Harry's**, 518 Church St., ($30), just up the way from Maple Leaf Gardens and popular with the hockey crowd.

The **Franz Liszt**, 603 Markham St., ($25), offers superior Hungarian food and a piano player, a little different from the usual strolling strings. **Csarda**, 720 Bay St., ($25), has gypsy musicians and tasty ujhazi soup, chicken vegetable with dumplings. **L'Europe**, 469 Bloor St. W., ($20), has gypsies, suckling pig and all that, and the unlicensed **Goulash Pot**, ($12), offers filling, tasty food and cheerful surroundings.

There are real bargains at the Portugese dining rooms. Don't be put off by the plain exterior appearance of **Imperio**, 349 College St. – inside there's folk guitar and fine shellfish.

Spanish? Try the mussels and guitar music at **Costa Del Sol**, 430 College St., ($25). **La Mamounia**, at 1280 Bay St., ($30), offers Moroccan couscous. **Bucharest**, 2140 Yonge St., near Eglinton subway station, ($30), has Romanian specialties like mititei, spicy beef sausages. **Cossacks**, 269 Queen St. W., ($25), has waiters dressed as, well, Cossacks, serving the dozen Russian entrées.

Here are some restaurants we think may be of special interest to the tourist:

La Chaumiere, 77 Charles St. E., (about $25) has sentimental associations for many Torontonians. It was one of the city's first fixed-price restaurants and its small dining rooms spread around in an old house were the site of wooings and intimate celebrations of special occasions. Besides a happy-go-lucky, friendly atmosphere, its great attraction is a two-tier hors d'oeuvre cart with a score of selections, from herring to winkles. You are encouraged to fill your plate. Among entrées, the duck is good. Line-ups on Friday and Saturday.

The kids will love the **Old Spaghetti Factory**, 54 Esplanade, and its sister establishment, the **Organ Grinder**, 58 Esplanade, down behind the O'Keefe Centre. Decor (an old streetcar, odd antique furniture, signs of all descriptions) and price are the main attractions at the Spaghetti Factory. Two adults can eat spaghetti and drink house wine for less than $15 here; the spaghetti is unexciting but it is filling. The pizzas at the Organ Grinder are quite good; the mammoth old pipe organs with which the place is furnished are fantastic. ($12). If you don't drink, you can get out of either place for about $3-$5 a person.

Not far away is **Graf Bobby**, 36 Wellington St. E., a German spot with good open-faced sandwiches and fine beer. ($10-$15).

Popular, but so roomy you usually don't have to wait is the **Old Fish Market**, 12 Market St. – cheerful and nautically decorated in an old warehouse. The fish is always fresh, the chowders excellent. At lunch you can keep it down to $10 or so a couple, with a beer or a drink. It's a good place to go for Saturday brunch or lunch if you visit the nearby St. Lawrence Market.

Ed Mirvish, the self-made millionaire who saved the Royal Alexandra Theatre, offers you a bargain in a restaurant complex next to the theatre. He throws in great fun too.

He started with **Ed's Warehouse**, 270 King St. W., ($22), specializing in great slabs of good beef and 1890s decor. Later he added **Old Ed's** and **Ed's Lobster**. They are real buys. Old Ed's offers only three main courses, but they are tasty and two hungry people will be filled for $10. Males have to wear jackets and ties.

Again for lunch, you might try **Mr. Greenjeans**, 120 Adelaide St. E., where diners are surrounded by plants. **Le Papillon**, 71 Jarvis St., which serves a variety of crepes, or **Café du Marche**, 47 Colborne. All are popular with young downtown lunchers and are reasonable.

Near the large department stores, just a step off Yonge St., is **Osaka House**, 12 Temperance St., a tiny place where shy, kimono-clad waitresses serve fixed price Japanese lunches to a clientele which includes many Japanese-Canadian businessmen. Osaka has a beer and sake license and lunch for two costs $6-$7.

Across the street at 15 Temperance St., **Maison Basque** ($25) is a very pleasant French restaurant. The tables are crowded, but the coquille St. Jacques or the fresh grilled grouper are worth it.

Toronto doesn't have as many brasserie-type restaurants as Montreal but for a taste of beverage room lunching you might try the basement room at the **Strathcona Hotel**, 60 York St., just up the road from the Royal York Hotel. Most patrons drink draught beer. The small lunch bar supplies daily specials and Chinese food, as well as hamburgers and fish and chips. About $1.50 a person should feed you. By the way, your children aren't allowed in to beverage rooms if they are under 18.

The best and perhaps only soul food in Toronto is served at the **Underground Railroad**, 225 King Street E. ($20). Ham hocks, ribs, corn bread and such-like in a place that is fitted out like a barn.

You may find the plastic grapes and pictures of galloping horses overpowering at the **Continental**, 521 Bloor St. W. But its excellent wooden platter (veal, chicken livers, pork, sauerkraut) and other Hungarian dishes make it a good representative of the central European eating spots in this midtown neck of the woods. No liquor license and two can dine for $12-$14. If you have to have a drink, **L'Europe** where the music is live, is a few steps away. Try its **Blue Cellar Room**, where the prices ($6-$8 a couple) draw beer-drinking students.

The **Croft**, 1311 Queen St. E., is a trifle out of the way but easily reached by car or streetcar (Queen E. line) and it has haggis. There are other dishes, of course, and the proprietor sometimes plays the bagpipes. The decor is tartan all the way, and some nights there is live Scottish entertainment. Thrifty, too. With a bit of beer, a couple might escape on a $10 bill.

Further out of the way, about 10 miles from downtown, is the **Guild Inn**, 201 Guildwood Parkway. It's a place for a restful few hours, carefully cooked vegetables and North American meals. ($25). The Guild was lovingly developed in a park setting by an owner who kept picking up friezes and other mementos of old Toronto as the city changed. Drive east on Kingston Rd. until you reach Guildwood Parkway, marked by tall stone pillars and a billboard proclaiming Guildwood Village. Since many downtown restaurants are closed on Sundays, you might try the

Guild for Sunday brunch, 11 A.M. to 3 P.M., adults $6.50, children under 10, $4.

You don't hear Torontonians talking as much these days about the **Old Mill**, 21 Old Mill Rd. ($40) as they did when Toronto was a wasteland for dinner and dancing spots. But it's still impressive, in a gracious, baronial way. Just off Bloor St. W., at the Humber River. The beef is fine, the dancing is Lombardo-ish. A place for quiet celebrating.

PLACES TO STAY Most of Toronto's first-class hotel rooms are new. They are also costly compared to many other cities.

The number of rooms in first-class hotels tripled in 15 years, from 6,000 in 1960 to more than 18,000 in 1976. By the latter year, there were 49 hotels classed as major by the city's tourist board.

Trouble was, a lot of those rooms were empty, with vacancy rates ranging up to 40% even during tourist months in recent years.

Rates of $40 and more for standard double rooms are common. (In the following listings we give the lowest rates for singles and doubles at the time of writing.)

However, Toronto is Canada's leading convention city and rooms in the hotel of your choice may be hard to get at any specific time. So check your local travel agent for full listings and reserve ahead.

Recently there has been a trend towards construction of hotels with relatively inexpensive room rates. The 808-room **Chelsea Inn**, 33 Gerrard St. W., in the heart of downtown, has been the most publicized. Its lowest rates are $25 single, $29 double. It is not as ornate as the plush inns but it is neat, comfortable, pleasant, with good restaurants and happy bars. Not far away, the **Bond Place Hotel**, 65 Dundas E., is smaller (293 rooms), and has even lower rates ($18 single, $20 double). Other new economy hotels include the **Carlton Inn**, 30 Carlton St., ($17 and $21), a neighbor to Maple Leaf Gardens; and the downtown **Ramada Inn**, at Carlton and Jarvis Sts.

These and most other Toronto hotels offer lower rates for groups and conventions.

Watch too for special weekend packages and other sales gimmicks. They change from time to time, but are worth taking advantage of.

The **Prince Hotel**, 900 York Mills Rd., one of the really luxurious new hotels, built by Japanese owners in its own park-like suburban setting, set aside 25% of its 406 rooms to go at $29 a night. Its regular rates start at $32 single, $40 double. The Prince has superb service, fine eating places, but you need a car or taxi to go downtown. Access is quck though, it is near the Don Valley Parkway, an expressway which hooks up with both Highway 401 and the Queen Elizabeth Way.

Most of the usual hotel chains are represented at Toronto. But check rates first to avoid surprises. You won't get a room at the **Don Valley Holiday Inn** ($32 single, $38 double) for what you are used to paying in Meadville, Pa.

There are plenty of motels on all approaches to the city. From outer suburbia, it is 15 or 20 miles to downtown. Motel rates generally are from $15 to $20 for one person, low $20s for two. The bigger motor hotels, many of which feature live entertainment, go up to around $30-$35 minimum for a double.

Airport row is one of the biggest and liveliest concentrations of hotels and entertainment. Rates are comparable with those in similar hotels downtown. Among them: **Skyline**, 655 Dixon Rd., ($29, $36); **Constellation**, 900 Dixon Rd., (where the late Prime Minister Lester Pearson, a knowing fellow about such things from his years as a diplomat and polititian, used to stay) ($28, $36); **Bristol Place**, 950 Dixon Rd., smaller, newer, ($34, $43); **Holiday Inn**, 970 Dixon Rd., noted for its buffet ($32, $38); **Howard Johnson**, 801 Dixon Rd., ($30, $34). If you are on a second honeymoon, and intend to spend much of your time at the swimming pool, and listening to music in the bar, you could do far worse than to stay at a hotel on the airport strip and sample the various nightclubs in nearby inns. The airport hotels are close to Woodbine race track, as are **Heritage Inn**, 385 Rexdale Blvd., ($20, $25) and the **Ascot Inn**, 534 Rexdale Bvd., ($21, $28) both small but comfortable and lively. You can walk across the road to the track from the Ascot.

There is no doubt about Toronto's number one hotel. The **Royal York**, 100 Front St. W., across the street from the railway station, has occupied that ranking for generations. Its 1600 rooms make it the biggest, and the turretted pile is a landmark, the only hotel among the half-dozen major buildings in Toronto's skyline. Rates at this flagship of the Canadian Pacific chain start at $33 single, $43 double.

If your relatives used to talk affectionately about the **King Edward**, 37 King St. E., so do a lot of Torontonians. It used to be second only to the Royal York. No longer. It shows its age. But it is still big (768 rooms), has a fine dining room, is handy as all get-out and its rates are low ($19, $29).

Second biggest now is the **Sheraton Centre**, 123 Queen St. W., with 1466 rooms. It's right across the street from City Hall Square, a minute's walk from the major department stores, and like the Royal York, it is a city within a city. It even has movie theaters, the one thing the Royal York lacks. It has rates to match ($34, $43).

Among other major mid- and down-town hotels

are the **Park Plaza**, 4 Avenue Rd., a distinguished hostelry, steps from chic shopping ($31, $39); **Hyatt Regency**, 21 Avenue Rd., ($37, $47); **Sutton Place**, 955 Bay St., ($35, $43); **Westbury**, 475 Yonge St., ($26, $33), just around the block from Maple Leaf Gardens; **Hotel Toronto**, 145 Richmond St. W., ($38, $48).

Perhaps the most beautiful hotel location is occupied by the **Harbour Castle-Hilton**, 1 Harbour Square, on the waterfront. Views are breath-taking. So are the prices. Singles not long ago started at $40, doubles at $48. Drinks and meals are priced to match.

Next prettiest may be the hillside spot where the **Inn on the Park** stands, overlooking hundreds of acres of green belt parkland. It is at 1100 Eglinton Ave. E., just a minute's drive west of the Don Valley Parkway. Rooms start at $33 and $45. Its dining rooms are renowned.

For quiet, older and dignified accommodation, you might try places like **Windsor Arms Hotel**, 22 St. Thomas St. ($18, $23), a short block from fashionable Bloor St., steps from Yorkville boutiques, and possessor of exquisite dining rooms. Or **Benvenuto Hotel**, 1 Benvenuto Place ($22, $28). Both are small. So is the **Waldorf Astoria**, 88 Charles St. W. ($19, $23) where visiting show-business folk often put up.

A special personal favorite is **The Guild Inn**, 201 Guildwood Parkway ($25, $31), out in the far reaches of eastern suburbia. Built by a man who cared about his guests, local history and beauty, it serves all three graciously. It is set in its own park near the bluffs looking out over Lake Ontario. Artists' workshops and pieces of old Toronto buildings are set up on the grounds. It is serene. But it is a long way from downtown.

THEATRE The city-owned **O'Keefe Centre** brings in major productions and international stars, at prices ranging up to $13 or $14 for the best seats. It is also the locale of the home stands of the Canadian National Ballet and the Canadian Opera Company. For the ballet especially, good seats for the more popular attractions are sold weeks or months in advance. Write O'Keefe Centre, Front and Yonge Sts., phone (416)-363-6633.

Discount merchandiser Ed Mirvish took the old **Royal Alexandra** some years ago, dolled it up and reclaimed its vintage charm. Its fare is mostly touring productions of Broadway shows, its prices a bit lower than the O'Keefe.

Next on the ladder is the city-owned **St. Lawrence Centre**, at 27 Front St. E., a neighbor of the O'Keefe. Its resident repertory theater, **Toronto Arts Production**, features players you also see at the Shaw Festival or the Stratford Festival. It is completely professional and it stages drama a bit farther out on the limb than the two main houses. Prices go up to $9 or so for the best seats. Phone (416)-366-7723.

The other three dozen theaters vary widely in experience, style and aims, from extemporaneous and often virtually incomprehensible, performances to disciplined productions of familiar standbys like the **Toronto Truck Theatre's** recent staging of Agatha Christie's *The Mousetrap*. Toronto Truck, which works from a small theater at 94 Belmont St. (922-0084) frequently chooses such popular fare.

Several other of the better known and established theater companies are: **Tarragon Theatre**, 30 Bridgman Ave., 531-1827; **Toronto Workshop Production**, 12 Alexander St., 925-8640; **New Theatre**, 736 Bathurst St., 364-5202; **Toronto Free Theatre**, 26 Berkeley St., 368-2856; **Bayview Playhouse**, 1605 Bayview Ave., 481-6191. Tops usually $6-$7 on weekends at any of these, lower at some, discounts for students and senior citizens.

Harbourfront, 235 Queen's Quay W., the park-complex funded by the federal government, frequently stages free plays, reviews and cabarets.

For drama and for musical concerts, there is always something doing at Toronto's half-dozen university and college campuses. Check them – and the regular theaters – in newspapers and local magazines.

SOUTHERN ONTARIO

Many attractions are within easy distance of Toronto. Just 98 miles southwest, **Stratford** and its world-famous Shakespearean Festival draws about 500,000 visitors, or 20 times the city's population, during the season from May to late October. It was just a dream a little over a quarter of a century ago. At that time Stratford was a sleepy town just sputtering along, getting old and not very healthy, a railroad center in a world that was using railways less and less. Then a local dreamer named Tom Patterson had a vision. Why not set up a Shakespearean theater in the town named for his Shakespeare's English birthplace?

Many people scoffed. But Patterson slowly sold his idea, first to local businessmen and then to Tyrone Guthrie, the world renowned director and producer from London. For the first season, in 1952, a tent was built. Guthrie persuaded Alec Guiness to star. And the crowds came. They have never stopped: regulars from Toronto, critics from New York and London, school groups, trains chartered by newspapers.

The festival now involves three theaters and all forms of drama, art and music from folk-singers to opera. International stars like James Mason, Maggie Smith, Jason Robards, Siobhan McKenna, are featured each year, backed by a splendid continuing company. While Shakespeare's major plays are the centerpieces, other dramatists such as Ibsen, Coward and Strindberg are also performed. Through July and August a music festival is held.

The tent theater has long since given way to a magnificent semicircular auditorium seating 2,258. Performances are given each day except Monday, at the main theater, with Wednesday and Saturday matinees, and daily except Monday at the Avon Theatre, with matinees on Wednesday, Saturday and Sunday.

Festival Theatre tickets range from $3.50 to $12.50, Avon Theatre from $3.50 to $10.50.

Up-to-date detailed brochures and order forms are available after March 1 each year from Stratford Festival, P. O. Box 520, Stratford, Ont., Canada N5A 6V2.

Many people make a leisurely event of a Festival visit. Parks and gardens range over 130 acres on the banks of the Avon River, near the Festival Theatre. You can laze in the sun, feed the dozens of swans and picnic.

Or you may dine at one of the fine restaurants which have evolved with the residence of hundreds of knowledgeable theater people and the visits of thousands of sophisticated playgoers. Two favorite dining rooms are the **Church Restaurant**, which serves French country fare in a converted church at the corner of Brunswick and Waterloo Sts., and the **Queen's Hotel**, 161 Ontario St., a charmingly-kept old hostelry. Dinner with wine will cost about $40-$45 for two at either place.

Most playgoers are day-trippers. Still, at the peak of the season, you should plan your accommodations well in advance. Biggest and popular hotels are the **Festival Motor Inn**, 1144 Ontario St., and the **Victorian Inn**, 10 Romeo St., each with over 100 rooms. Doubles there range up to $40. Smaller motels, including such Shakespearean names as the **As You Like It**, and the **Swan**, charge up to $30 or so double.

KITCHENER-WATERLOO (pop. 171,000) is the center of one of Ontario's most colorful areas, the land of Amish and Mennonite farmers, German cooking and Oktoberfest. The city is 18 miles east of Stratford, 80 miles southwest of Toronto.

Oktoberfest, a nine-day party of beer, bratwurst and oom-pah-pah music in early October, is the biggest celebration of the German tradition in North America. It draws 350,000 people annually. Busloads pile in from the United States and all over Ontario. Clubs which are private the rest of the year open their doors, serve up sausage, sauerkraut, pigs' tails, and rivers of beer. Noise is unconfined. Hotel rooms are reserved as much as a year in advance. Many visitors stay in rooms temporarily rented out in private homes. Write the Kitchener-Waterloo Chamber of Commerce, 67 King St. E., Kitchener for Oktoberfest information.

The German tradition runs deep. Kitchener was founded in 1799 and was called Berlin until 1916, when anti-German feeling in the midst of World War I caused the change to a name taken from a British military hero. In the countryside, many farms are owned by Amish and Mennonite people, gentle, hard-working folk, many of whom shun modern conveniences like electricity and television and still drive horse-drawn buggies.

A good place to meet them, see their crafts and taste their foods is at the weekly farmers' markets on Saturday mornings at **St. Jacob's** and **Elmira,** or at the larger markets in Kitchener and Waterloo. The biggest, at Kitchener, is also open Wednesday mornings. On Saturdays, get there early. Many Torontonians make the trip each week to buy cheese, sausages, home baking and fresh vegetables. The **Kitchener market** is just behind Eaton's department store on King St., the city's main street, in the center of town.

The venerable **Walper House** at 1 King St. is one of the finest German dining rooms in North America. Another favorite eating place is the **Breslau Inn**, at

Breslau, just east of Waterloo, where a family of four or five can lunch on mouthwatering spareribs and other delicacies and get change from a $20 bill.

At nearby **Elmira** (pop. 5,000), you can go on a tour of Mennonite country offered by the Chamber of Commerce. Brubacher's general store in Elmira is charming. Fifty thousand persons go every year to Elmira for the Maple Syrup Festival on an April weekend when the sap is running. Just outside Elmira is **West Montrose**, which once thought it would outdistance Kitchener. Now it has only 70 residents and Ontario's last covered bridge, over the Grand river.

Tiny **Elora** (pop. 2,000) has a spectacular view of the Elora Gorge, pleasantly restored arts and crafts businesses, Drimmies Mill beside the Grand River Falls, converted into a luxurious inn and dining room – and an irresistible love story.

Florence Nightingale's lover and first cousin, the Rev. John Smithurst, came to Elora and obscurity from his English home when the church forbade their marriage. She went to the Crimean War and a place in legend. Neither ever married. In 1852, a beautiful communion set was received mysteriously and anonymously at St. John's Anglican Church. It was, so it was discovered, Miss Nightingale's gift to the love she forsook, and it can still be seen at the church.

At **Brantford** you can visit the home of Alexander Graham Bell, who invented the telephone, and visit various museums dedicated to the area's Mohawk Indian history. During the first three weekends in August, Indian culture and history is enacted in a pageant in a forest ampitheater on the **Six Nations Indian Reserve.**

A major tourist draw is the **African Lion Safari and Game Farm** at **Rockton**, 20 miles northwest of Hamilton, where African animals roam free in a 500-acre park. You drive among them, and monkeys will clamber on your car to the delight of the small fry. Hours 10 A.M. to 5.30 P.M. in July and August; noon to 4.30 P.M. weekdays and 10 A.M. to 4.30 P.M. weekends the rest of the year. Closed Christmas. Adults $3, ages 3-17, $1.50.

The metropolis of southwestern Ontario is **London** (pop. 244,000), kept prosperous by breweries, insurance firm head offices and a major university. The kids love **Storybook Gardens**, a theme park and zoo open in 350-acre Springbank Park from mid-April to mid-October. Adults, 60 cents, under 12 years, 15 cents. The 110-year-old **Western Fair** is held for 9 days in mid-September. It is Canada's second-largest agricultural exhibition. First-class harness racing is conducted at the fair grounds during most of the year. The **Royal Canadian Regiment Museum** at Wolseley Barracks, depicting the regiment's history from the Riel Rebellion through both World Wars and Korea, is one of Canada's most extensive military museums.

Some other attractions in southwestern Ontario include:

The 300-acre bird sanctuary at **Kingsville** 35 miles south of Detroit, founded by Jack Miner in 1904. It's free. Best times to see migrating birds: first two weeks of March, first two weeks of November.

Point Pelee National Park and **Colasanti Cactus Garden**, near **Leamington**. The park is a 4,000 acre sandpit with 14 miles of beaches and a mile-long boardwalk through the marsh, the most southerly part of the Canadian mainland. Vehicle entry fee is $2.

Chatham and **Dresden** figured largely in the Underground Railroad which brought thousands of slaves to Canada and freedom before the U.S. Civil War. Many descendants of slaves still live here. At Chatham, John Brown plotted his raid on Harper's

Ferry. Several museums are dedicated to this heritage, including **Uncle Tom's Cabin Museum** at Dresden, the home of Rev. Josiah Henson, original Uncle Tom of Harriet Beecher Stowe's novel. Open May 1 – Oct. 31, adults $1.50, ages 6-12, 50 cents. At nearby **Oil Springs** the Oil Museum of Canada is on the site of North America's first commercialized oil well. Mid-May through October, adults $1.25, children 35 cents and up.

NIAGARA TO TORONTO **Niagara Falls** has been around a long time but it is still one of the wonders of the world and a sight the tourist shouldn't miss. Indian travellers thought it was great, so have millions of visitors since.

Except, one must say, Oscar Wilde. The English wit said the "wonder would be if the water fell up." And, he added, the Falls must be the bride's second great disappointment when she gets up after her first night of marriage. Oscar, of course, would say almost anything to get a laugh. Those millions of gallons tumbling over the 176-foot high Canadian Falls and the 184-foot high American Falls are awesome. The view is better from the Canadian side, Canadians always say.

Moreover, the Falls is the focal point of one of Canada's best-developed parks system, strung along the 35-mile Niagara Parkway from **Fort Erie** on Lake Erie, site of Ontario's prettiest race track, to **Niagara-on-the-Lake** at the mouth of Lake Ontario. Beautiful homes, riverside picnic tables, floral clocks, historical monuments entice you to stop repeatedly.

There's a bit of a bizarre atmosphere to the city of Niagara Falls, (pop. 65,000). Wax and other commercial museums abound, Boris Karloff, Houdini, House of Frankenstein, Ripley's Believe It or Not and Cars of the Greats, automobiles which belonged to Al Capone, Clark Gable, Mussolini and other notables. Charges run from $2 to $3 for adults.

But nature's showerbath reigns. You can see it from all angles: from high above, from down under, from cable car and from helicopters. It's not a bad idea to take a look from the shore at the top, too. Some facilities: **Great Gorge Trip**, River Rd., just north of the Whirlpool Rapids bridge. An elevator takes you to a boardwalk beside the rapids at river level. $1.75, under 11 free with parents. **Horseshoe Falls Incline Railway**, cable cars, 20 cents one way. **Maid of the Mist** boat rides to base of the falls, $3, ages 6-12, $1.50, waterproof clothing provided. **Table Rock House** – an elevator descends for a close-up of the Horseshoe Falls and Niagara river, to tunnels leading to observation platforms. Adults $2.10, ages 7-14, 75 cents, under 7, 25 cents. **Whirlpool Aerocar**, cable car over the Niagara Gorge and back. Round trip $1.60, ages 7-14, 75 cents, under 7, 25 cents.

The Skylon Tower, overlooking the falls, which are especially impressive during the 3-4 hours they are lighted after dusk, offers a revolving dining room, lounge and observation decks 520 feet up. Adults $2.75, ages 12-18, $1.25, ages 6-11, $1.

The Niagara Parks Commission has developed beautiful free attractions, including 196-acre Queen Victoria Park, right at the Falls, with notable floral displays; the commission greenhouses one-half mile south of Horseshoe Falls; a floral clock with thousands of blooms at Sir Adam Beck-Niagara Generating Station; and Queenston Heights Park, 7 miles north of Horseshoe Falls. It contains a 210-foot monument to the British general Sir Isaac Brock, a hero of the War of 1812, who was killed here and is interred beneath the monument. You can walk up the inside if you are fit enough.

Marineland and Game Farm, 7657 Portage Rd., is a commercial venture which has become second only to the Falls themselves. There are hundreds of animals in a 75-acre park. You can walk among deer and feed them. The main show is a genuinely thrilling performance by trained dolphins, sea lions and whale, several times a day. The performance area is open daily from 9 A.M. to dusk all year, the game farm the same hours from May 1-Oct. 31. Adults $4.25, ages 4-12, $1.50.

You might call **Niagara-on-the-Lake** a white-painters' paradise except that its beauty goes very deep. It is one of the best-preserved 19th century towns (pop. 12,500) in North America. But it is a monument that is alive. Unlike Williamsburg or Upper Canada Village, people live in those gorgeous restored houses. The town was the first capital of Upper Canada and was completely razed by American invaders during the War of 1812. Some residents are descendants of the people who rebuilt it and many are actively upset about the extent to which their town is being pushed as a tourist attraction.

You must walk along Queen St., see the 1866 apothecary shop, McClellands Store, which has been operating since 1835, the fudge shop where they make it while you watch, and the shop where Bill Greaves sells home-made jams in the place his family has operated for four generations.

Fort George is one of the province's more interesting military posts. It was built in the 1790s, occupied by the Americans and destroyed in 1813, rebuilt by 1815, abandoned and eventually restored in the 1930s. Open daily from mid-May to October, adults $1, ages 7-12, 50 cents, family rate $3.

The **Shaw Festival** is a highly-rated theatrical season from late May to mid-September, featuring plays by George Bernard Shaw and his contemporaries.

They are performed by an accomplished repertory company. For information, write the Shaw Festival, Niagara-on-the-Lake, or phone 416-468-3201; Toronto, 416-361-1544.

In both cities good bets for dining are the leading hotels: in Niagara Falls the venerable but updated **Sheraton Brock** and **Sheraton Foxhead** (doubles $21.50 to $48.50 and $27.50 to $68.50 respectively); in Niagara-on-the-Lake, the beautifully restored **Prince of Wales Inn**, and the **Pillar and Post**. The Niagara Falls area alone has more than 160 hotels and motels.

Heading towards Toronto from Niagara Falls, you are in the vineland of Ontario. Grapes, orchards and wineries abound. **St. Catharines** holds a 10-day annual Grape and Wine Festival in late September. If you have time, stay off the Queen Elizabeth Way and take highway 8 as far as Stoney Creek.

Most travellers whiz by **Hamilton**, Ontario's third largest city, with 306,000 residents. That is too bad. While the steel plants' smokestacks symbolize Hamilton's place as Canada's Pittsburgh, a lunch-bucket town, the city also has much to offer the visitor.

It's symphony orchestra is among the most imaginative in Canada in devising ways to take music to the people. **Hamilton Place**, an $11 million cultural center across from modernistic city hall, includes a 2,183-seat theater where international artists perform.

Most of Hamilton's tourist attractions are within walking distance of each other in the compact downtown. The country's biggest open-air market for farmers is held Tuesday, Thursday and Saturday at James St. N. and York St. The **Canadian Football Hall of Fame**, adults $1, under 14, 25 cents, is in City Hall Plaza. Nearby is **Whitehern House**, an elegantly restored Georgian residence, adults 75 cents, children 25 cents.

Dundurn Castle, on a hillside on York Blvd., is a magnificently-restored 36-room mansion which was the home of Sir Allan Napier McNab, prime minister of the United Provinces of Canada from 1845 to 1856. Adults $1.50, under 12, 25 cents. Concerts, festivals, theater, a summer sound and light show, are performed here.

But Hamilton's great showplace is the spectacular **Royal Botanical Gardens**, 2,000 acres of flowers, natural parkland and a 1200-acre wildlife sanctuary with marsh and wooded ravines called Cootes Paradise.

If you are driving in Hamilton, be alert for one-way streets. The city has a lot of them and they move traffic along.

EAST TO LOYALIST COUNTRY Eastern Ontario is limestone houses and rolling farms, where the Loyalists settled after their flight north from the American Revolution. It is sand dunes and yachting, forts and pioneer villages, the Thousand Islands and the Seaway and, at the far end, a French-Canadian presence.

But first, as you go east from Toronto, you hit the end of the industrialized Golden Horseshoe. Oshawa (pop. 100,000) is General Motors town. R. S. McLaughlin turned his family's buggy company into GM of Canada and built a husky city. **The Canadian Automotive Museum**, 99 Simcoe St. S., has a fine collection of antique cars on view. Adults $1.50, students 11-18, 50 cents, open from 9 A.M. to 5 P.M. Monday through Friday, 10 A.M. to 6 P.M. Saturday, Sundays noon to 6 P.M.

The horse is represented at Canada's largest thoroughbred breeding farm in Canada, E. P. Taylor's

1320-acre **Windfields**, where fine stallions stand. It is open to visitors, free, weekdays 1 to 4 P.M., 2½ miles north of Oshawa, Simcoe St. N.

A few miles northeast is **Mosport**, Canada's major car-racing track, which draws up to 50,000 for major events from April to October, including Formula 5,000 in June and Formula 1 Grand Prix in October.

If you use Highway 2 instead of superhighway 401, you will pass through gracious old towns like **Port Hope**, whose residents celebrate Old Tyme Christmas all through December each year, dressing in period costumes and riding in sleighs.

At **Brighton** is the entrance to **Presqu'ile Provincial Park**, 2,000 acres of marsh, woodland and beaches on Lake Ontario. There are free guided tours by canoe through the marsh at dawn in summer. Presqu'ile is a great place to view bird migrations, and there is an aquarium and a natural history museum. $1.50 vehicle entry, camping $3.50, with electricity, $4.

Belleville, a center of Loyalist settlement at the mouth of the Moria river on the Bay of Quinte, is the gateway to **Quinte's Isle** and **Picton**. There are miles of spectacular sand dunes on the Isle. You'll find six museums of early days, and many legends. It is said that a clear lake, 200 feet above Lake Ontario at Lake of the Mountain Provincial Park, is fed underground, direct from Niagara Falls. At 1,700-acre **Tyendinaga Indian Reserve**, just off the Isle, the original landing of the Mohawks is re-enacted in tribal dress.

To the north, **Peterborough** (pop. 58,000) is an old lumber town that is the major link in the 240 mile Trent-Severn canal system from Lake Ontario to Georgian Bay. A hydraulic lift lock, which takes pleasure craft 65 feet straight up, is said to be the largest in the world. At nearby **Lakefield** is the private boys' school which was attended for one academic year by Prince Andrew, second son of Queen Elizabeth.

Rockhounds love the area around **Madoc** and **Bancroft**, where you can find examples of 80% of all Canada's minerals.

Early in August each year, thousands of rockhounds from all over North America gather for Bancroft's Gemboree, a five-day festival of rockswapping, square dancing and corn roasts. Visitors are welcome at Princess Sodalite Mine, 2 miles east. **Eldorado Gold**, site of Ontario's first gold strike, had 19 hotels in 1866; now its whole population is 48.

WAY DOWN EAST Kingston, the Thousand Islands and the **St. Lawrence Seaway**, and **Upper Canada Village** symbolize eastern Ontario.

Kingston (pop. 62,000) is the archetypical city of the area. With limestone houses and a sense of the past, located where the St. Lawrence flows into Lake Ontario, it is a thriving city with 12 legitimate theater groups, a leading university, Queen's Royal Military College, and an excellent open-air market every Tuesday, Thursday and Saturday. But its heart is in the past. It knows the things that are solid and lasting.

The market is outside the 1843 city hall, a magnificent domed building of cut limestone, built while Kingston was capital of the United Provinces of Canada. Then as now, **Old Fort Henry** looked out over Kingston. It is busy still, as an important military museum visited by thousands of tourists weekly. During summer the well-schooled Fort Henry Guard performs 19th century drills, fires off muzzle-loading cannon and plays fifes and drums. The colorful Sunset Retreat is performed at 7.30 P.M. Wednesdays and Saturdays. Adults $2, ages 6-15, 75 cents.

Other military sights include the museum in **Murney Tower**, built in 1846, in Macdonald Park, adults 50 cents, children 25 cents; **Fort Frederick Museum** at Royal Military College, adults $1, ages 8-16, 25 cents; **Royal Canadian Signals Museum**, at Vimy Barracks, open daily but Saturday all year, adults 50 cents, children 25 cents.

Kingston is big on museums. It has a restored pumping station, a woodworking museum, a marine museum and the International Hockey Hall of Fame. Bellevue House, an 1840 villa in Tuscan style, once was the home of Sir John A. Macdonald, Canada's first prime minister.

A good way to see the town is to take a tour train which leaves from a spot just south of the city hall hourly from 10 A.M. to 7 P.M. in the summer. Fare for the 10-mile ride, adults $2.50, children over 5, $1.

More than most cities, Kingston has kept its history alive. Lawyers' offices are clustered in 100-year-old buildings. Many shops also reflect the past, like **Cooke's Old World Shop**, a gourmet grocery with the wide counters and tin ceilings of a century ago.

Across the street, incidentally, is a dandy place to eat where we always break on our drives to Montreal. **Murphy's** is a family-run place above a fish store, with no decor and wobbly tables but a huge selection of seafood. It is unlicensed.

From Kingston you can board boat tours of the Thousand Islands. Other cruises leave from **Gananoque, Ivy Lea, Rockport** and **Lancaster**. Most motels and many stores sell tickets and make reservations. Fares range from about $4 to $6, depending on the length of the tours, which vary from 2½ to 4 hours.

The river means so much to Gananoque that you can even go to church there on summer Sundays. A non-denominational service is conducted from a pulpit formed by rocks at Half Moon Bay, with the congregation in small boats. A summer resort now, as it was for the Indians before the white man came, Gananoque is one end of the Thousand Islands Parkway.

At **Ivy Lea** (pop. 65) turn off for **Hill Island** and the Thousand Islands bridges to the U.S. On Hill Island is **Skytown**, a new complex with a wax museum, aquarium and a 400-foot observation tower from which you can see for 40 miles. The elevator ride up costs adults $1.75, students $1. ages 5-12, 50 cents.

East of the Thousand Islands is **Morrisburg** (pop. 2,100), one of the communities which had to be moved when the St. Lawrence Seaway was built. Seven miles east of it on highway 2 is **Upper Canada Village**, Canada's largest restored village, in full working order.

Upper Canada Village is one of those don't-miss attractions. Nearly every town in Ontario has a restored pioneer house or village but this one, developed by the Ontario government, is a super-star.

There are over 40 buildings, illustrating every phase of life in those bygone days. An articulate and friendly staff, in period costume, operates the woollen mill, blacksmith's shop, inn, sawmill and other enterprises. You can travel by foot, stage-coach, boat or ox-cart over corduroy roads and canals.

Every aspect bemuses the visitor. The difficulties of farming in an unmechanized age and a largely uncleared country emerge graphically, for example, at a field dotted with treestumps, with wheat sown between.

Expect to spend hours here. You can eat full meals in the Village, or buy snacks, or pack a picnic. The Village is open daily from 9:30 A.M. to 6:30 P.M. June 15 to Labor Day, and from 9:30 A.M. to 5 P.M. from May 15 to June 14 and from Labor Day to Oct. 15.

Adults $2.50, ages 6-15, 75 cents. Ask for the family rate.

If you buy your ticket less than 3 hours before closing time, have it validated before leaving the village to use again the next day.

THE OTTAWA VALLEY The valley, northwest from Ottawa, is worth visiting for its legends of tough lumbermen, its Gaelic heritage, and its rugged scenery.

At **Almonte** (pop. 3700) on the Mississippi river, is the **Mill of Kintail**, a museum of pioneer artifacts and of sculptures by Robert Tait McKenzie, a surgeon and sculptor who converted the 1830 stone mill to a studio and summer house.

Find the place they call Magnetic Hill at **Dacre** (pop. 58). Point your car downhill, release the brakes, and the car will roll back up the hill. That's why they call it Magnetic Hill.

Untamed forests and streams surround **Renfrew**. See them from **Champlain Lookout**, 400 feet above the countryside. It is at **Storyland**, where more than 200 storybook characters, many of them animated, are set in woodland. Open daily mid-May to early October, adults $1.50, children 4-12, 75 cents.

A tropical sea hundreds of millions of years ago left twisting caves, now called Bonnechere Caves, at **Eganville**. Guided tours daily from May to October, adults $2, ages 5-12, $1. Ontario's largest totem pole is at **Pembroke**, first Canadian city to light its streets by electricity.

Chalk River, once a lumbering town, now is the site of Canada's Nuclear Research Centre, which welcomes visitors weekdays in summer. A few miles southeast, guided half-hour walking tours are offered at **Petawawa Forest Experimental Station,** where forestry research started in Canada in 1918.

COTTAGE COUNTRY In the summer, a wide band of Ontario belongs to Toronto, Ohio, and Pennsylvania people. This is cottage country, a wildly varied belt across the northern end of industrialized southern Ontario. It ranges from wide, flat, sandy beaches to crowded resort areas with a touch of the honky-tonk, to tranquil, cool, deep lakes and lonely almost untamed woods. The headlights of the unending stream of cars driving into cottage country, to Bracebridge or Minden or Wasaga, from Toronto on a Friday evening have aptly been called a "river of gold."

For generations city dwellers have been in love with Ontario's lake country. Years ago they would arrive by train at places like Bala, walk to big old lodges and hotels, break out their straw skimmers and white gowns, and listen to soft music on a summer's night.

Today there are still many lodges, less formal and ornate but more luxurious and comfortable. But most visitors to cottage country go to cottages. Instead of skimmers and white dresses, they are in jeans and shorts and bikinis. The open air is still the attraction, but relatively sedate pastimes like walking and croquet have given way to water-skiing, fishing, boating, golfing. Cottage country is action country.

Waterfront cottages almost anywhere in southern Ontario will rent for $200 or more a week for an average three-bedroom with indoor facilities. The best way to find them is to pick out the kind of locality you want and subscribe briefly to the local newspaper and its classified advertisements.

You can expect to pay $250 or more per week at a

high-class lodge for accommodation and all meals. Many of these have tennis courts, golf privileges, planned activities like barbecues, dances and parties throughout the week. Consult a travel agent. Rates go as high as $575 a week, for instance, at Honey Harbor's Delawana Inn.

From the left side of your map of Ontario, here is a very general description of some major cottage areas:

Lake Huron is typified by **Sauble Beach** and other established areas on wide sandy beaches. Often crowded.

On southern **Georgian Bay**, the shoreline differs widely within a few miles, from the pebbles at Thornbury to the shale rock at Craigleith, 8 miles east, to the spectacular sand beaches at Wasaga, just another 20 miles.

The **Lake Simcoe-Lake Couchiching** area, just 60-80 miles north of Toronto on superhighways, is so handy to the big city that it is often quite crowded with day-trippers as well as cottagers. The lakes are large, shallow and usually warm – almost soupy for swimming in summer. Boats crowd them.

North of the latter area is **Muskoka**, rugged gateway to the pre-Cambrian shield, rocky, pine-treed. Smaller lakes, deep, clear, colder. Long a favorite cottage area.

Haliburton and the **Kawarthas**, to the east, are much similar. The area around Minden and Haliburton has a unique aspect: probably more Unidentified Flying Objects have been reported thereabouts than in any other part of Canada.

Costs in cottage country tend to be somewhat higher than in the south. You don't get as many specials in the food stores. In recent years, movement to these areas of capable entrepreneurs who are seeking more than just maximum profits has benefited visitors. You don't have to settle for greasy spoon restaurants. Every area has its gourmet dining rooms now, like the Spike and Spoon in **Collingwood** or the Bala Bay Lodge in **Bala**. Ask any local person for directions.

Some of the best dining is at the major lodges: **Deerhurst, Delawana Inn, Muskoka Sands, Cleveland's House,** are simply examples. Many admit non-guests for dining and some require reservations for use of the dining room.

The resort towns often have specialty shops worth visiting – most of them seem to be home bakeries. There is something about warm buns and cool nights that go together.

There are also summer theaters in many cottage resort areas, and lake cruises. Check locally. Ontario cottage country offers too many specific attractions to list fully but here are some:

Barrie is only 56 miles from Toronto by superhighway 400. It is the gateway to Lake Simcoe, which is 30 miles long. **Simcoe County Museum**, open every day except for Mondays in winter, adults $1, children 25 cents, is one of the better displays of pioneer life. **Springwater Provincial Park** is a particularly attractive picnic ground, with deer, raccoons, beaver and other animals on view in natural surroundings. $1.50 per vehicle.

A few miles north in **Orillia**, on Lake Couchiching, the 19-room lakeshore mansion of the great humorist, Stephen Leacock, is open daily in summer, adults $1, children and students 25 cents and up.

The Muskoka Cavalcade of Color, when leaves change, late in September or early in October, is great fun, especially in **Gravenhurst, Bracebridge** and **Huntsville**, which put on street dances, turkey dinners and fireworks. All three are great summer towns, too.

Santa's Village, at **Bracebridge**, is an 18-acre park where children can meet Santa Claus all summer long, visit his workshop, ride a paddlewheel boat and a small train. Daily 10 A.M. to 6 P.M. from mid-June to Labor Day, weekends only for a month earlier and a month later. Adults $1.75, under 12, 50 cents. But take more money; your kids will see lots of ways to spend it.

At **Gravenhurst** there are free band concerts from a barge in Gull Lake on summer Sunday evenings. You can also visit the home of Dr. Norman Bethune, a controversial Canadian who is venerated by modern China, where he died while tending Mao's sick during the revolution. You may run into a Chinese diplomat there; it's a must visit for them when they come to Canada.

Midland is the present-day site of a Jesuit mission established in 1639. **Sainte-Marie-among-the-Hurons**, the reconstructed mission where the Jesuit Martyrs lived in the early 17th century, is a must visit. Archaeologists have painstakingly put together this fascinating look at Indian life of that day, adults $1.50, students 75 cents, under 12, 25 cents.

Across the road is the **Martyrs' Shrine**, run by the Jesuits as a memorial to the missionaries killed by Indians between 1642 and 1649. These eight men were the first on this continent to be canonized by the Roman Catholic Church. There is a miniature of the Lourdes Grotto, a hillside Stations of the Cross, and a flower-planted island. Admission $1 per car. There is also a first-rate **Huron Indian Village** at **Little Lake Park**, adults $1.50, ages 8-14, 35 cents.

Neighboring the Martyrs Shrine, the **Wye Marsh Wildlife Centre** offers a spectacular look at the secret world of the marshland, with guided tours, boardwalks, an underwater window and an observation tower. Adults 50 cents, children, 25 cents.

The **Collingwood** area of Georgian Bay at the base of Blue Mountain, the highest part of the Niagara Es-

carpment has a wide variety of activities. Collingwood itself began as, and still is, a shipbuilding center. But the region is one of Ontario's busiest recreational zones, both summer and winter. **Blue
Mountain Park** and **Georgian Peaks** are both well-
known ski centers, with chalet villages, ski-lifts and
runs of all degrees of difficulty.

The ski-lifts operate in summer as well, taking visitors to the top of Blue Mountain, 1500 feet high, to
look out over Georgian Bay and the countryside. The
Scenic Caves nearby are intricate fissures once fre-
quented by a Huron tribe. You will find snow and ice
until mid-summer in some deep spots and if you are
overweight, beware Fat Man's Misery, a narrow slit
that many have to bypass. Adults $2.25, ages 6-14,
$1. A new attraction that goes with the Blue Moun-
tain chair lift is a 3,000-foot-long summer slide down
a cement chute on a fiberglass sled. Adults, $2, chil-
dren $1.25.

Wasaga Beach, a few miles east of Collingwood,
swells from its permanent population of 2,000 to
scores of thousands on summer weekends. Main attraction is a sweeping 9-mile sand beach and a gay
carnival-like main drag. There's an impressive lakes
museum on **Nancy Island**, which formed around the
British schooner *Nancy* after it sank in 1814. Adults
$1, children 25 cents, family rate $2.50. You can see
one of the province's better zoos with elephants, hip-
pos, jaguars, wallabies and about 800 animals on a
50-acre site, mostly natural bush. Adults $2, children
and students, 25 cents to $1.50.

Just west of Collingwood, there are spectacular
views in the **Beaver Valley**, particularly at Eugenia
Falls, where there is an 80-foot waterfall in a conser-
vation area with picnic, boating and hiking facilities.

The only marine railway of its kind left in North
America is near **Port Severn**. It is the last big lift in

the 240-mile Trent-Severn waterway which links Lake Ontario to Georgian Bay. Each boat is put on a railcar and hauled up an inclined railway.

Owen Sound (pop. 20,000) boasts the surprisingly extensive **Tom Thomson Memorial Art Gallery**, with many of the works of one of Canada's favorite painters, who gave us a new look at our outdoors.

Go north from there to **Tobermory**, (pop. 336) at the tip of the Bruce Peninsula, which looks like a quiet fishing village but in fact is a bustling recreational area. Because at least 50 known wrecks of ships are in nearby waters, Tobermory is a magnet for scuba divers. Take a water taxi to **Flower Pot Island**, four miles north, an off-shore National Park with caves and remarkable water-worn rock chimneys that look like giant flower pots.

From Tobermory, a 600-passenger car ferry makes the two-hour trip to **Manitoulin Island** four times daily in summer. It is a beautiful trip to a beautiful place. Manitoulin, at the north end of Lake Huron, is believed to be the world's largest island in fresh water, nearly 110 miles long and varying from 3 to 47 miles in width. The people are friendly and it's uncrowded. There are six Indian reservations, several free museums, serenity and great fishing for pike, bass, muskellunge and other varieties. **The Centennial Museum** near Little Current is on the site of one of North America's oldest civilizations, where artifacts dating back 3,000 years have been discovered.

ALGONQUIN PARK This unspoiled wilderness where you can hear the howl of a wolf or the cry of the loon is one of Ontario's great treasures. Yet it is only 180 miles from Toronto. The park covers 2,900 square miles – or 1,862,402 acres – from just east of Huntsville to just west of Pembroke.

But there is only one through road, Highway 60. It runs for 37 miles across the southwest corner, and along it are three lodges, 8 campgrounds and picnic areas. The interior of the park is relatively inaccessible – you have to pack in to many places – and therefore offers good fishing and canoeing. Motors are not allowed in the park's interior; and firearms are forbidden. Fee is $2 per boat per day or $20 for up to 16 days.

An excellent way to orient yourself is by visiting the park museum, at Mile 13 on highway 60 which tells the story of the park's history, geology and wildlife. It is open daily from June 12 to Sept. 4 and is free. It is open only on weekends in late May, when the park opens, and from Labor Day to mid-October, when it closes.

Another free museum is the **Pioneer Logging Exhibit**, at Mile 37, near the eastern entrance to the park.

Rates at the three lodges are: Arowhon Pines, $69 to $124 double a day, and Killarney, $58 to $72 double, both including all meals, and Bartlett's, $50 to $60 a day double, with some meals.

THE NORTH – FAR AND NEAR Open spaces, awesome scenery, big game, moose and bear, and big fish, vast forests and hidden lakes, portages, backpacks, beaver, ice. The north. That's all still part of it. But that's not all the north is today. A century ago the only way in was by canoe. Today the roads are good, provincial parks and camping spots frequent, the restaurants growing more sophisticated. You can get turf'n surf in New Liskeard; go to rock festivals in Sudbury.

Just to touch on a few major places:

North Bay (pop. 54,000) is a traditional jumping-off place for fishermen, hunters and trappers. Canada's major fur auctions are held here. There are excellent daily 6-hour cruises in a modern 300-passenger ship on the route of the voyageurs to the Upper French river daily in summer. The Winter Carnival is typical of winter fairs held in northern cities like **Cochrane** and **Kirkland Lake**. It lasts four days and includes dog-sled races, ice-fishing, snowmobile contests, pancake breakfasts and many social events. Late February or early March. Check with the Ontario Travel, Queen's Park, Toronto, Ontario, Canada M7A 2E5 for annual details on this and other winter carnivals.

Six miles south of North Bay on Highway 11 is the **Quints Museum**, the original log farmhouse which was the birthplace of the Dionne quintuplets who made little **Callander** famous. Two are dead, the others live elsewhere, and other multiple births have since occurred. But the Dionnes, born here in 1934, are still the famous ones. Open daily from late May to early October, adults 75 cents, students 25 cents, children 10 cents, under 6 free with adult.

In the north, **Sudbury** (pop. 97,000) counts as a metropolis, but one with economic problems. A world glut of nickel has slowed down giant International Nickel, the city's main employer. Until very recently, Sudbury was regarded as one of the most polluted areas in Canada. U.S. astronauts came here to practice some routines in a locale described as being as close to the barren surface of the moon as could be found. Steps to fight pollution, including a new giant smokestack at Inco, have helped.

Slowed as the northern giant is, much of its tourist attraction still relates to its vast mineral resources. The pouring of slag, like tongues of fire, is spectacular in the evening. You can tour the mines. Or explore the replica of a working mine underground at

Canadian Centennial Numismatic Park, where you can also see a 30-foot-high stainless steel Canadian five cent piece, a 10-foot Kennedy half dollar. Open daily May to October, adults $1.50, students $1, under 12, 50 cents.

You can also tour mines near **Cobalt**. Enquire at the **Cobalt Mining Museum**, which includes the world's best display of native silver. Open daily May 1 to Oct. 31, adults $1, children 50 cents. Cobalt is small (pop. 2200) but has a strong hold on the affections of Ontarians. According to legend, the town's silver rush started in 1903 when blacksmith Fred Larose threw a hammer at a fox, missed and nicked a rock which revealed silver, the clue to the world's richest silver vein. In 1977, 20% of the town's homes – including that of the mayor – were destroyed by a fire, but the town is rebuilding. Stop in for a drink at the **Miner's Home Tavern**. It doesn't look like much but it is a friendly place. If you're anywhere near, come to the week-long miners' festival of fiddling, step-dancing, rock-breaking and other festivities early in August.

Charming for itself, set around 55-acre Commando Lake, **Cochrane** (pop. 4,800), is where you catch the **Polar Bear Express**, a unique and exciting train trip to the Arctic tidewater at **Moosonee**, on James Bay, which is part of Hudson Bay. The express trip is 4½ hours, 186 miles, through untouched wilderness where only trappers and Indians live. Daily at 8 A.M. Saturday through Thursday in summer, leaving Moosonee for return trip at 5:30 P.M. Round trip $18, ages 5-11, $9.

Better yet, take the slow local which carries trappers, hunters, Indians, to the few stations en route. This means a two-day trip, staying overnight at a lodge in Moosonee.

The train is the only way to get to Moosonee (pop.

1,800), which grew from a nearby Hudson's Bay Company post established in 1673. You can see several 18th century buildings at the site of the old post. St. Thomas Church is fascinating: it has altar cloths of moosehide, prayer books in the Cree language, and holes drilled in the floor. In the 19th century, the church almost floated away during a flood; the holes were drilled to let the water in so that next time the church won't sail off.

Timmins-Porcupine and **Kirkland Lake** are other towns filled with mining lore. The Porcupine region is the biggest gold producer in the western hemisphere. You can visit mines in these and other areas, including the regions around Lake Superior to the west. Among these are **Elliot Lake** (pop. 4,000) Canada's center of uranium mining. **Bruce Mines** (pop. 480) where Cornish miners opened a copper mine in 1846, has one of the best mine museums. Curiously, it also houses the doll's house of the Marquis of Queensbury. The son of the man who formulated the rules of boxing, he ran the mines at one time. Open daily in summer, free.

From **Sault Ste. Marie**, the Algoma Central Railway runs the spectacular **Agawa Canyon Wilderness Tour**. Every day at 8 A.M. from mid-May to mid-October the train pulls out for the 10-hour return trip to the beautiful canyon. It snakes through ravines and across high trestle bridges to the canyon, where you are deposited for a two-hour visit. The train has a restaurant car or you may take a picnic basket. This trip is sensational in fall. Round trip $12, children from age 5 to high school, $6. From January to March, the same trip is made on weekends only, at 8:30 A.M., without the stopover.

"**The Soo**" (pop. 80,000), is a steel and shipping city which faces its matching Michigan city across the St. Mary's river. The Soo Locks connect Lake Superior with Lake Huron. The rapids were discovered by French explorers in 1622 and the Jesuit, Marquette, founded a permanent mission in 1669. Cruise lines operate two-hour boat trips through the locks, $4.50 adult, ages 6-12, $2.50. There is skiing nearby, and the city hosts two major festivals: the Algoma Fall Festival, 2½ weeks of music, theater, film, art and dance in late September, and the Bon Soo Winter Carnival in late January.

Eighty miles north of the Soo is **Lake Superior Provincial Park**, 340,478 acres. It is rugged country but highway 17 runs through it.

It takes you to **Wawa**, (pop. 5000), five miles north of the park. Wawa, or "wild goose" in Ojibway, was a fur-trading post before 1700, later the site of three gold rushes. Magpie High Falls, which is 75 feet high, freezes solid in winter.

When you get north of Lake Superior, you are north, period. There is a lot of empty space up there. And a lot that is going on. Lots of provincial parks, plenty of outdoor activities. **Thunder Bay** was once called The Lakehead, or the two cities of Fort William and Prince Arthur. They merged in 1969. Three generations ago, Prime Minister Wilfrid Laurier called it the Chicago of the North. It's not, never has been, likely never will be. But it is an interesting place and a big one (pop. 116,000).

It is at the head of navigation of Lake Superior, as far into the continent as the big ships can go. Its major skyline is the rows of tall grain elevators which can store 105 million bushels of grain. In summer, you can tour some of the elevators and the huge paper mills in town.

You'll also be shown the Sleeping Giant, a huge rock peninsula that rises from the water of Thunder Bay and looks like a sleeping giant, Nanibijou, the Ojibway "Great Spirit." The legend is that Nanibijou lived on Mt. McKay, now part of the Ojibway reservation. To reward the Ojibways for their loyalty, Nanibijou told them of a rich silver mine but said that if any white man learned of it, they would perish and he would turn to stone. An Indian did tell the white man. As the white man's canoes drew near, a storm broke and the interlopers drowned. In the morning, there was Nanibijou, turned to stone, sleeping across the mouth of Thunder Bay.

Mount McKay is still there, of course, now the center of a burgeoning ski industry – there are five ski resorts within 10 miles of town.

Thunder Bay, once mostly muscle and industry, is rapidly expanding as a recreational area. The provincial government has reconstructed **Old Fort William** to show what it was like during the days the North West Company held its annual "Great Rendezvous" of fur traders and trappers, when the nearest city was 1,000 miles away and you had to use canoes to get there. There are 40 buildings and an expert staff to help you test-fire a musket or help build a birchbark canoe. It is the northern equivalent of famed Upper Canada Village. Daily 10 A.M. to 6 P.M. May 15-Oct. 15, adults $2, students $1, ages 6-12, free.

The city is especially rich in parks. Kids love 100-acre **Centennial Park** on the Current river, which is free. It has a reproduced logging camp, an animal farm, and a cookhouse serving lumberjack meals. Also free are **Boulevard Lake Park**, a 1,000-acre park surrounding Boulevard Lake and offering beach, tennis courts, boat rentals, playgrounds, and **Chippewa Park**, 300 acres a few miles south on Lake Superior which has a zoo and camping.

Thunder Bay Amethyst Mines, 35 miles east of the city, was discovered accidentally when a forest road was being built. Now it is one of the biggest in north

America. You can visit it free but you will be charged for any specimens you collect.

Kakabeka Falls (pop. 350), 18 miles west of Thunder Bay on highway 17, has a dramatic 128-foot falls. And a stirring legend. An Ojibway princess who was captured by the Sioux pretended to lead them to her people. Instead, she steered them – and herself – over the falls.

West to the Manitoba border, the tourist passes through more rugged country, replete with parks and with small towns proud of their local history and museums.

Most striking is **Quetico Provincial Park**, 1,148,000 acres of wilderness a few miles east of **Atikokan**. It links up with Superior Park in Minnesota.

Kenora (pop. 10,952) gives access to Lake of the Woods, one of the best fishing and hunting areas in the province, which has 14,600 islands. Every year, early in August, the International Lake of the Woods Regatta and the Lake of the Woods International Pow-Wow are both held on the same weekend. The regatta is an 88-mile sailboat race celebrated with dances and art shows. Indians from as far away as the U.S. southwest come to the pow-wow and there are competitions for drummers and dancers.

THE PRAIRIES

"Breadbasket to the world; drag strip to its neighbors."

Wheat from the Canadian prairie provinces – Manitoba, Saskatchewan and Alberta – has shown up in one form or another on tables from Paris to Peking and from Moscow to New Delhi. Prairie-raised beef is almost as well travelled. Oil from these provinces fuels the nation and its cars. Yet, except for the Rocky mountains on its western fringe, it remains one of the most ignored regions of Canada, leapfrogged every week by thousands of Canadians heading west to the sea or east to the bright lights of Montreal and Toronto. Summer vacationers using the family car treat the prairies just as lightly, as a sort of drag strip to greener sightseeing pastures on either side. Even Canadians who have crossed the prairies too often dismiss it as a pancake-flat sea of wheat, glowing golden in the summer sun but downright boring after the first two hundred miles.

One reason for this is that the main route across Canada – the Trans-Canada Highway – slices across the prairie provinces at their flattest and dullest belt. Only those lighthouses of the west, the grain elevators, relieve the monotony over much of the route. If you're making the trip by car by all means use the alternate Yellowhead Highway – linking Portage la Prairie in Manitoba with Prince Rupert, B.C. – in one direction. It takes you through rolling hill country, dotted with lakes and ponds inhabited by wild ducks. Along either route, plan some sidetrips. The real rewards of a prairie visit lie off the main highways.

And before you head out, get a few things straight. Only a small portion of these three provinces is flat prairie. Canada's most popular mountains, the Rockies, lie largely along the western border of Alberta. Manitoba has some 100,000 lakes and 440 miles of seacoast on Hudson Bay. At Cypress Hills in Saskatchewan, you find mountains 4,500 feet high just 35 miles from the U.S. border and near Prince Albert, in the center of the province, there's a national park that opens up a 1,500-square mile forest wilderness of lakes, streams and hills to the visitor. You will also find surprises among prairie cities – Edmonton is building its own subway; Winnipeg has a renowned ballet and summer theater in the park; Regina's Centre of the Arts is a theater complex that wouldn't look out of place in New York.

Moreover, because many prairie people are only a step or two removed from pioneers, they are among the most open and friendly natives you'll meet in Canada. Put them right next to the Newfies in that regard. Their rodeos and folk festivals are lively and inviting, their manners informal all the way. So don't keep on trucking past those prairie grain elevators. Stop at one and ask the manager to show you around. We've done that a half dozen times – even got introduced to a local farmer once who insisted on taking us home to lunch. By the way, farms are really farms in this part of the world – one that covers a couple of square miles isn't even unusual. In Saskatchewan they say a farmer needs to pack a lunch just to plough to the end of one furrow.

But let's not get carried away. Much of the prairies – at least the portion that can easily be reached by road – isn't a showstopper. Distances are great and a bit of advance planning is needed to ensure that you don't waste your precious holiday time on less-than-inspiring sidetrips. Here's a province-by-province guide to the high points – no pun intended.

WEATHER REPORT   Except for vacationers heading for skiing in the Rockies, late spring, summer and early fall are very much the best time for a visit. Prairie cities are notoriously cold in winter. Edmonton, Regina and Winnipeg rarely get up to the freezing mark in January and February. If you've wondered why so many of those hockey stars you see in Boston, Toronto or New York are from the prairie provinces – that's the reason. They had to keep skating or freeze to death. Prairie summers on the other hand are invariably sunny and bright, with the days reaching into the 70s and 80s. Regina, for example, gets 40 more hours of July sunshine than Toronto, on average, and 90 more hours than Halifax. Humidity is also lower than in the rest of Canada.

MANITOBA

"Cinderella of the Confederation."

John Norquay, Manitoba
premier in 1884.

Looking down from atop the domed Manitoba Legislative Building in Winnipeg is a beloved statue known as the Golden Boy. He symbolizes the Manitoba of yesterday in more ways than one. Naturally he is carrying a sheaf of wheat under one arm, but there's more to his story than that. Manitoba commissioned a Frenchman named Charles Gardet to create the Golden Boy prior to the outbreak of World War I. The factory where Gardet worked was hit by a bomb early in the war and the Golden Boy was one of the few survivors. He was loaded into the hold of a ship heading for America, but – wouldn't you know it – the ship was commandeered to carry troops and the Golden Boy spent the war sailing back and forth with them through treacherous waters before finally being delivered to his new homeland. That's the way things were right from the start for Manitoba, too. Survival was something she had to work at.

The province, all 251,000 square miles of it, began as a private preserve of the Hudson's Bay Company, a fur trading conglomerate that in 1670 was deeded rights to half of what is now Canada by King Charles II of England. It remained the happy hunting ground of Indian and Métis (French-Indian) trappers until 1812 when Lord Selkirk bought into the company and began attempts to settle impoverished Scottish farmers at the junction of the Red and Assiniboine

Rivers, where Winnipeg now stands. These would-be settlers immediately found themselves in direct conflict with the Métis who, egged on by rival Northwest Company fur traders and seeing their free-spirited life style threatened, clashed with the settlers and in one incident killed 22 of them. But a tiny agricultural colony, the beginnings of today's Manitoba, finally got a foothold in 1817. In 1869, when the Canadian government bought the entire northwest from the Hudson's Bay Company, a second major confrontation with the threatened Métis took place. This time they were led by a visionary school teacher named Louis Riel, still one of the most controversial characters in Canadian history. Was he saint, villain, martyr or madman? It depends on whom you talk to. This first Riel Rebellion and the provisional government he set up failed when troops were sent out from the east, and in 1870 the province of Manitoba was born.

The new settlement remained small until the Canadian Pacific railroad was pushed west to Winnipeg in 1881, bringing with it hoards of newcomers – Ukrainians, Poles, Germans, even Icelanders whose descendants still make their home at Gimli. That same railway also carried large shipments of wheat east as the prairies began to play its key role in Canadian nationhood. But struggles for survival continued. Rivers flooded, sometimes leaving Winnipeg's streets knee deep in dreaded Red River "gumbo." Manitoba was to suffer along with the rest of the world in the Great Depression – only more so. For the collapse in the economy here was accompanied by one of the worst droughts in history. Farmers, the dust on their faces turned to mud by stubborn tears, watched their precious topsoil blow away as the searing sun opened cracks they could barely step across in the parched earth. But enough of that; now let's

take a look at this western survivor as she looks today.

WHAT TO SEE Winnipeg, the capital, is the
country's most underrated city – a culturally rich and
lusty kind of town – the Chicago of Canada though
without its U.S. counterpart's tawdry crime record.
Canada's fourth largest city, with a population of
570,000, Winnipeg is the country's rail center and
headquarters for major meat packers and grain buy-
ers. Yet in the bright prairie sun, with its new cluster
of skyscrapers visible for miles around on the flat
prairie it inhabits, Winnipeg stands out like a real-life
Oz. And, indeed, it is a place where theater, ballet
and folk festivals flourish, where paddlewheelers ply
the rivers in summer and where body-rub parlors
make house calls. The rest of Canada generally
downplays the place, largely because of its notorious
winter weather – where 20 below zero isn't regarded
as worth talking about. The famous Arctic explorer
Stefansson, himself a Manitoba native, said it was
colder crossing the corner of Portage and Main (the
heart of the city) than it was at the North Pole. But
we'll assume you'll do your sightseeing during a summer visit and start you off this way:

Head first for the handsome **Legislative Building**, a
domed, neoclassical edifice (bordered by Broadway
Ave., Kennedy and Osbourne Sts. and the Assiniboine River) that will remind you of the best U.S.
state capitols. Two bronze buffalo guard the marble
staircase, and fossils dimple the Manitoba limestone
of which the place is constructed. Free tours show
you around between 9 a.m. and 4 p.m. daily. The surrounding grounds are just as handsome and studded
with statues of Scots, Ukrainian and Icelandic heroes

– plus, of course, the omnipresent widow of Windsor, sour old Queen Victoria.

A short walk away, at the corner of Portage and Memorial Blvd., is the **Winnipeg Art Gallery**, shaped like a wedge of cheese but an absolute sensation of a place. Here you'll find the largest collection of much-coveted Eskimo art in the country, as well as Canadian and European masters. The coolest place in town on a hot summer day and easily the best art gallery in all of western Canada. Free and open daily, except Mondays.

Then head for Main St. and the **Centennial Centre complex**, the city's 100th birthday present and a surprise package for any visitor. The No. 1 attraction there is the **Manitoba Museum of Man and Nature**, 555 Main St. It uses ultramodern electronic techniques to give you and your children a quick glimpse at prairie life past and present. You don't just walk in; you arrive on a simulated space ship about to land in this part of the world. Dioramas bring back the day of the buffalo and the age of the fur trade, besides detailing the struggle for survival mentioned earlier. Anyone over five pays 50 cents admission. It and the planetarium it operates are open daily.

The Centennial Centre also houses a huge concert hall and a theater, the homes of the splendid Royal Winnipeg Ballet, the Manitoba Opera and the Winnipeg Symphony. The **Manitoba Theatre Centre** is nearby at 174 Market St. Any of these is worth an evening out – if you're lucky enough to find them in town and not on tour.

Now it's time for a break, which one can take in fine style by heading out on day, or evening, paddle-wheel cruises on the Red River. (Gray Line will pick you up at your hotel or you can head north on Main St. to the dock which is just off Redwood Ave.) The riverboats aren't actually propelled by their paddlewheels but they look so much like the real thing that you almost expect to see Mark Twain on the bridge. Cruises run from $2.75 to $3.50. There is also a longer (seven-hour) cruise to Lower Fort Garry, described later.

The railway played a key role in Winnipeg's history and you can see the **Countess of Dufferin**, first steam engine to reach the west, on Main St. near the Centennial Centre. Other sights that may interest someone on a longer stay include: **Kildonan Park**, off north Main St., where musicals are presented in summer on the outdoor Rainbow Stage; **Assiniboine Park**, on the banks of the river of the same name in west Winnipeg, with fine English gardens and a small zoo; the **Grain Exchange** at 167 Lombard Ave. where a visitor's gallery overlooks the trading floor as tons of wheat are bought and sold (it's open weekdays 9.30 A.M. to 1.15 P.M.); the **Ukrainian Cultural Centre**, also near the Centennial Centre, with a stock of artifacts, paintings and costumes these vibrant settlers brought to the west.

Before leaving, cross the bridge into **St. Boniface** at least once. Although now technically part of Winnipeg this is a much different corner of the west, a community that was founded by French-speaking Canadians and one where streets bear French names and institutions have a distinct Gallic flavor. You can best feel this at **St. Boniface Cathedral** on Rue Tache. The original cathedral, one of the largest in the west, was gutted by a disastrous fire in 1968. But the walls have been left standing like a Roman ruin, surrounding the contemporary cathedral which has been erected within. In the adjoining graveyard, you will find the grave of Louis Riel, mentioned earlier. He was brought back to St. Boniface for burial after being hanged in Regina following the failure of the ill-fated second rebellion he led on behalf of Métis' rights.

Lower Fort Garry, on the banks of the Red River, 19 miles north of Winnipeg (via Highway 9), is not to be missed by history buffs. It is the only stone fort from the fur trade days which remains in its original condition. Costumed characters demonstrate how life was lived in the west in those wild days. It is open daily from May until October (adults $2, children 50 cents). At nearby Selkirk, you may get a glimpse of the M.S. Selkirk II, a prairie cruise ship which makes week-long and weekend trips on Lake Winnipeg from June to October. You can get details on sailings from P.O. Box 1701, Winnipeg.

To the west of Winnipeg, the city of Brandon won't command your attention for too long but due south on Highway 10 you come to the **International Peace Gardens**, 2,300 acres of formal gardens and parkland, lying on both sides of the border with the U.S. It is a tribute to the long, undefended – except by Customs Officers – border between the two countries. A music camp and school of fine arts is held there each summer.

If you decide to visit Manitoba's northland, you can drive to **Flin Flon**, 450 miles north of Brandon, and to **The Pas** along Highway 10. The latter is still the home of a colorful crew of trappers, prospectors, lumbermen and miners, while Flin Flon is the jumping off place for canoeing and fishing trips into the wilderness. These two towns, by the way, are included in Canadian National's summer railway tours to **Churchill** on Hudson Bay (CN Passenger Sales offices in Winnipeg and other major cities can give details).

Churchill is Canada's northernmost deepsea port and the landing place of early Manitoba settlers. More than 1,000 rail miles from Winnipeg, Churchill is not a noted Canadian beauty spot, though herds of whales are sometimes spotted in the nearby frigid waters of the bay. This is an active port during summer despite its remoteness, with grain going out and a variety of goods arriving for shipment south by rail. Fort Prince of Wales, the 200-year-old restored ruins of a British fortress, overlooks the harbor. Despite its mighty cannons and 14-foot walls this fortress fell to the French in 1782 without a shot being fired. It can be visited by boat tour when the unpredictable weather is in the right mood.

Manitoba has one national park and 10 provincial parks, two of which are outstanding. **Riding Mountain National Park**, covering 1,150 square miles of lakes and forest, 165 miles northwest of Winnipeg, offers camping, hiking and trail riding in a preserve that's alive with elk, moose and deer, not to mention the wild ducks and geese that inhabit so much of northern Manitoba. **Whiteshell Provincial Park**, 90 miles east of Winnipeg on the Trans-Canada Highway, has more than 200 lakes, countless streams and waterfalls. Pike, walleye, lake trout and smallmouth bass abound. **Grand Beach provincial park** offers camping at Manitoba's favorite beach, just an hour's drive north of Winnipeg.

HOW TO GET THERE Most visitors arrive by car, either travelling the Trans-Canada Highway or from neighboring North Dakota and Minnesota. The Trans-Canada cuts across the southern portion of the province, the No. 1 trunk road among some 10,000 miles of Manitoba arteries. Roads are non-existent in much of the north – prospectors, lumbermen, fly-in fishermen, trappers and hunters don't need them.

Both CP Air and Air Canada fly to Winnipeg from other parts of the country, and Northwest Orient, North Central and Frontier Airlines fly from U.S. points. Trans Air flies to the northern part of the province. CP and CN trains serve the province, especially as part of trans-continental routes. Major cross-country bus routes pass through the province along the Trans-Canada and there is good bus service from neighboring U.S. points.

WHERE TO STAY   The best accommodation is in Winnipeg where the plush **Winnipeg Inn** is in a class by itself among the luxury hotels. Moreover, it is just a few steps from Portage and Main, the heart of town. This ultra-modern hotel stands above the **Lombard Place** shopping concourse, handy in winter. It has one of the city's best restaurants, the **Velvet Glove**; well-appointed rooms; sauna; pool; nightclub – the works. (Singles from $33, doubles from $41). Other top-line hostelries include: CN's gently aging **Fort Garry**, 222 Broadway, recently refurbished and also the possessor of a first-rate restaurant, the **Factor's Table.** Room rates run from $29 single, $37 double. CP's **Northstar Inn**, which starts high in the sky above an immense indoor parking garage at 288 Portage Ave., has a dining room, coffee shop, indoor pool, cocktail lounge and sauna. Rates are $32 single, $40 double. For budgeters we suggest the **Gordon Downtowner** on the Kennedy St. entertainment strip. Singles start at $18 and doubles at $22, there's a budget-priced restaurant and coffee shop and a lively beverage room next door where drinks are half the price the big hotel lounges charge. Some of the rooms even have individual saunas – or did the last time we stopped by. Biggest hotel in town is the **Holiday Inn**, attached to the city's new convention center. Singles start at $30, doubles at $37. The ancient **Marlborough**, from railway days, on Smith St., just north of Portage has also been redone. The price is right there, with singles starting at $18 and doubles at

$24. **The International Inn**, 1808 Wellington Ave., out by the city's international airport, is a lively spot ($20 single, $29 double), with the same assortment of facilities as the in-town biggies, plus a theater restaurant. Motels around the periphery of Winnipeg are generally reasonably priced, with doubles available for as little as $16. In most of the rest of the province you have to depend on motels and motor hotels, though Brandon has CP's first rate **Red Oak Inn** ($24 single, $32 double) with complete facilities.

In the far north hotels are naturally a little more rudimentary. **The Tamarack** ($20 double) is handy in **The Pas** and the **Oreland Motel** ($15 double) at **Flin Flon**, even has color TV. There are three hotels at **Churchill** – the **Hudson, Churchill** and **Polar** – which should, of course, be booked before you fly or take the train there. You can get a complete priced list of accommodations, including the many fly-in lodges of the north, by writing to the Manitoba Department of Tourism, 200 Vaughan St., Winnipeg, and asking for its Accommodation Guide.

It's also worth keeping in mind that this is farm country much of the way. You can book your family on a farm holiday and even help swill the pigs and milk the cows. Write Manitoba Farm Vacations, 347 Assiniboine Ave., Winnipeg for details.

WHERE TO EAT Used to be that you were out of luck unless a steak dinner was your idea of dining adventure. But things are fast improving, especially in Winnipeg where Greek, Indian, Japanese and continental restaurants have arrived. But our favorite dining spot is still **Hy's Steak Loft**, 216 Kennedy St. This is part of a distinctive chain that came out of the west to make its mark even in Toronto. Winnipeg's **Steak Loft**, with the usual – for Hy's – paintings of horrendous nobility, oaken walls and never-read shelves of books, is perhaps the best of the lot. You can still get a steak dinner – soup, salad, baked potato and garlic toast for $9 to $12. The wine list is one of the most extensive in Winnipeg. The **Velvet Glove** in The Winnipeg Inn offers lavish service and prices to match, backed by a top-notch wine cellar. The intimate **Old Swiss Inn** on Edmonton St. offers veal dishes to remember and serves up the best fondues in town. At lunch you can get by for under $5, including drinks. The **Old Spaghetti Factory**, 291 Bannatyne St., doesn't pretend to make the world's best spaghetti but it's a low-priced fun place for the family. The **Factor's Table** in the Fort Garry Hotel, mentioned earlier, offers a refined setting for its excellent steak tartare. **Ichi Ban**, 189 Carlton St., where the Japanese chef prepares the tempura, shrimp or chicken, at your table is a dazzling place with exciting food. The **Hollow Mug Theatre Restaurant** at the International Inn doesn't serve a memorable meal, in our opinion, but the entertainment is usually more so. The **Town 'n Country Cabaret** on the Kennedy Strip, presents name groups at its dinner shows. We think the best hamburgers in town are served by **Junior's** at 170 Main St. In Brandon, the **Suburban** on Victoria Ave., is a first-rate place to stop for fine homemade cooking.

NIGHTLIFE In Winnipeg it's a rousing mixture of cultural, contemporary and lusty; elsewhere in the province it's almost non-existent. Of the many cultural presentations, the **Royal Winnipeg Ballet** performances are justifiably most renowned. Trouble is that the Royal's season usually runs from October to May, a time when few tourists are in town. The hotel and cabaret dinner shows, mentioned earlier, compete for attention with a number of strip joints and body rub parlors (largely on the Kennedy Strip) that advertise house calls – hotel, too. We know, dear reader, that doesn't interest you; it's presented merely as a social note. **Folklorama**, a festival in mid-August in which various ethnic groups put on entertainment at pavilions scattered about the city, is worth taking in if you're in town then.

SPECTATOR SPORTS They're big here. The beloved **Blue Bombers** play football at **Winnipeg Stadium** in fall, the **Jets** play hockey at **Winnipeg Arena** in winter, the ponies run at **Assiniboia Downs** from early May to the middle of August and **harness racing** is held at the same track from the end of August until late October.

WHERE TO SHOP In Winnipeg, **Portage Avenue**, especially the dozen blocks west of Main, is very much the center of things, anchored by Eaton's and the Hudson's Bay Co. department stores. The **Odjig** shop at 331 Donald St. offers prints by Canada's Indian artists. The **Winnipeg Art Gallery** also sells crafts as does the **Crafts Guild of Manitoba**, 183 Kennedy St.

WHERE TO GET HELP WITH YOUR TRIP Best source of additional information is the Manitoba Dept. of Tourism, 200 Vaughan St., Winnipeg, Man. R3C 1T5. It sends out free accommodation guides, canoe maps, fishing and hunting guides and other specialized information. They have welcome stations at highway border points, issuing the same information. If your trip is taking you to other parts of Canada, too, write to the Canadian Government Office of Tourism, 150 Kent St., Ottawa.

SASKATCHEWAN

"The Lord said 'let there be wheat' and Saskatchewan was born."

Canadian humorist Stephen Leacock.

The prospect of a visit to Saskatchewan doesn't excite too many travellers heading west – any more than a visit to Kansas or Nebraska would thrill a visitor to the U.S. For this middle prairie province, one of only two in Canada that doesn't boast a seacoast, is the heart of agricultural Canada. Farm products account for nearly half its livelihood and most of its 940,000 citizens are in one way or another involved with the good earth. Saskatchewan works harder than most at welcoming visitors but can't really overcome the fact that it doesn't have a single major tourist attraction. The people are friendly, the towns sunny and bright in summer, the parklands plentiful and relaxing, lakes and ponds alive with ducks and fish – but there are no awesome mountains, no manmade wonders, no cities one is dying to see. But then Saskatchewan is only a lifetime old, an infant of civilization. There are plenty of oldtimers around who can still remember the day in 1905 when their province was born.

Naturally, its history goes back much further than that. For centuries before the coming of the white man, Indian tribes came to the grasslands, just north of what is now the U.S. border, to hunt the great buffalo herds. Then in 1670, the 251,700 square miles that now make up the province became part of the immense tract of wilderness deeded by Charles II of England to fur-trading Hudson's Bay Company.

However, as buffalo hunters and trappers aren't the kind that stay put, there wasn't a permanent settlement of any kind in Saskatchewan until Cumberland House (now an historic park) was established by Samuel Hearne in 1774.

Saskatchewan remained a lawless no-man's land where whisky traders fleeced the Indians out of their buffalo hides until Canada purchased the northwest from the Hudson's Bay Company in 1870. Law and order was administered by the scarlet-tuniced Northwest Mounted Police (now the Royal Canadian Mounted Police or "Mounties"). The force made the trek west in 1874, finally establishing its headquarters at Regina, which was later to become Saskatchewan's capital. But significant settlement came only with the arrival of the Canadian Pacific Railway a few years later. Instant towns sprang up beside the track and a steady stream of farmers, attracted by free land grants, followed. But, as in Manitoba, the new settlers soon found themselves in conflict with the Métis (French-Indian people) who felt the intruders were about to steal their land.

The Métis were buffalo hunters and their free-spirited way of life had already been dealt a blow by the indiscriminate slaughter of the great herds that once roamed the prairies. Early chroniclers tell of trains stopping in the middle of nowhere to allow mindless passengers the thrill of firing at will at the helpless beasts. The resounding culture clash came at Batoche in the Riel Rebellion of 1885. Louis Riel, who had led an ill-fated uprising against eastern settlers on Manitoba's Red River 15 years earlier, answered pleas from fellow Métis to return from exile in the U.S. and lead them in a last ditch stand against the intruders who, they had every reason to believe, were about to usurp their lands along the South Saskatchewan River. Riel's small force, under his com-

mander-in-chief Gabriel Dumont, were overwhelmed
by an army dispatched from the east under Major-
Gen. Middleton. In the last moments of the battle,
the Métis were using nails and bits of scrap to charge
their guns. Meanwhile, Middleton's force had a gatling gun, forerunner of the machine-gun, which a
U.S. firm was anxious to try in battle. Riel was
hanged at the Mounties' barracks in Regina while
Gabriel Dumont fled to the U.S. where he joined Buffalo Bill's wild west show.

One of the great pities of Batoche is that it didn't
really solve much. The Indians and Métis of the prairies are still having difficulties adjusting to the white
man's ways. Too many end up on the skid rows of
Regina and Winnipeg; too many are still the object
of deep-seated prejudice. Westerners talk about their
"Indian problem" in much the same way that easterners talk about the "Quebec problem." And no one
seems to have a good solution for either.

Hollywood took a crack at telling the story of Batoche in the 1930s when Cecil B. DeMille produced
Northwest Mounted Police, starring Gary Cooper as
the Texas Ranger who saved Canada from the rene-
gades. Naturally DeMille got the whole thing
backwards – even had the gatling gun in the hands of
the Métis. When Fred Anderson, the man who had
shown DeMille around Batoche, wrote to complain,
DeMille fired back a letter saying, "Your version may
be right but mine will sell a lot more theater tickets."

Batoche, 30 miles south of Prince Albert, is certainly a worthwhile stop, especially for those using
the close-by Yellowhead Highway to cross Saskatchewan. A national historic site has been established
at the tragic battleground. Look at the exterior of the
Rectory of St. Antoine de Padoue, where the Métis
were holed up, and you'll still see scars from the gatling gun. An interpretive program describes the bat-

tle. Nearby is the grave of Gabriel Dumont, who quietly returned to his home after his Buffalo Bill days ended.

Now on to modern day Saskatchewan which, by the way, is a Cree Indian word meaning "swift flowing." It was first applied to the river that cuts across the province, then to the land that surrounds it.

WHAT TO SEE **Regina**, the capital, has fewer than 150,000 citizens, but is still the largest of the 11 cities in the province. It was originally called Wascana, an Indian word meaning "pile of bones." That wouldn't do, so Princess Louise, wife of the governor general and a daughter of Queen Victoria, suggested Regina in honor of mother – and so it is today, the queen city of the prairies. It started out treeless, resulting in an absolute fetish for planting by almost everyone. Today it's easy to identify the older parts of town by the height of the trees that surround the homes.

The place to head when you hit town is **Wascana Centre**, 2,000 acres of parkland in the heart of the city. Here, surrounding a man-made lake on Wascana Creek, you can visit the handsome **Legislative Building** with three small art galleries and the **Museum of Natural History**, which though it appears old-fashioned compared with Winnipeg's ultramodern Museum of Man and Nature, still does a fine job of showing you the prairies both before and after man arrived. Also in the center is the prairie homestead of **John Diefenbaker**, the first westerner to become Prime Minister. Dief is revered in these parts as "the Abe Lincoln of Canada" and Saskatchewan natives invariably enter the cabin hat in hand and head bowed. Still, its simple furnishings offer a fine vignette of "make-do" pioneer life on the prairies. The

Saskatchewan Centre of the Arts, also in Wascana, is a splendid, modern theater the likes of which you would hardly expect to see in so small a city. Surrounding these institutions are landscaped gardens and a park filled with all sorts of waterfowl. All in all, it's a great oasis in a trip through the heart of the wheatlands. Moreover, none of the buildings charge admission except the theater.

Regina is no longer the headquarters of the Royal Canadian Mounted Police – that was moved to Ottawa long ago. But it is still the main training center for the force and you can watch drill squads of ramrod stiff men and women cadets on parade at 1 P.M. daily at the **R.C.M.P. barracks** on the edge of town. But the most interesting thing at the base is the **Mountie Museum**, which traces the history of the force from the days it rode into the west to bring law and order, through the times when they mushed by dogsled across frozen northern wastes to its present F.B.I.-like sophistication.

The museum is a modern showcase, opened in 1973 to celebrate the force's 100th birthday. One of the more gruesome displays is a collection of ropes claimed to have been used to hang Louis Riel after the failure of the Northwest Rebellion. You can also see pay notices from the time Mounties were paid 50 cents a day to maintain the peace. By the way, you'll notice that Mounties aren't quite as popular in Regina as they are elsewhere. Cadets love to go to Saskatchewan Roughrider football games en bloc and cheer for the other team – and that, pardner, is something you just don't do in these parts. Moreover, in their role as provincial police here and in most other provinces, they don't patrol highways in red tunics on horseback – but in unmarked cruisers. The museum is free and is open from 8 A.M. to 9 P.M. during summer.

Saskatoon, the second city, has a much nicer setting than Regina, cuddling the banks of the South Saskatchewan River, in rolling hill country. There are enough pubs in town today to make one forget that Saskatoon was settled by temperance workers from Ontario. The **Western Development Museum,** 2610 Lorne Ave., displays a street from a pioneer prairie village as its focal point. The **Mendel Art Gallery,** 950 Spadina Cres. E., has an interesting collection of Eskimo sculpture and Canadian paintings for people staying around town for the day. It is open daily and free.

Saskatchewan has only one national park but it's a dilly. Covering 1,496 square miles, **Prince Albert National Park** is two thirds the size of the entire province of Prince Edward Island and is sprinkled with hundreds of lakes and streams. To reach the recreational center of the park, you drive 55 miles north from the city of Prince Albert to the Waskesiu townsite. There, besides camping and trailer sites, you'll find an 18-hole golf course, motorboat and canoe rentals, a riding stable, nature trails, tennis courts, laundromats, beach and playground areas – in short, everything the pampered camper could want. Yet it is set amid pristine woodlands with enough interconnecting lakes to permit escape from the world. There's a $2 fee for non-campers who want to slip in for the day to do some fishing. Serviced campsites cost $6 and unserviced ones $3. The **Lune Wildlife Exhibit** on River St. is worth a peek when you pass through Prince Albert. Admission is $1 for adults, 50 cents for students.

Several other outdoor areas have special appeal. **Cypress Hills Provincial Park** takes you into an area where mountains 4,500 feet high rise sharply from the surrounding ranchlands of southeastern Saskatchewan. The **Qu'Appelle Valley,** whose praises were sung by the noted Canadian poet Pauline Johnson, parallels the Trans-Canada Highway just east of Regina. Lakes along the Qu'Appelle River, easily reached by roads running north from the highway, offer top-notch fishing and there are beaches, picnic sites and golf courses for anyone who wants to take a break on his trek east or west. If you have children, take them for a look at the fish display in Fort Qu'Appelle's hatchery. It's free. **La Ronge**, 150 miles north of Prince Albert on Highway 2, takes you to God's country. There are a couple of islands for every square mile of nearby Lac La Ronge – and there are 500 square miles in all. Motels, cabins and a provincial park campground offer accommodations. By the way, Saskatchewan provincial parks are among the best in the country. Several, including Cypress Hills, offer modestly priced cabins as well as campsites.

If you haven't had enough of the Mounties when you've visited their Regina headquarters, you can see five of their earliest buildings at **Fort Battleford** national historic park at the town of Battleford, northwest of Saskatoon. And when you visit **Batoche**, mentioned earlier, make a short hop over to **Duck Lake**, where one of the great old characters of the west, Fred Anderson, established a museum in an abandoned schoolhouse. It's got a specimen of just about everything ever used in the west and some of Louis Riel's letters to his followers. Should they have hanged Riel? I asked Fred Anderson who had lived with Batoche for most of his life. "No," he said, "today they would have said he was insane."

HOW TO GET THERE   The Trans-Canada Highway cuts 400 miles across the southern half of the province and there are border information stations at either end. The alternate Yellowhead Highway route cuts through Saskatoon to the north and is much more pleasant to drive than its trans-continental counterpart. Several highways cross the 49th parallel from neighboring Montana and North Dakota. Canadian Pacific's trans-continental trains more or less parallel the Trans-Canada route and Canadian National's go through Saskatoon like the Yellowhead. Air Canada flies into Regina and Saskatoon, and Transair serves several Saskatchewan communities from within the province and from other parts of the prairies.

WHERE TO STAY The downtown **Regina Inn** (singles from $25, doubles from $30) is a big city hotel in a small-town atmosphere. It's got everything you could expect, including rooms with balconies, a heated pool, coffee shop and two restaurants and a large attached shopping complex. Right across the street at 1717 Victoria Ave., the **Westward Motor Inn** ($17 single, $21 double) is a better-than-average budget choice, offering nightly entertainment. The new **Sheraton Centre Motor Inn**, just along Victoria St. from the other two, is another pleasing pad, with rates from $28 single and $33 double. Also in the heart of town is Canadian Pacific's aging **Hotel Saskatchewan**, at Victoria and Scarth. Given the fact that it hasn't aged as well as most other hotels in that chain, we would opt for any of the above mentioned at the price ($27 single, $33 double). On the outskirts of town, the **Landmark**, the **Bell City, Holiday Inn** and **Vagabond**, all on the Albert St. strip, are pleasant and bouncy at night. In Saskatoon, the vintage **Bessborough** at Spadina and 21st St. is still charming and comfortable ($22 single, $28 double). Motels across the province are inexpensive by eastern Canada standards, with doubles even in newish places generally available in the $16 to $20 range. As we mentioned before, some provincial parks offer cabins as well as campsites. And don't forget this is the heart of Canada's farmland, so opportunities to spend a week in the country abound. You can get a list of the growing number of Saskatchewan farms that accept guests from Travel Information, Department of Tourism, P.O. Box 7105, Regina, Sask. S4P 0B5.

WHERE TO EAT   Get to like steaks or Chinese food – found in every prairie town – or move on. **L'Habitant**, 2169 Lorne St. in Regina, is generally regarded as the province's top steak house and has a first-rate wine cellar to back it up. **Golf's Steak House**, 1945 Victoria Ave., is its closest rival. The **Chinese Palace** on the Trans-Canada, just south of town, lets you choose between steaks and a wide variety of oriental dishes. Golf's also has a Saskatoon outlet along 21st St. One warning: When you say "rare" out west, you get a steak that has only flirted with flame.

NIGHTLIFE   Lively but uninspiring – though the motels and hotels mentioned above do offer lounge entertainment and there's a theater restaurant in the **Regina Inn.**

SPECTATOR SPORTS   Despite its size, Regina manages to field a first-rate Canadian Football League team, the Roughriders. Summer thoroughbred racing is held in Regina.

WHERE TO SHOP   Indian artifacts are the top buys and you'll find them even in smaller towns. Get a free Saskatchewan Travel Guide from the address listed below and you'll find every craft shop in the province listed. The **Regina Native Arts and Crafts Co-op**, 636 Victoria, has a fine collection of hand-sewn moccasins, jewelry and dolls. The **Canadian Craft Shop** at the Regina Inn offers crafts from across Canada, including Eskimo soapstone carvings and Indian artifacts. But pricey. **The Battleford Native Handicrafts Co-op** on 24th St. E. is Indian-owned and offers artifacts made by Cree, Saulteaux, Stoney and Chippewyan tribes of the province. **The Prairie Pottery** in Saskatoon offers handcrafted vessels made from native clays and the **Saskatchewan Council for Crippled Children and Adults** in the same city has a large selection of ceramics among its offerings.

WHERE TO GET HELP WITH YOUR TRIP Best source is the travel guide, distributed free by Travel Information, Dept. of Tourism, P.O. Box 7105, Regina, Sask. S4P 0B5

ALBERTA

"Worthy the daughter of our English kings"

The Marquis of Lorne, a governor general, on naming Alberta in honor of his wife, a daughter of Queen Victoria.

Travellers may rush through Saskatchewan. They may even rush through Manitoba. But no one rushes through Alberta. They stop as if they had suddenly run into the side of a mountain – which, of course, is exactly the case. A magnificent chain of the Rocky Mountains rises out of the prairie foothills all along the western border of this sparkling province. They're not Canada's highest mountains, by any means, but they're her most famous and in many ways her most spectacular. For Alberta's Rockies cradle two immense national parks; readily accessible glaciers; highly visible moose, elk and bear; snow-capped peaks that appear close enough to touch; a couple of castle-like hotels; motels and campsites; emerald green lakes; countless streams and waterfalls – all of them linked by a beautifully engineered highway running north and south along the spine of the Rockies. Niagara Falls may have the numbers to prove it is Canada's No. 1 attraction, but we would put Alberta's Rockies even ahead of the great cataract on Canada's list of natural wonders.

The Rockies have awed travellers since the westward-moving fur traders came upon them and wondered how the hell they'd get through to the wealth of pelts they knew must lie on the other side. Finally, in 1793, Alexander Mackenzie of the Northwest Company found a pass on his historic trans-continental journey. (The passes he and other explorers discovered are, by the way, still the ones used by the railways and trans-continental highways to cross the Great Divide.) It was these same fur traders who brought the first vestiges of the white man's civilization to the Indians in the interior of Alberta – the plains and badlands where dinosaurs once roamed. The province was part of the vast tract of land deeded to the Hudson's Bay Company in 1670, but that claim was always hotly contested, first by the French who were the earliest to reach Alberta, then by the Northwest Company, on behalf of whom Mackenzie had made his epic journey. As in the case of Saskatchewan and Manitoba, significant settlement came only after Canada bought the west from the Hudson's Bay Company and the railroad and peace-keeping Northwest Mounted Police arrived on the scene. Alberta was administered as a territory until 1905 when it received provincial status and took one of the names of the same Princess Louise who had talked the authorities into naming Regina in honor of her mother, Queen Victoria.

Villages sprang up around former fur-trading forts and homesteaders from Britain and Europe, especially the Ukraine, poured in to carve farms and ranches out of the wilderness. Alberta's terrain is much different from the other two prairie provinces. Besides possessing 10,000-foot mountains, she offers rich farmland even north of Edmonton – in an area which gets less than 120 frost-free days a year. The province played a quiet agricultural role in Canada's economy until 1947 when vast oil fields were discovered near Edmonton. Almost overnight thousands of wells sprouted amid waving fields of wheat. There are 7,000 in the Edmonton area alone and they supply Canada with most of its oil and natural gas. With the new wealth came a new "we can lick the world" spirit, evidenced by the modern skyscrapers of Edmonton and Calgary. Oil also has pleasant side effects for the visitor – this is the one province in Canada which doesn't impose a retail sales tax. Both Edmonton and Calgary are very much worth a visit – but even they play second fiddle to the Rockies, so let's hit those lofty peaks first.

WHAT TO SEE You can reach the Rockies from either east or west along two major routes – the Trans-Canada Highway or the more northerly Yellowhead. No matter which way you come there is one requisite trip to make – the 142-mile drive along the **Icefield Parkway**, which links Banff and Jasper National Parks. We've driven through Switzerland and sailed up the Nile, but we would still put this Banff-Jasper trip ahead of all the others. The first time we made it we came on a herd of big-horn sheep fighting a tong war right in the middle of the highway. They'd get a running start at either side of the road and meet head on in the middle – a stunning sight to behold. A few miles along we spotted a black bear leading her cubs across the highway and giving the straggler a cuff on the ear that sent it somersaulting across the pavement. There were moose munching at the edge of the road, children throwing snowballs at each other in July, all amid the staggering grandeur of snow-capped peaks etched against a deep blue sky. Later we picked up a young hitchhiker who turned out to be Swiss. He had grown up in the shadow of the Alps but was obviously overwhelmed by his Rockies experience: "I have seen two wild bears in my life," he told us, "One this morning and one just a few minutes ago. Man has conquered the Alps – these mountains are still in the wilderness."

And chances are good they'll stay that way. For

Alberta's Rockies are embraced and protected by
two national parks that are more than three times the
size of the whole province of Prince Edward Island.
Jasper, to the north covers 4,200 square miles and
Banff 2,560. Townsites, bearing the same names as
the parks themselves lie at either end of the Icefield
Parkway and supply most of the accommodation and
tourist services in the parks. Banff is just an 80-mile
drive from Calgary along the Trans-Canada and 40
miles to the west of that is Canada's showplace **Lake
Louise**, a mile high and alternately deep blue or green
from the rich glacial waters that feed it. As a backdrop, Lake Louise has the Victoria glacier, a river of
ice several hundred feet thick. Louise and the other
lakes of Banff and Jasper are too cold for even the
hardiest swimmer but at **Upper Hot Springs**, near
Banff, natural springs pour 100-degree waters into an
outdoor pool and there are similar hot springs at
Miette, north of Jasper, with an outdoor pool. Larger
motels and hotels in the park also have heated pools.
The castle-like **Banff Springs Hotel** and **Chateau Lake
Louise**, both owned by Canadian Pacific, and **Jasper
Park Lodge**, Canadian National's superb resort, are
Rockies' institutions, with facilities to match the best
big-city hotels and a setting no other hotel in the
country can match.

Keep in mind that this is also Canada's prime ski
area – many hotels and motels stay open all year and
the summer visitors benefit from cable and gondola
lifts, designed to carry skiers to the upper slopes but
also available in summer to take rubberneckers to
new heights. Lifts, charging from $2.50 to $3.50 operate at **Mt. Norquay, Lake Louise, Sulphur Mountain**
– all in the Banff area – and at **Jasper's Whistler's
Mountain**.

There are a couple hundred miles of roads through
the parks – but do yourself a favor and get off them

once in a while. There are plenty of marked walking trails that someone in average condition can manage and there are day and weeklong trail riding expeditions.

Here are some other things to see as you drive about the two parks: **The Columbia Icefield** covers 160 square miles of the Rockies to a depth of 3,000 feet, supplying waters that flow into the Pacific, Arctic and Atlantic oceans (via Hudson Bay, in case you were wondering). **The Athabasca Glacier**, just one finger of this incredible mass, comes right down to the edge of the Icefield Parkway. Here you'll find children making snowballs in July. When the weather isn't too blustery, you can take rides onto the glacier in a tank-like snowmobile. You can also drive the road to **Maligne Lake**, south of Jasper, where boat cruises are offered amid the mountains – in summer only, of course, and even then you need a sweater for these glacier-fed waters. The Banff Springs golf course often has something duffers won't find elsewhere – elk on the fairways.

By the way, this is a major wildlife santuary but don't get the idea you're dealing with tame animals just because they have grown used to humans. Every year someone gets injured, even killed, because he knelt down to snap a picture of a moose who was camera-shy or got in between a mother bear and her cubs. When you walk the trails here it's a good idea to hang a can with a few stones in it from your belt. The rattle will keep you from catching some grizzly unawares, an incident few live to tell about.

In both Jasper and Banff, several shops rent auto-tape tours in the $10 range to guide you around both parks and help you pick out the various peaks.

One oddity about the Canadian Rockies: Although the peaks in Alberta are more famous, the highest

Rocky of them all is Mount Robson (12,972 feet), across the border in British Columbia.

You won't find it easy to pull yourself away from the mountains but when you do, here are some of the other things Alberta offers:

Edmonton, the capital, is a city of less than 500,000 which is building its own subway and getting ready to host the 1978 Commonwealth Games. That gives you an idea of the kind of spirit – and money – there is in this well-oiled metropolis of the north. The boom from oil has brought sophisticated trappings – skyscrapers and ultramodern indoor shopping centers, fancy restaurants and showplace museums – but Edmonton is still a frontier town at heart.

Stroll along Jasper Ave., the broad main drag, during the day and you'll see store windows filled with New York and Paris fashions. Stroll along late at night when the pubs are getting out and you have to duck the whooping bodies that come hurtling out the swinging doors. For Edmonton is not only rolling in its own oil but has become the main supplier of men and materials for Canada's new Arctic oil explorations. In a way it is reliving the riotous times when this was the jumping off point for men who went mucking for gold in the Klondike.

A first-rate place to start your visit is at **Old Fort Edmonton**, a reconstruction of the Hudson's Bay Company post on the banks of the North Saskatchewan River where the city had its beginnings. Costumed guides show you how the trader and his family lived and how they cheated the Indians when they brought in their furs. The fort is just part of an impressive plan to tell Edmonton's story. Original buildings have been collected from various parts of the city and region and are being rebuilt on streets typical of 1885, 1905 and 1920. Open daily in summer, the fort charges adults $1, children 50 cents. It's closed between Oct. 11 and May 21.

Modern Edmonton straddles this same river valley, with part of the downtown looking down from sheer bluffs. Along the banks lies the city's pride and joy, 17 miles of parkland sprinkled with picnic sites, golf courses and ponds. A few years back four glass pyramids were built in the valley as a unique botanical garden, each section featuring plants from a different climatic zone. This **Muttart Conservatory** is something very special for a city situated so far north that one can count on only 117 frost-free days a year. It is open daily.

The ultramodern **Provincial Museum and Archives**, 12845 102nd Ave., is one of the finest centennial projects anywhere in the country. Marvellously airy and alive, it takes you through Alberta from Indian and fur trade days to the present. The Indian and natural history sections are especially well conceived. Open daily, no admission charge.

We weren't expecting much at the **Edmonton Art Gallery** – but it turned out to be a real sleeper, especially for anyone interested in Canadian art. The Group of Seven, Krieghoff and Emily Carr are all represented. The gallery on Sir Winston Churchill Square is open daily. No admission charge.

The domed **Alberta Legislative Building**, overlooking the river on the original site of Fort Edmonton, was constructed in the shape of a cross. Its carillon gives recitals at noon and on Sunday afternoons. The adjoining formal gardens are the loveliest in Edmonton and there is a bandshell where concerts and rock sessions take place during summer. **McDougall Church**, 101 St. and 100th Ave. was erected in 1871, the first building outside the walls of the fort. Now it's a free museum filled with pioneer memorabilia. Closed Mondays. If you've got children with you by all means take them to the fun **Storyland Valley Zoo,** on the riverbanks at Buena Vista Rd. and 134th St. It's filled with small approachable animals (adults 50 cents, children 25 cents). The **Jubilee Auditorium,** built to commemorate the province's 50th anniversary, is where you see live theater and the **Queen Elizabeth Planetarium** in Coronation Park, west of Highway 2 on Highway 16, is where you'll see more famous stars. Open daily. Adults $1, children 25 cents.

Edmontonians are said to be Canada's most avid gamblers. You better believe it. Out beside Northlands Park, the bullring that serves as a horse racing track in these parts, there's a place called the **Silver Slipper** where you can try your luck at the blackjack tables. The Silver Slipper is the center of things during the latter half of July when the city lets its hair down for the annual Klondike Days festival, really the best time of all to visit. During the rest of the year, service clubs and the like are allowed to take over the Silver Slipper to raise money – and you are welcome to help.

By the way, **Klondike Days**, a gay nineties affair that recalls the era when the muckers for gold poured through town, is timed so it won't clash with the more famous **Calgary Stampede**, always held early in July. So with a little planning you can take in both the big whoop-ups on a single trip. Dates change each year so its best to check Travel Alberta, 10255 104th St., Edmonton, T5J 1B1, when planning a trip.

Before leaving the Edmonton area, animal lovers should head 20 miles southeast on Highway 14 to Al Oeming's **Alberta Game Farm.** You'll know you've reached it when you see llamas grazing beside cattle in nearby fields. Here tigers, leopards, zebras, rhinos and a host of endangered species thrive in a climate that can hit 50 below in winter and go for weeks without rising above the freezing mark. Open daily. Adults $2.50, children $1.

Calgary is not so much a sister city to Edmonton as a hated rival. Slightly smaller, it still wrankles over the decision that made Edmonton the provincial capital. A visitor who comes at Stampede time in early July might get the idea he's in an overgrown cow town – street dancing, chuckwagon breakfasts, 10-gallon hats and cowboy boots tend to create that sort of impression. But anyone who takes the time will find a city of rising skyscrapers, growing sophistication and oil-based wealth. In the center of town, the **Calgary Tower** rises 626 feet as a symbol of those things – though, more importantly for the visitor, its observation tower (adults $1.50, children 75 cents) provides a superb view of the nearby Rocky Mountains and foothills. On a clear day that is.

No one arriving with young children should miss the **Calgary Zoo** and **Dinosaur Park** at Memorial Drive and 12th St. E. Life-sized replicas of the gigantic creatures that once made the Alberta plains their home loom above you and there's a fine display of live animals including ones your youngsters can pet. They – and you – will also like **Heritage Park**, off Highway 2 on the west side of town. A trading post, 1896 western opera house, paddlewheeler, and blacksmith shop are among the late 19th century exhibits that fill this re-created village. Open daily. Adults $1, children 35 cents. **Stampede Park** is where the action is during the big annual festival early in July. Chuckwagon races are the big hit, though a full card of rodeo events is also presented. Thoroughbred horse racing takes place there at other times during the summer.

More formal entertainment is found at the **Jubilee Theatre**, a twin of the one in Edmonton, and like the capital, Calgary also has a planetarium. Still and all, the nicest thing about the place is that it's just an hour and a half's drive from Banff.

The **Alberta Badlands** are also very much worth a look. To get to them head 90 miles northeast from Calgary (along the Trans-Canada and Highway 9) to Drumheller from where the Dinosaur Trail leads into one of the eeriest areas of Canada. Here, amid strange mushroom-shaped hoodoos, eroded from hills in the surrounding valley, have been found many dinosaur skeletons and fossils of other prehistoric animals. One of them is exhibited at the **Drumheller Museum**, on 1st St. E. in Drumheller. It's free and open daily in summer. **Dinosaur Provincial Park**, just north of the Trans-Canada Highway at Brooks unveils another section of the badlands and exhibits skeletons found in the area.

Alberta has another national park, **Waterton Lakes**. It's no match for Banff or Jasper – but it would be the star of the show in most other places. Straddling 200 square miles of mountains and lakes on the U.S. border, Waterton is actually part of the gigantic Waterton-Glacier International Peace Park, extending down into neighboring Montana. **Red Rock Canyon**, especially caught at sunrise, is a highlight for hikers. International launches cruise the mountain-rimmed park lake system in summer. The park townsite has hotels and motels, besides campsites. Campers also will find well-equipped sites in 40 provincial parks scattered about the province.

HOW TO GET THERE You can cross Alberta by either the Trans-Canada (Highway 1 going through Calgary) or the Yellowhead route (Highway 16 going through Edmonton). Through the mountains, the Yellowhead provides less arduous slopes for someone pulling a heavy trailer but doesn't seem to get you as close to the peaks as the Trans-Canada's **Rogers' Pass**. You can, of course, change routes by many north-south connecting roads – the trick is to manage your trip so that you get to drive the Icefield Parkway on one segment. One very special road in Alberta is the **Mackenzie Highway**, the only road leading into the Northwest Territories.

Air service is excellent to both Edmonton and Calgary, with Air Canada, CP Air, Pacific Western, Western Airlines, Hughes Air West and Northwest Orient all flying into the province. The main rail lines of Canadian National and Canadian Pacific serve Edmonton and Calgary respectively. Alberta is one of only two provinces without a seacoast so you can't catch a ship to anywhere.

WHERE TO STAY Edmonton, Calgary, Banff and Jasper are all major centers of accommodation. Edmonton alone has more than 70 hotels and motels. Here's a rundown:

EDMONTON Plush but pricey is Canadian Pacific's **Chateau Lacombe**, a circular tower atop the river bluffs just a few steps from the heart of town. It has a revolving rooftop restaurant, dining room and coffee shop. Singles from $31, doubles from $39. Rival Canadian National's vintage **Hotel Macdonald**, 10065 100th St., ($30 single, $36 double) and Western International's **Edmonton Plaza**, 10135 100th St., ($31 single, $39 double) are the other downtown luxury hotels – and they're both good ones. Less pricey and central is the **Sheraton-Caravan** on 104th St., $27 single, $31 double. There are large pockets of motels on Highway 2, on the southern approach to the city from Calgary, and on Highway 16 and 16A, both east and west of town. Rates for a double run from $14 up.

CALGARY The downtown biggies here are the new **Four Seasons**, 19th Ave. and Centre Sts., ($28 single, $38 double), the vintage **Palliser**, 1133 9th Ave., ($27 single, $34 double), the **Calgary Inn**, 320 4th Ave. S.W. ($30 single, $38 double) and the **International**, 220 4th Ave. S.W. ($34 single, and $42 double). We give the Four Seasons a big edge on the others, with one of the best restaurants in town, **Trader's**, right on the premises. It also adjoins the city's new convention center. The **Empress** on 6th Ave. S.W. is a good bet for those seeking a cheaper in-town pad ($19 single, $22 double). Large pockets of motels are found west on the Trans-Canada and on Highway 2, south of town.

BANFF If you can afford the **Banff Springs** ($36 single, $42 double) or **Chateau Lake Louise** (same rates), you're on top of the world. There's a wide range of choice at Banff townsite itself but, as you might expect, everything's quite a bit more expensive than elsewhere in Alberta. Expect to pay $25 to $30 for a double at nicer motels.

JASPER It costs $102 to $118 for a couple to stay at **Jasper Park Lodge** – with two meals thrown in. It's almost worth it. For this is a world class resort on the edge of Lac Beauvert. At Jasper townsite you'll pay $25 up for a double.

Elsewhere in Alberta, prices are extremely reasonable, from $16. Many ranches and farms across the province now take guests. You can get a list from Alberta Great West Vacation Association, Box 185, Bentley, Alberta.

WHERE TO EAT Steak houses are the standby here as throughout the west. But there is growing sophistication in dining in both Edmonton and Calgary – even outside the plush new hotels.

EDMONTON **The Great Escape** at 9602 82nd Ave. set Edmonton on its ear when it opened a few years back. You had to reserve weeks in advance to try many-coursed meals featuring paella, spareribs or curry. The original owners are gone but it's still a fine dining experience. Expensive, count on paying $25 up with wine. You can even things out the next day by eating at **Primo's**, 10123 106 St., where the chicken is spicy but the prices nicey. **La Ronde**, the revolving restaurant atop the Chateau Lacombe, has food which, while we don't think it matches the view, is a notch above the usual fare in these twirling terraces. Steaks and beef, from $7 up. **Oliver's**, 11730 Jasper Ave., is a good seafood choice and the **Japanese Village**, 10126 100th St. and **Fujiyama**, 10125 121st St., are first-rate Japanese steak houses. The **Old Spaghetti Factory**, 10220 103rd St., might not have you raving over its pasta but its fun decor and ambience will keep the family happy at a price you can afford. The **New World**, 10120 97th St., is a first-rate Chinese restaurant.

CALGARY We usually avoid hotel restaurants. But in Calgary we always have one meal in **Trader's** where the smoked B.C. salmon is worth the lofty prices. You can balance your food budget the next day at **Taj Mahal,** 4816 Macleod Trail, one of the best Indian restaurants in the west where you can fill up on curries and sweets for under $5, wine included. **Hy's,** part of the reputed steak house chain we've mentioned earlier is located at 316 4th Ave. S.W. The steaks from $9 to $12 aren't all that pricey when you take into account the salad, onion soup, garlic toast and baked potato that come along with them. **The Silver Dragon,** 106 3rd Ave., is a long-time Calgary favorite.

NIGHTLIFE   Lively in Calgary and Edmonton and in Banff where the Banff School of Fine Arts helps draw a young crowd and puts on a summer arts festival. The big city hotels have entertainment in their lounges and there are more than enough discos to ruin anyone's hearing.

SPECTATOR SPORTS   Football, with a long-standing rivalry between the Edmonton Eskimos and Calgary Stampeders, is the biggest game in both towns. Horse racing meets spend time in each city during summer as part of an active prairie circuit.

WHERE TO SHOP   The good news, as we said before, is that no sales tax is tacked on to the price in oil-rich Alberta. The **Edmonton Centre,** with a six-story Woodward's department store and four dozen other shops is a good starting place in the capital, as is the **Palliser Square mall** in the heart of Calgary. Eskimo and Indian crafts are the best souvenir items. **Cottage Crafts,** in Calgary's Mayfair Shopping Centre, **Arctic Arts,** 10064 104th St., Edmonton, and **The Quest** in Banff are good places to browse.

WHERE TO GET HELP WITH YOUR TRIP   Travel Alberta, 10255 104th St., Edmonton, Alberta, T5J 1B1, is the top source for maps and a free travel guide listing accommodation across the province. The Yellowhead Interprovincial Highway Association, 907 McLeod Building, Edmonton, will send a detailed map of its route through the west. If you are also going to other parts of Canada, contact the Canadian Government Office of Tourism, 150 Kent St., Ottawa.

BRITISH COLUMBIA

"A sea of mountains by a mountain of a sea"

Now we come to the pot at the end of Canada's rainbow – British Columbia. And, indeed, it does overflow with tourist gold. This third largest province is ribbed with mountains stretching almost three miles into the sky and covered with towering forests that supply more than half its livelihood. Yet British Columbia – or B.C. as it is invariably known – also finds room for Texas-sized ranches, fruit-growing valleys as lush as California's fjord country that rivals Norway's and a city with a setting even San Francisco can't match.

Sprawled across 366,255 square miles, between the Rockies and the blue Pacific, British Columbia is the most ruggedly beautiful of Canada's 10 provinces yet, in places, offers the country's most benign climate. For while many of her peaks are permanently snow-capped, Victoria, her small-townish capital, is sunnier than New York or Toronto in summer and warm enough in winter to make golf possible 12 months of the year. In spring, the mild southwestern corner of British Columbia bursts into bloom as the rest of the country digs out of yet another snowfall. Little wonder British Columbians take to the outdoors like small boys to a swimming hole. Even for those in the center of the province's larger cities, the wilderness is just an hour's drive away. There's no better way to become acquainted with the drama of this place than to drive its mountain highways, although even beautifully paved ones rarely offer anything between you and oblivion. Guard rails seem to be placed only at spots where a car plunging over a cliff might descend on some unsuspecting home or hamlet down below.

Beautiful as it is, however, British Columbia didn't much impress the first white man to see it. Sir Francis Drake took time off from plundering galleons on the Spanish Main to seek a northwest sea passage across the New World in the late 16th century. If he bothered to land on any of the coastal B.C. islands or along its fjord-indented coast, he didn't bother to mention it. So, the highly developed coastal Indians were left to themselves for another 200 years until the Spanish, entrenched in the U.S. southwest started to send feelers up this way, beating England's famed Captain Cook, who landed on Vancouver Island in 1778, by just a few years. Meanwhile, the Russians had moved across the Bering Strait into Alaska and were working down along the coast. A treaty known as the Nootka Convention settled rival claims to this new land in 1790 and a year later, Captain George Vancouver, who had sailed with Cook, landed and claimed Vancouver Island for Britain. While these events were taking place at sea, those intrepid fur traders, pushing westward across the prairies, finally found a pass through the mountains.

Alexander Mackenzie of the Northwest fur trading company arrived in 1793, on the first sea-to-sea journey ever made across Canada. At his heels came explorers David Thompson and Simon Fraser and the stalwarts who were dispatched to man fur-trading outposts. They had the run of the place until gold was discovered in 1856. To control the ensuing rush, Britain, which had declared Vancouver Island a colony in 1849, did the same for mainland B.C. In 1866, the two colonies were united and five years later agreed to join the new country of Canada on the promise that a railway would be pushed west to link the Atlantic and the Pacific.

That railway finally made it in 1887 but, as many a Vancouverite will tell you, it didn't completely erase the barrier the mountains create between British Columbia and the rest of the country. They still look on their province as not just different from the rest of the country, but as better. And, indeed, we Canadians from other parts of the country do secretly envy them. Many of us have "emigrated" to Vancouver. If not, we've watched our children hitch or hop a bus west to what has become regarded as a sort of lotus land for the young. (The one unfortunate aspect of this is that Vancouver has become the drug capital of Canada.)

So here we go into a province which provides several of the highlights on a trip to Canada.

WEATHER REPORT British Columbia dishes up a mixed bag indeed. In Vancouver or Victoria you can go golfing and skiing on the same day, for snow remains on mountain peaks in spring even on days when the sun turns the fairways emerald green. And while you can ski into June on the slopes of Whistler Mountain, in B.C.'s Garibaldi Provincial Park you can winter in Victoria, the capital, in French Riviera comfort – at least with regard to weather. The average temperature in January is 41 degrees Fahrenheit (5 degrees Celsius). Not balmy but not fur coat weather either.

Vancouver gets altogether too much rain for our liking – though the summer of '77 was unusually dry. It should be noted, however, that Victoria is generally much sunnier than the province's big city. In an average summer Victoria gets 140 more hours of sunshine than Vancouver and 75 more hours than Toronto.

Cities in the interior are much colder and snowier in winter than these moderate coastal ones, and much hotter in summer. Kamloops, for example, reaches into the 80s F (25-plus C) in July and August and dips to below 20 F on winter nights.

VANCOUVER

WHAT TO SEE **Vancouver**, Canada's third largest metropolis, with 1.2 million people around and about, boasts the most spectacular setting of any North American city. Put it right up there with Rio or Hong Kong in this regard. Snowcapped peaks rise all about you and chances are that the place where you are standing to view them also looks out across a finger of the blue Pacific. Beaches and yacht harbors lie just a short walk from downtown office towers. Lush landscaped gardens front even the most ordinary of houses – and mansions too, of course. Great ocean liners sail into the very heart of town.

What Vancouver's planners – or were there any? – have done with the magnificent setting won't leave you quite so enthralled. Put Montreal or Toronto, or Quebec City amid those lofty peaks and people would begin describing any of them as the most beautiful city in the world. Vancouver misses any such ranking, especially on its downtown peninsula which, on a drizzly day, resembles a futuristic ghost town of shapeless, grey highrises that stand out as an insult to the surroundings.

However, at one place, just a short walk from downtown hotels, Vancouver does hit the peaks it should have. They call it **Stanley Park** and it is as beautiful a piece of in-city real estate as you will find anywhere in Canada. As you might suspect, most of it was put there by nature – not by man. Bordered by the sea on three sides, it is forested by towering evergreens, yet laced with 50 miles of roads and trails. It's used, really used, by just about everybody. Cricket matches, band concerts, cycling and picnicking cause traffic jams on the roads leading to Stanley Park from the first warm weekend of spring on. Amid the trees and the totem poles are a rose garden; a fun zoo where polar bears from the north pole and penguins from the south pole have each found new homes, and Canada's best public aquarium where killer whales and dolphins perform several times a day. Most things in the park are free, but you pay $2.50 for adults and 75 cents for children to see the aquarium. In summer it's open daily 9.30 a.m. to 9 p.m., shorter hours at other times. Phone 682-1118 for opening times and feeding schedules.

North America's second largest **Chinatown** (after San Francisco's) occupies a good chunk of downtown Vancouver. It is filled not only with restaurants but with shops where the city's Chinese still come to buy pressed duck and other oriental treasures. You get to Chinatown by walking a few blocks east from the center of town along Pender St.

Just to the north, between Chinatown and the city's bustling deep-sea harbor, is **Gastown**, the area where the city had its beginnings as a boisterous shacktown. Named for Gassy Jack Deighton, a noted pioneer and windbag, Gastown had become the heart of Vancouver's skid row until restoration forces redid it a few years back.

Its refurbished warehouses, faced with beautiful old brick and illuminated by gaslight-style fixtures, now house an array of boutiques and restaurants. Because of its bohemian personality, the restored Gastown once was the mecca for young people from across the country who pour into Vancouver each summer. Too often, however, a visitor had to step over spaced-out or guitar-playing youths as he made his way about. Gastown seems to have got rid of much of its unwashed and unwanted element these days – but, in so doing, it has met with the same fate as so many Greenwich Village style "old towns,"

from Atlanta to San Francisco. It has become sterile.
Interesting but not much fun.

The heart of town, centered along Georgia St. between Burrard and Granville, is, on the other hand,
very much alive. Sprouting new skyscrapers, hotels
and shopping malls, it has radically changed in appearance during the past five or six years. Two blocks
south of Georgia St. is **Robsonstrasse**, thus called because the city hoped its German flavor would make it
into a major tourist attraction. It hasn't, although
there are a few fancy shops and some worthwhile restaurants along it, just a short walk from major hotels.

It's the outdoorsy, non-urban aspects of Vancouver
that grab most visitors. When the sun shines in winter
you can ski on North Vancouver's **Grouse Mountain**
in the morning and golf at one of the many public
courses in the afternoon. In summer you can go out
to **Horseshoe Bay** for a bit of salmon fishing and then,
just a few blocks from your hotel, go swimming in
English Bay. In between seasons, there's even the odd
day when a hardy type can do all these things on one
and the same day. Grouse Mountain is worth the
short drive from downtown, winter or summer – but
on clear days only. This 4,100-foot peak looks directly down on the city and an all-year-round skyride
takes you to a striking chalet, at the 3,700-foot level,
where you can dine with a rooftop view matched by
no other city on the continent. Fare on the aerial cars
is $4 for adults and $2.75 for children under 12. Ski
rentals are available there during the season. Also in
North Vancouver is the remarkable **Capilano suspen-
sion bridge**, strung 210 feet above the Capilano River,
from one sheer canyon wall to the other. Claiming to
be the world's longest suspended foot bridge, it sways
gently, but noticeably enough to give even the coolest
visitor pause. You pay $2 for adults, 50 cents for chil-
dren to walk across and, hopefully, back.

A trip out to **Horseshoe Bay** (from where the car ferries leave for Vancouver Island) is a really great one for a landlubber who wants to try his hand at salmon fishing. No need to bring a rod – just an old pair of slacks and a sweater. **Sewell's boat rentals**, at the dock, has been outfitting visitors, from prime ministers on down, as long as anyone can remember. They'll show you how to bait your hook and put you out to sea in a modern outboard on Howe Sound, a corner of the Pacific that seems to be surrounded on all sides by mountain peaks. A glorious day even if you don't get a bite and a couple can do the whole thing for under $20. You can also get a rare view of the city's imposing skyline and a look at its great harbor on the **Yukon Belle** and **Yukon Queen**, sternwheelers operated by Harbour Ferries Ltd.

Vancouver is noted for its gardens, more beautiful ones per square foot than you'll find anywhere else in Canada. The **British Properties**, across the Lions Gate Bridge from downtown, is an area of marvellous mansions with gardens to match. More formal gardens can be seen at **Queen Elizabeth Park**, Cambie St. and W. 33rd St., at the **Van Dusen Botanical Display**, 37th and Oak St. and at the **Japanese Friendship Gardens** on Royal Ave. in adjoining New Westminster.

Indoor Vancouver isn't nearly so exciting. But then you must remember that this is a young city, not yet a century old. The **Vancouver Art Gallery** (free admission) remains justifiably unsung, though it does contain the country's foremost collection of Emily Carr paintings. Far and away the most interesting museum in town – at least in our books – is the new **Museum of Anthropology** on a cliff overlooking the sea along Marine Drive, on the campus of the University of British Columbia. It houses a smashing collection of Indian artifacts, of especially high quality on this coast; a towering display of beautifully carved totem poles, as well as 10,000 pieces collected in Asia, Africa and South America. On the way you can visit the **Maritime Museum** (adults 50 cents, children 25 cents) and the **Centennial Museum** (same rate) in Vanier Park. Star of the former is the St. Roch, the sturdy little Royal Canadian Mounted Police vessel which made history in the early 1940s by sailing through the Arctic Northwest Passage in both directions. The other Vanier Park museum houses an extensive collection of British Columbia artifacts, but it's a bit of a ho-hummer for anyone who has seen the new Museum of Anthropology. Just outside the city, in neighboring Burnaby you can see how this area got its start at **Heritage Village**, a collection of shops and homes from the 1890-1920 era.

Vancouver is a sports-crazy town, too. When someone isn't sailing his boat he's watching professional football, hockey, horse racing, lacrosse or even cricket. The B.C. Lions football club plays at Empire Stadium in **Exhibition Park**, a complex which also houses the race track where nags run in day and evening meetings from spring to autumn. The Vancouver Canucks, a sorry lot at best, play at the Pacific Coliseum. New Westminster is the lacrosse hotbed – try Queens Park there. You can see cricket played in Stanley Park.

WHERE TO STAY   In the luxury class we give the **Hyatt Regency**, rising above Royal Centre on Burrard St. an edge over the others. Many rooms have balconies and refrigerators and there's an immense shopping center and lobby area. Hyatt's **Truffles** dining room (expensive) is one of the best in the city. Also rooftop dining and coffeeshop. Singles from $32, doubles from $42. Until Hyatt came along we preferred the **Bayshore Inn,** where the late Howard Hughes resided when he was hiding out in Vancouver. The Bayshore, 1601 W. Georgia St. is slightly west of the downtown, looking out on the waterfront. You can arrive by car or boat – or even by air. $37 single, $47 double. Canadian National's **Hotel Vancouver** is the traditionalist's luxury hotel here. $35 single, $45 double. In the heart of downtown at 900 W. Georgia St., it has recently been lavishly refurbished. The **Four Seasons** (single $30, double $40) at Georgia and Howe is another downtown stickout, as is the **Sheraton-Landmark** (single $20, double $25) west of the town center at 1400 Robson. We've always had a soft spot for the **Blue Horizon**, which traditionally charged the least among the name hotels in Vancouver (single $24, double $29). At 1225 Robson, it features suite-like rooms with balconies and refrigerators. There are motel rows on all major highways leading into Vancouver from the east and south, with rates generally in the $20 double and up range for closer-in, modern pads.

VICTORIA AND VANCOUVER ISLAND

Now we'll move on to the spots most summer visitors to this west coast metropolis head for – Victoria and Vancouver Island. It's easy enough to get there, with a steady stream of car and passenger ferries making the crossing each day from Horseshoe Bay, just northwest of downtown Vancouver and from Tsawwassen, just south of the city. Crossings take from an hour and 40 minutes up. We say "up" because there can be two-hour waits during July and August, as people pour across to the island.

You'll see why they do when you get to this sometimes-wild-and-woolly, sometimes-gentle chunk of real estate, one of the protective chain of islands that guards the B.C. coast. Some of them are barely large enough to support a cottage but Vancouver Island is immense – at 12,500 square miles, six times as large as the east coast province of Prince Edward Island.

Victoria, the B.C. capital, is the principal city on the island and one which generally vies with Fredericton in far-off New Brunswick as the country's prettiest city. Indeed, it is a garden of a place, with baskets of blooms cascading down from lamposts in summer, the sea at its doorstep, fountains setting off European-style squares, Victorian mansions rising behind stately trees and boats bobbing in the sunlight.

Sunlight, by the way, is one of the big attractions of Victoria, which over the years has become a major retirement center for many sea captains who came this way and liked what they saw. Eastern Canadians tend to lump the whole west coast into one soggy basket, picturing a land of leaden skies, cities of upraised umbrellas. Victoria, however, is an exception, getting

140 hours more sunshine during an average summer than Vancouver does. Sea breezes cool it then and also keep it from getting frosty in winter when days generally reach into the mid 40s (7 Celsius) even in deepest February. Like many western cities, Victoria got its start as a Hudson's Bay Company post during the fur trade era. It was boosted into prominence when it became the main supply center for the Caribou goldrush in the interior of B.C. That was enough to ensure that it would become the capital when the province joined the rest of the country – but the coming of the railway from the east ensured that rival Vancouver on the mainland would get most of the industry and most of the influx of settlers. So today, there are just 220,000 people living in and around Victoria, though on a summer day you'll meet at least twice that many on its tourist-packed streets.

The good news about Victoria is that its recent success in tourism has made it more than a retirement center. It has become much livelier of late, even boosts an eatery or two that gourmets take seriously. Through it all, however, it has managed to remain a "little piece of England," and even works at the title. Afternoon tea, complete with buttered scones and jam, is still a tradition at the chateau-like **Empress Hotel**. And when he has had tea just about every Victoria householder goes out to do a bit of gardening.

Victoria is centered around an inner harbor where from a single dock-side perch one can take in the ivy-covered Empress, and the domed Parliament Buildings, done by the same architect; millionaires' yachts, totem poles; horsedrawn tourist wagons; pedestrian malls, and a parade of arriving and departing ferry boats and float planes. On a sunny day, such sights can't help but cast a euphoric spell on the visitor and he carries it with him as he strolls through a downtown where former warehouse districts have been restored to handsome squares where old men sit feeding pigeons they know by name.

With the lesson of Vancouver staring it in the face from across the Strait of Georgia, Victoria is not about to give in to the skyscraper mania that has devoured so many cities. It has strict height regulations and even the handful of buildings that have risen a dozen storeys stand out like a sore thumb that many Victorians would like to see amputated. Pollution isn't a problem here either. Even today it remains mostly a market gardening and supply center for the island and, of course, the home of the provincial government and the coterie of civil servants that entails.

This is also very much a port city. Not only do ferries pour over from Seattle and Port Angeles in neighboring Washington, but scores of cruise ships sailing the Inside Passage to Alaska call here each summer. Cruise passengers pour ashore and head for downtown shops stacked with (you guessed it) English china and woollens not to mention Canadian Indian artifacts, some authentic, some made in Hong Kong.

Victoria's No. 1 tourist attraction isn't even in town. **Butchart Gardens**, 12 miles to the north, is a former limestone quarry that has been transformed into a beauty spot of international acclaim. A mélange of Italian, Japanese, English and sunken gardens, it is illuminated at night and set off by a spectacular 70-foot-high fountain. It is open daily. Adults pay $3 and children 75 cents in summer. In winter the admission charge is dropped. In town, **Beacon Hill Park** is 150 acres of flowerbeds, lakes and greenery that's free for the seeing.

Because so many tourists now make the scene, Victoria has the usual jumble of car museums, imitation thatched cottages, frontier towns, wax museums and the like. But they are mostly unobtrusive and you don't have to bother with them unless you have children in tow. One place you should head for, however, is the **Provincial Museum**. A beautifully conceived centennial project, this museum is one of those involvement-type showcases telling you all you need to know about the way life evolved on this coast, both before and after the white man arrived. If you've ever wondered whether they could really build a better lightbulb if they wanted, take a look at the Parliament Building when it is illuminated at night. Some of the bulbs setting off its fine Victorian lines have been in constant use since 1912.

The **Marine Museum** in restored Bastion Square is housed in a former courthouse and is really worthwhile for those with a nautical bent. Its pride and joy is the Indian war canoe, *Tilikum*, in which Captain J. C. Voss made an incredible sea journey via the Pacific from Victoria to Margate, England. It was found rotting in the mud of the Thames and rescued through the efforts of some of those old salts who have made Victoria their home. The museum is also chock full of a raft (if you'll pardon the pun) of ship models, from square riggers on. The price is right – 50 cents for adults, 25 cents for children.

Victoria's island home isn't anywhere near as gentle as the capital itself. Much of it is the terrain of lumberjacks and fishermen. Douglas firs that were tall before Columbus arrived in America still cast shadows across interior roads. Mountains on the island aren't as gargantuan as those on the mainland – but they'll do. Especially since you drive through them on former logging trails that are now paved but still boobytrapped with switchback turns. Vancouver Island is the site of one of Canada's newest national parks, **Pacific Rim**. It's on the west coast of the island facing straight off to Japan with nothing in between but cold, blue Pacific – 46 degrees (7 Celsius) at

Pacific Rim's beaches. Since logging began on the island, one broad beach here is lined with silver drift logs, tens of thousands of them that have drifted ashore and bleached in the sun. If you're lucky on a visit to this magnificent piece of wilderness, you'll catch sight of one of the family of grey whales that spends its summer vacation there.

The island is streaked with mountain streams where you can try your luck. **Campbell River** in the heart of tall timber country is one of the most famous fishing centers in the west. The roster of its Tyee Club includes fishermen who have made the pilgrimage here from all over the world.

WHERE TO STAY   Victoria: The Ivy-covered, chateau-like **Empress Hotel** is one of the most famous in the west – though we think many of the rooms aren't worth the $35 single, $45 double rates. Finding your room is no mean trick if you get stuck off in some remote corner. But you can forgive it all its failings for its setting right on the Inner Harbor across from the Parliament Buildings. Victorians say more government decisions are made in the Empress dining room and bar than across the street in the legislature. The **Executive House** (single $26, double $32), 777 Douglas St. is almost as central, offers free parking and contains the always reliable **Hy's Steak House**. Less central but equipped with both a coffee shop and restaurant is the **Colony Motor Hotel** (single $19, double $21), 2852 Douglas St. Other highly rated suburban spreads in Victoria are the **Oak Bay Beach Hotel** ($25 double) at 1175 Beach Drive and **Royal Oak Inn** (single $22, double $26), 4680 Elk Lake Dr.

WHAT ELSE TO SEE IN B.C.

Now, let's head back to the mainland where among other things 4 magnificent national parks and some 50 provincial parks await.

As you may have gathered from the chapter on Alberta, the authors would head for Banff or Jasper if we were to be allowed a crack at only one or two of the country's national parks. But B.C.'s mainland outdoor treasure houses – **Glacier, Kootenay, Yoho and Mount Revelstoke** aren't far behind when it comes to gorgeous scenery – and they are much less trammelled. The first three cover more than 500 square miles each and Mount Revelstoke offers 100 square miles in which to roam. All four lie along the Trans-Canada Highway or a few miles off it. **Yoho**, just west of Banff, is the Cree Indian word used to express astonishment and wonder. You'll use it, too, when you get a close-up of Yoho's 1,000-foot high waterfalls and emerald green mountain lakes. The **Kootenay** preserve is entered at Radium Hot Springs and allows you to drive 65 miles with mountains on either side. If anything, **Glacier** in the heart of the Selkirk mountains, is even more splendid, with 10,000-foot high peaks overlooking campsites and mountain passes and fingers of glaciers reaching down into alpine meadows. You can stop for a picnic just off the Trans-Canada on your way through Mount Revelstoke or, in summer, drive a gravel road to the summit of the peak that gives the park its name. B.C.'s provincial parks are also among the best in the country. **Garibaldi**, the pick of the lot, has been developed for both skiing and summer recreation – which can be one and the same. Occasionally some of the slopes are still in use late into June. Garibaldi and its Whistler Mountain ski resort are only a 75-mile drive from Vancouver.

Barkerville is the pick of the historic sites in this province. This storied ghost town was the largest city east of Chicago and north of San Francisco in the 1860s after naval deserter Billy Barker struck gold. The rush had barely started when the gold petered out, leaving the place deserted and untouched for almost a century until the British Columbia government decided to save some 100 of the best preserved buildings. It put costumed characters into some of the shops and revived the old Theatre Royal with period melodramas. In summer you can take in performances twice daily (adults $1.50, children 75 cents). You can also ride the stagecoach or pan for gold. The park is open all year and it's free.

A similar, though inferior, presentation of the way things were is offered at **Fort Steele**, northeast of Cranbrook in the Kootenay region. This historic park is open only in summer and is free.

Now, remember the homemade quote with which we started this chapter. British Columbia is mountains, but it is also intimately involved with the world's largest sea. So, although there are few coastal highways because of the fjord-cut nature of the coastline, there is nonetheless an active coastal "bus service." A large fleet of car and passenger ferries carries it out. Besides running off to Vancouver Island and the closer Gulf Islands, B.C. ferries also carry traffic up and down the coast to Prince Rupert, just south of Alaska, using the Inside Passage. This route is so-called because it runs between the mainland and off-coast islands, avoiding the full sweep of the Pacific. We've seen Norway's fjord country and we wouldn't give it too much of a scenic edge over this trip. Often, as the ferry sails amid the islands you can see snowcapped peaks on every side. As you may imagine, these ferries are not the punkydunk type you may have seen on inland lakes and rivers. They are big, ocean-going vessels, with dining and sleeping facilities.

The **ferries** make the run to Prince Rupert from **Kelsey Bay on Vancouver Island**. To get there you take the ferry from Horseshoe Bay, north of Vancouver, to Nanaimo and drive to Kelsey. Or, you can drive to Prince Rupert from the east along the aforementioned Yellowhead Highway route that crosses the prairies and B.C. From Prince Rupert you also can take the Alaska ferry service north to Ports on the Alaska Panhandle. The B.C. ferries are the budget way (about $150 for two persons and a car) to see this coast. You can, of course, do the Inside Passage on a variety of cruise ships, at many times the rate. These sail from Vancouver and from U.S. west coast ports.

Back inland some of these other stops may interest you: **Hell's Gate**, seven miles south of **Boston Bar** on the Trans-Canada route to Vancouver, lies at the narrowest point of the Fraser River canyon. Indians used to drive pegs into the canyon walls to get through. Now modern man runs two major railways and the country's No. 1 highway through the same space. It's a dramatic setting for a fish ladder built to help salmon reach their spawning ground. There's also an aerial tramway.

Penticton is the heart of B.C.'s lush fruit-growing area, with a big peach festival in the first week of August and a square dance jamboree the next week. The Okanagan summer school of arts is held there in July. The **Okanagan game farm,** five miles south on Highway 97 (adults $1.50, children 50 cents) supplies natural surroundings for a variety of African and American animals. If you go to Prince Rupert to catch a ferry north or south, take a look at the free **Museum**

of Northern British Columbia's fine display of coastal Indian carvings and other artifacts.

WHERE TO STAY **Vancouver** and **Victoria** have by far the best selection of hotels and motels in the province but communities along the Trans-Canada have become better endowed in the past few years. **Guest Ranch** accommodation is also available in several parts of the interior, and there are plenty of private and government-run campsites in all parts of the province, except the far north and remote coastal areas.

The best way to get a line on ranch accommodation and hotel and motel accommodation in smaller centers is to write for a copy of the "Green Book," the free British Columbia Tourist Accommodation directory, obtainable from Tourism British Columbia, 1117 Wharf St., Victoria, British Columbia V8W 2Z2.

WHERE TO EAT Easterners used to laugh at Vancouver restaurants – but no one laughs anymore. They're good, getting better and prices are certainly lower than in Toronto. We could find dining-out happiness simply by travelling between two of the best, right next door to each other and owned by the same man, Umberto Menghi. **Umberto's**, 1380 Hornby St., housed in a converted mansion, is one of the finest Italian restaurants we've found anywhere – including Rome. The scallopini or rack of lamb in martini sauce are unforgivably good – at least for weight watchers. **La Cantina**, next door, does all sorts of seafood dishes – almost as well. For seafood on a budget try the **Only Fish and Oyster Cafe**, 20 East Hastings St., in business since 1912 dishing up thicker-than-stew clam chowder, 45 cents; or fried salmon $3.95; The **William Tell**, 722 Richards St., is as expensive as the **Only** is cheap, but serves from a long list of Swiss specialties with old-world care and courtesy. Start with snails, go on to the escalope de veau or the spring lamb, choose a suitable wine and you won't get out for under $20. But it will be worth it. You couldn't eat your way through the Chinese restaurants in Vancouver – there are dozens of good ones. The way Vancouver differs from most cities in this regard, however, is that you can get the real thing and forget the sweet and sours here.

The **Kwangchow**, 251 E. Pender St. offers fine Cantonese fare and **Yang's**, 4186 Main St. is noted for its spicy northern Chinese dishes. For Japanese food it's hard to beat the **Aki**, 374 Powell St. and for Greek meals served with a flair, **Orestes**, 3116 W. Broadway.

Of the hotel restaurants, **Truffles** in the Hyatt is the best we've found in the no-holds-barred price range, though both the **Panorama Roof** and **Timber Club** in the Hotel Vancouver are contenders for the big-buck diner. The **Old Spaghetti Factory**, 53 Water St. in Gastown, won't make you forget Umberto's but the price is right ($2 to $7 for dinner) and it's a fun family place. **Muck-a-muck**, 1724 Davie St. derives its name from the Haida Indian word for food. Steamed black cod and barbecued salmon are typical fare.

Victoria offers a much more limited choice to diners but if you like German cooking you'll enjoy the **Burgermeister**, 732 Johnson St. You can dine in the $6 to $7 range, including homemade soup and a choice of schnitzels. The **Edwardian Dining Room** of the Empress Hotel impresses the roast beef lover on an expense account but those on a slightly more limited budget should head for **Hy's in the Executive Hotel. The Wig and Dickie** at the Wilson Motor Inn supplies theater to dine by and the **Shah Jahan**, 1010

Fort St., is a new and nicely priced Indian restaurant. **Maiko Gardens** in Bastion Square is a first-rate Japanese eaterie for sukiyaki lovers.

WHERE TO SHOP Indian wood carvings, usually richly decorated with homemade paints and B.C. jade products are the real finds in B.C. **Maple Leaf House**, 142 Water St., is a part of Woodward's department store facing into Gastown. It offers Indian jewelry, painting and carvings as well as other handcrafted articles from B.C. **Canadian Art Products**, 976 Granville St. specializes in Indian products as does **Mrs. Willard Sparrow** in her shop at 6508 Salish Drive. Indian and Chinese shops in the Gastown and Chinatown districts offer an array of oriental goods. In Victoria, Government St. is lined with shops selling china and woollens from Britain and a variety of good and phony souvenirs. **The Quest** is one Government St. shop that traditionally offers top Canadian handicrafts. There are shops in both the Vancouver and Victoria art galleries.

NIGHTLIFE In Vancouver it has improved dramatically; in Victoria, noticeably; elsewhere imperceptibly. Used to be that the **Cave** on Hornby St. was the only place where you could see live entertainment in Vancouver. Only trouble was that every time we got there Mitzi Gaynor was making another comeback. She still is – but now there are dozens of competing nightspots. And **Oil Can Harry's**, 752 Thurlow, is now only one of several jazz spots. You can hear Dixieland at the **Hot Jazz Society**, 36 E. Broadway. **Annabelle's**, 670 Howe St. and **Pharoah's** in Gastown are among the more active discos.

Theater has also come to life in Vancouver where

more than a dozen big and small companies now put on regular performances. The **Queen Elizabeth Theater**, 649 Cambie St. is the largest – home of the Playhouse Theatre Company (with a September to May season), the opera and symphony. **The Arts Club Theatre**, 1181 Seymour St., produces plays during the winter and musicals in summer. Theater in the park – a summer season of musicals – is presented at the **Malkin Bowl** in Stanley Park.

WHERE TO GET HELP WITH YOUR TRIP   For an accommodation guide, maps and other detailed information on the province, write to Tourism British Columbia, Ministry of the Provincial Secretary and Travel Industry, 1117 Wharf St., Victoria B.C. V8W 2Z2.

For information on Vancouver, contact the Greater Vancouver Convention and Visitors Bureau, 650 Burrard St., Vancouver.

For information on Victoria, contact Greater Victoria Visitors Information Centre, 786 Government St., Victoria.

If your trip is taking you to other parts of Canada, contact the Canadian Government Office of Tourism, 150 Kent St., Ottawa, Ont. K1A OH6.

THE TRUE NORTH

"But can't you hear the Wild? – it's calling you."

Robert Service

Actually, only a relative handful of visitors – or Canadians for that matter – answers the call of the True North. Yet it covers a third of the big land, sprawling across two vast territories from the 60th parallel to within a few hundred miles of the North Pole. The Northwest Territories alone contain 1,304,903 square miles – an area larger than all the U.S. states east of the Mississippi. And, when and if the Yukon Territory ever becomes a full-fledged province, at 207,076 square miles, it will be larger than four of the others.

Yet fewer than 60,000 inhabitants call this last frontier home, and they are mostly native peoples, Indians and Eskimos living in remote outposts. Of late, as you may have read, they have been joined by hundreds of prospectors, especially oilmen seeking the new wealth of the Arctic. This greatly increased interest in Canada's Arctic has been accompanied by a greater awareness on the part of native peoples of the value of the rugged land they have had to themselves through the centuries, largely because no one else was interested. "Native claims" has become a household phrase in Canada as Indians and Eskimos, using the education gained in the white man's northern schools, insist on compensation for the disruption of their hunting grounds. The explorations and technologies necessary in the Arctic to fuel North American factories, cities and automobiles seem light years away from their way of life. For in the northern reaches of the territories, some of these native Canadians still live much as they did when the first white man, Martin Frobisher, came this way in 1576, seeking a water route to the Orient – the fabled Northwest Passage that wasn't finally discovered until 1845. Meanwhile, the Northwest Territories were largely left to the fur traders and those peoples who in prehistoric times had crossed the Bering Strait from Siberia to trade one frosty homeland for another.

In the Yukon that icy isolation came to a sudden end in 1896 when gold was discovered on Bonanza Creek, a tributary of the Klondike River. Muckers for gold, as Robert Service called them, endured unbelievable hardships in their lust for instant wealth. Landing at Skagway in Alaska, they clawed their way up mountains and rafted hundreds of miles along icy and treacherous rivers to reach the Klondike. The original tent city set up at Dawson, headquarters for the strike, grew into a "metropolis" of 30,000. In a decade more than $100 million in gold was scratched from the Klondike. Then the bubble burst. The gold petered out and Dawson became all but a ghost town – though almost 1,000 people still call it home. The far north was again left to the hardy people who had learned to live in peace with it and remained under direct rule of the federal government, although a greater degree of self-government has now been won, with elected councils sharing in decisions.

Even Canadians, who should know better, often dismiss the territories as a frozen wasteland. And indeed temperatures of 70 below have been recorded. But in summer this is the land of the midnight sun, a magnificent terrain that's ablaze with pink and purple wildflowers, a land where caribou roam in big game numbers that can be matched only in East Africa. Few areas of the world are capable of leaving the nature lover more awestruck. Visitors to lodges in the far north sight, as a matter of course, grizzly bear, arctic wolves, musk ox, seals and lemmings, as well as 50 varieties of birds, including eagles, hawks, owls, and loons. Permanent icecaps, treeless tundra, sheer cliffs, mountain ranges, trout-filled lakes and streams, dramatic seacoasts, mighty rivers, broad valleys and thick forests all find a home here. Isolation keeps the crowds away, preserving this land as a vast natural wilderness.

WEATHER REPORT Temperatures of -70 degrees below (-57 C) have been recorded but this is not a land of eternal snows. In fact, on very rare occasions, temperatures as high as 100 degrees have also occurred. The territories encompass both arctic and sub-arctic regions. The former is an area in which the mean daily temperature during the warmest month doesn't exceed 50 degrees. The northern regions all fit into this coolish-in-summer and unbearable-in-winter category. The Mackenzie valley area of the Northwest Territory, however, is sub-arctic, more like the northern prairies. Don't show up in July wearing a parka; you'll likely pass sunbathers on the way in from the airport. But do come with a sweater even in summer – in "southerly" Yellowknife, where days in July usually average in the 60s, night temperatures close to the freezing mark have been recorded. Best advice for a winter visitor: Don't go.

HOW TO GET THERE Only two highways lead into Canada's far north. The Alaska Highway enters the Yukon from British Columbia and the Mackenzie Highway reaches into the southern part of the Northwest Territories from Alberta. Both are all-weather gravel roads, which, though well maintained, are a real test for both car and driver. It's a good idea to carry a spare fan belt, an extra spare tire and to cover headlights with a protective plastic covering and your grill with a wire mesh. It's a 947-mile drive from Edmonton to Yellowknife, capital of the Northwest Territories, 1,780 miles from Vancouver, 3,577 from New York and 3,180 from Toronto. There is bus service to the NWT from Edmonton with Canadian Coachways, 10202 102nd St., Edmonton.

The Alaska Highway, by the way, was started in 1942 as a wartime measure after the Japanese invaded the Aleutian Islands, and completed in just eight months. It is still the main artery in the Yukon, passing through Whitehorse, the territorial capital, on its way to Fairbanks, Alaska. There is a surprisingly large network of other roads, leading off to Dawson City and to Haines, Alaska, where you can link up with the Alaska car ferries.

The far north may also, of course, be reached by commercial jets and charter planes, from several large Canadian cities. CP Air connects Whitehorse in the Yukon with Vancouver. Nordair flies daily (except Saturday) to Frobisher Bay on Baffin Island in the east; Transair flies from Winnipeg to Yellowknife, via Churchill, Manitoba; and Pacific Western Airlines flies both to Yellowknife and Inuvik in the western Arctic. Airlines within the territories make connecting flights to even the remotest outposts.

Air distances within the territories are enormous. It's 1,160 miles from Yellowknife to Cape Dorset, 1,405 from Yellowknife to Frobisher.

In summer for the past few years, an outfit called Holiday Travel (188 University Ave., Toronto) has flown overnight jet trips to Frobisher Bay, on the edge of the Arctic from Toronto and packed its planes. Passengers get only a few hours in the north to rub elbows with a few sleepy Eskimos and buy their wares – but in one recent year 1,500 people paid $199 each to make the trip.

Travel agents sell a variety of tours which include the Yukon or Northwest Territories, or both, in their itineraries.

WHAT TO SEE First the Northwest Territories. Don't expect big city amenities – though there are a few in Yellowknife. But do expect an unforgettable wilderness show, especially if you have the money to fly into far-flung outposts. From Frobisher, where the jets land daily from the south, you can take a short si-detrip by plane to Pangnirtung where hardy types hike the **Pangnirtung Pass** in **Baffin Island National Park**. Here glaciers flow down from a permanent ice-cap on one side while sheer cliffs of multi-colored rock rise 2,000 to 3,000 feet on the other.

In the western Arctic, a few hundred people each year get an unforgettable wildlife experience at a na-ture lodge on **Cambridge Bay**, run by a former Moun-tie, Glenn Warner and his wife Trish. Warner was mushing across the frozen wastes by dogsled when he came on the abandoned Hudson's Bay Co. trading post which he has turned into a lodge for nature-lov-ers only – no hunters need apply. Here you can see a herd of up to 1,000 caribou, spot a grizzly or an arctic wolf, explore a fjord or observe the Eskimo lifestyle up close. The Warners have the shortest resort season in the country – mid-June to mid-August. Guests pay $1,375 all-inclusive to spend a week at the lodge. That includes pickup by plane and return to Yellow-knife. Travel agents can book you into the **Warner's Bathurst Inlet Naturalists Lodge.**

By road you can reach **Yellowknife**, the territorial capital and by far the largest community in the Northwest Territories, with a population of 10,000.

It's got a highrise hotel with color TV in every room, a golf course, movie theater and modern shopping centers – but that makes it sound much more "civilized" than it actually is. This is one of the main educational centers in the north and a jumping-off point for fly-in fishing and hunting trips. Also reachable by car is **Wood Buffalo National Park**, where the largest herd of buffalo on the continent roams in safety. This park was established in 1922 to protect Canada's only remaining herd of wood bison, which then numbered only 1,500. Later 6,000 plains buffalo were moved to the park to produce the present hybrid herd of 7,000.

Though the park's road system doesn't – thank God – go anywhere near him, the whooping crane also makes its summer home here. This near-extinct big bird (only about 50 survive in the wild) flies all the way to Texas to spend its winters where you can see all that's left at the **Aransas Wildlife Refuge**, near **Corpus Christi**.

Rae, **Hay River** and **Fort Simpson** are other communities you can reach by car – but none of them quite match the other sights on the Mackenzie Highway system, such as **Alexandra Falls**, where, when you can cast a line at the foot of a far-north Niagara, you know that you're in god's country. There are campgrounds located at several points along the Mackenzie system.

Fly-in destinations include: **Inuvik**, the largest community in the western Arctic and the main supply base for oil exploration; **Aklavik**, an Eskimo community well-known for its excellent handicrafts, and **Cape Dorset**, the main art center of the eastern Arctic and one that is famous for its soapstone carvings.

Now to the **Yukon** where most visitors want at least a peek at **Dawson City** where a few of the gold rush buildings, including the **Red Feather Saloon** and the cabin where Robert Service worked, still stand. The **Palace Grand Theatre** presents mining town entertainment and melodrama Tuesday to Sunday at 8 P.M. in summer. Tickets range from $2.50 to $4.

Whitehorse, the territorial capital with 12,000 inhabitants, lies on a bend of the Yukon River. You can take river excursions on the Schwatka riverboat, $8 adults, $4 children. Whitehorse is also the terminus of the famed **White Pass and Yukon Railway**, a narrow gauge line built at the height of the gold rush and following the trail of '98 through some of the most gorgeous scenery in all of Canada. There is daily service between Whitehorse and Skagway, where you can connect with Alaska car ferries. One-way fare is $30 for adults, half that for children under 12. The **W.D. MacBride Museum**, on First Ave. gives you a quick insight into gold rush days, with newspapers, books and guns from those rollicking times and even a cabin said to belong to Sam McGee, the ill-fated hero of one of Service's poems. Adults $1, children under 12, free.

Haines Junction, at the junction of the Alaska Highway and Haines Highway to Skagway, lies on the fringe of spectacular **Kluane National Park**. The nearby Elias mountain range is awesome, with Mount Logan, Canada's highest at 19,850 feet, among the peaks. The icefields of this range date back to the last ice age.

WHERE TO STAY Yellowknife has most of the tourist accommodation in the Northwest Territories. The downtown **Explorer Hotel**, with 120 rooms each with color TV, is a big city pad with a good restaurant, lounge and nightly entertainment. Unfortunately it also has big city prices. Single $48.50, double $53.50. The **Yellowknife Inn**, also in the center of town, has 162 old and new rooms, starting at $44 single, $49 double. The **Northland Motel** on Franklin Rd. charges $22 single, $25 double. The downtown **Gold Range Hotel** has private baths in some of its rooms. Rates start at $12 single, $15 double. In Hay River and Inuvik there is small choice in accommodations, and in most other communities the hotel or motel where you hit the pillow will likely be the only one in town.

In the Yukon, Whitehorse is the main accommodation center. The **Whitehorse TraveLodge**, Second Ave. and Wood St., is the best equipped. (Singles $32, doubles $36.) The **Ben-Elle Motel**, 411 Main St. is also first-rate. (Singles $31, doubles $36.) The **Sandman Motor Inn** on Second Ave. (singles $27, doubles $33) and the **Edgewater Hotel**, First Ave. and Main St. (singles $21, doubles $25) are okay, too.

In Dawson City, the **Eldorado**, Third Ave. and Princess St. (singles $27, doubles $33) and the **Gold City Motor Inn**, Fifth Ave. and Harper St. (singles $24, doubles $28) are fine. **Haines Junction** and **Watson Lake** also have modern accommodation.

Many visitors to both the territories, however, depend on campgrounds and there are a good scattering of them along both far-north highways. If you're going to camp, bring plenty of insect repellent.

WHERE TO EAT   The best meals in the north are cooked by a campfire. However, the **Yellowknife Inn** in Yellowknife has fresh arctic char on its menu at times and the downtown **Hoist Room** serves good steaks. In the Yukon, the **Cellar Dining Lounge** in Whitehorse's Edgewater Hotel features fresh Alaska King Crab as does the **Golden Garter** in the Main St. Mall.

WHERE TO SHOP Indian and Eskimo crafts are the top buys – though they have zoomed up in price during the past five years. You can buy stone, whalebone and ivory carvings at co-ops and crafts centers in even the smallest communities in the Northwest Territories. Eskimo parkas and other fur garments are also sold through the same sources. **Northern Images** in Yellowknife is a first-rate crafts shop.

In Whitehorse, **Yukon Indian Craft** on Main St. has a good selection of Indian handiwork.

NIGHTLIFE Bring your own.

HUNTING AND FISHING NOTE Both these territories offer superb fishing and big game hunting. In the Northwest Territories, a visitor can still get a license to hunt buffalo – or even a polar bear. Which thrills some people. Frankly, it makes us sick.

WHERE TO GET HELP WITH YOUR TRIP Travel Arctic, Yellowknife, N.W.T., Canada X1A 2L9 puts out an excellent detailed Explorer's Guide to the territories which will be sent to you free for the asking. Get maps from the same source.

For the Yukon, write to the Department of Travel and Information, P. O. Box 2703, Third Ave. and Steele St., Whitehorse.

If you are going to other parts of Canada too, contact the Canadian Government Office of Tourism, 150 Kent St., Ottawa, Canada.

CALENDAR OF ANNUAL SPECIAL EVENTS

Despite the months of cold weather in Canada the people who live here have learned to adjust to winter and there are dozens of winter carnivals of various kinds. In some places it is a matter of making virtue of necessity; that's all they have to offer the tourist.

The tourism departments in each province will smother you with information if you just ask. Quarterly listings of events are issued in advance of each season by the Canadian Government Office of Tourism, 240 Sparks St., Ottawa, Canada, K1A 0H6. They are incredibly detailed. Here is a calendar of the biggest events:

JANUARY

Toronto International Boat Show, in mid-month, runs for 9 days each year at the Coliseum at the Canadian National Exhibition grounds. Hundreds of thousands of water bugs go to see what's new, from dinghies to luxury yachts.

FEBRUARY

Quebec Winter Carnival at Quebec City usually starts in mid February. It is Canada's Mardi Gras. Ice sculptures, sports, outdoor parties with a wind-up parade put it in the same colorful class as the Rose Bowl parade. Reserve hotel rooms at least 6 months in advance or settle for rooms in temporary lodgings.

International Pee Wee Hockey Tournament at Quebec City coincides with the winter carnival. Hundreds of 12-year-old miniature Bobby Hulls with thousands of parents and fans converge for hard-hitting, high-scoring games that determine the best of the best in that age group.

Montreal, National Boat Show, Place Bonaventure, late in the month.

The Pas, Manitoba, Northern Manitoba Trappers' Festival, one of the most colorful winter carnivals featuring dogsled and snowmobile races.

Winter carnivals in every province. Check locally.

MARCH

Montreal, **Camping Show,** Place Bonaventure.

Maple Syrup Festival, Elmira, Ont., late March or early April, visits to the woods, pancake breakfast in the streets, tours of Mennonite community.

Indoor Rodeos in several Alberta cities.

Winter carnivals in Northwest Territories and Yukon.

APRIL

Canadians go out and look at the green starting to come.

Tuktoyaktuk. (That is a place, not a typographer's error.) Traditional Eskimo games at a jamboree in this Northwest Territories settlement.

MAY

Niagara Blossom Festival, on the Niagara Peninsula in southern Ontario, centered on St. Catharines, about two weeks in mid-month. Just drive and see the bursting blossoms, billions of them.

Niagara-on-the-Lake, Ont., opening of summer-long **Shaw Festival** of plays by George Bernard Shaw and his contemporaries.

New Hamburg, Ont., **Mennonite Relief Sale,** quilts, preserves, crafts. Internationally famous event. Last Saturday of month.

Outdoor rodeos start in western Canada. Check provinces.

JUNE

Stratford Shakespearean Festival begins its annual, internationally acclaimed season of plays and music, early in month.

Metro Toronto Caravan, perhaps the city's best fun event, runs for 9 days towards the end of the month. Hundreds of thousands of visitors go to miniature foreign "cities" set up by 50 ethnic groups to demonstrate food, crafts, culture.

Toronto Woodbine Race Track hosts the **Queen's Plate,** Canada's equivalent of the Kentucky Derby, to determine the champion home-bred 3-year-old. Last Saturday of month.

Matane, Quebec, **Shrimp Festival,** an eight-day fête late in the month in honor of the tasty creature.

JULY

Calgary Exhibition and Stampede, 9 days starting in the second week of July, is Canada's biggest rodeo and one of the country's great fairs. The whole city goes 10-gallon.

Edmonton follows immediately with its 10-day **Klondike Days.** Both cities blossom out as well with miniature-Vegas casinos for gambling.

Highland Games are held in a number of cities, particularly Ontario and the Atlantic Provinces.

Canadian Open Golf Championship, only Canadian golf tourney on the major U.S. circuit, is held in mid-July at a permanent site, Glen Abbey Golf Course at Oakville, Ont.

Ottawa Summer Festival of music and arts begins.

Toronto Caribana, five-day fête of Caribbean food, music, dance, on Toronto Island, late in month.

St. John's Nfld., **Summer Festival of the Arts.**

Summerside, P.E.I., **Lobster Carnival,** 8 days starting July 1.

Halifax, **Neptune Theatre Summer Festival** begins.

AUGUST

The month for the big exhibitions, similar to state fairs in the U.S. Some of the biggest: Toronto, **Canadian National Exhibition,** the very biggest, from about Aug. 17 to Labor Day. Canada's biggest midway, biggest agricultural competition, biggest air show, biggest, biggest . . . . Ottawa, **Central Canada Exhibition,** 9 days late in month. Quebec city, **Quebec Exhibition**, 10 days leading up to Labor Day. Vancouver, **Pacific National Exhibition,** two weeks to Labor Day.

Brantford, Ont., **Six Nations Indian Pageant,** first three weekends in month.

Charlottetown, **Old Home Week,** second week in August, Islanders come back to the land of Anne of Green Gables to eat lobster, race harness horses, and gab.

Banff Festival of the Arts, in the Rocky Mountain resort area, most of the month.

SEPTEMBER

St. Catharines, Ont. Grape and Wine Festival, mid-September, nine days of parades, wine-tasting, and general merriment.

OCTOBER

Kitchener-Waterloo Oktoberfest, biggest North American celebration of the fall beer festival, an 8-day spree the second week of October. Many hotel rooms are reserved a year in advance. German clubs open their facilities for public partying every night, for a fee of course. Oom-pah-pah bands, dancing, sausages and good fellowship.

Smaller **Oktoberfests** are now held in other cities across Canada, with particularly big ones at Vancouver and Winnipeg.

NOVEMBER

Royal Agricultural Winter Fair, Toronto, featuring international horse-jumping competitions for 8 days in mid-month.

The **Grey Cup,** symbol of Canada's professional

football championship, is awarded to winner of final play-off game, last Sunday in November, at conclusion of a boisterous and, for many, drunken week of festivities. The locale shifts each year. In 1978, it will be held in Toronto on Nov. 26.

DECEMBER

Everything, it seems revolves around Christmas. At London, Ont., for instance, there is **Winter Wonderland** at Victoria Park, aglow with Christmas lights and decorations, and offering night skating. And everywhere, concerts.

DATE DUE